007856

OPERATIONAL RESEARCH
SOCIETY LIBRARY
(at)
LYON PLAYFAIR LIBRARY
IMPERIAL COLLEGE, S.W.7.

IMPERIAL COLLEGE, LONDON, S.W.7

D1341967

| AUTHOR (AS UNDERLINED) |
| CLASS No. 658.5 |
| COPY No. |
| ACCESSION No. 007856 |

PRODUCTION CONTROL:

A Quantitative Approach

John E. Biegel

Department of Industrial Engineering
Syracuse University

Prentice-Hall, Inc.   Englewood Cliffs, N.J.   1963

PRENTICE-HALL INTERNATIONAL, INC., *London*
PRENTICE-HALL OF AUSTRALIA, PTY., LTD., *Sydney*
PRENTICE-HALL OF CANADA, LTD., *Toronto*
PRENTICE-HALL FRANCE, S.A.R.L., *Paris*
PRENTICE-HALL OF JAPAN, INC., *Tokyo*
PRENTICE-HALL DE MEXICO, S.A., *Mexico City*

(ORS)

TS

157

B52

© 1963 by PRENTICE-HALL, INC., Englewood Cliffs,
N.J. All rights reserved. No part of this book may be
reproduced in any form, by mimeograph or any other
means, without permission in writing from the publisher.

658. 5

007856

Library of Congress Card Catalog No. 63–9171

Printed in the United States of America

72514—C

To

JERRI
STEVE
DALE
KURT

They
Withstood
and
They
Understood

Preface

While teaching production control to engineering and business students, I have felt a definite need for a quantitative approach to the subject. Such text material has been lacking; thus, my aim is to provide a logical, analytical approach to an area that readily lends itself to such methodology.

In recent years, production control has assumed a position of increasing prominence in business thinking. This increasing emphasis has resulted in growth. The advent of the computer has, no doubt, been partially responsible for the current status of the field. Further, the computer will continue to inspire the development of new quantitative techniques and the application of existing techniques.

With the increase in capacity for handling and analyzing quantitative data comes a need for the utilization of statistical techniques. Certainly, the basic data being used, the forecast, is not sufficiently accurate for precise determinations. However, the statistical techniques provide methods of determining the most likely values and estimates of their error. I am a firm believer in the application of the appropriate techniques, such as averages, standard deviations, regression lines, control charts, etc.

With these ideas in mind, I have attempted to present a logical, understandable application of statistical techniques to the important areas of production and inventory planning and control. I have deliberately omitted the organizational and managerial aspects of the area. I feel that such discussions are more logically a subject for a treatise on management and administration. Further, I hope the treatment is sufficiently clear to permit the average student or practitioner to understand the methods and the reason for their use. However, a sound foundation in statistics is desirable. A knowledge of calculus may prove helpful but is certainly not absolutely essential.

If I am able to convince the reader that production control can be treated quantitatively, I will feel successful.

I am indebted to many people for their direct and indirect assistance and guidance in writing this book. Some of these people are Professor Wallace J. Richardson, Lehigh University; and Professor C. A. Anderson, North Carolina State College for helpful comments on the manuscript; Professor Bert H. Norem, Syracuse University for his continued encouragement; Mrs. F. E. (Alice) Hares and Mrs. K. W. (Mildred) Haskins for typing the manuscript; and my brother, James, for providing the material for Chapter 12. And last but not least, the four co-authors whose contribution was not so much in the writing as in the forebearance of a busy and somewhat irritable husband and father; Jerri, Steve, Dale, and Kurt.

JOHN E. BIEGEL

Contents

1. **The Nature of Production Control**   1

1.1. Introduction   1
1.2. Functions of Production Control   2
1.3. The Manufacturing Process   4
1.4. Illustration of Production Control Problems   5
1.5. The Varying Nature of the Production Control Problem   6
1.6. Summary   7

2. **Functions and Documents in the Manufacturing Enterprise**   8

2.1. Introduction   8
2.2. Manufacturing Functions   9
2.3. Engineering Functions   9
2.4. Control Functions   10
2.5. Support Functions   11
2.6. Documents   12
2.7. Interrelationship of Functions and Documents   13
2.8. Summary   13

3. **Forecasting**   16

3.1. Introduction   16
3.2. Sales Characteristics Affecting Forecasts   17
3.3. Uses of Forecasts   17
3.4. Types of Forecasts   18
3.5. Forecast Accuracy is Essential   21

3.6. Example 1: Level Demand with Random Variations   22
3.7. Example 2: An Upward Trend with Random Variations   24
3.8. Example 3: Cyclic Demand with Random Variations   29
3.9. Example 4: Cyclic Demand Following an Upward Trend with
       Random Variations Superimposed   32
3.10. The Moving Average as a Forecasting Method   34
3.11. The Weighted-Average Forecast   35
3.12. Other Statistical Techniques   36
3.13. Determination of the Periodicity of Demand Data   41
3.14. The Total-Demand Forecast   43
3.15. Summary   43

4. Controlling the Forecast   44

4.1. Introduction   44
4.2. The Moving-Range Chart   44
4.3. Use of the Moving-Range Chart to Determine the Appropriateness
      of the Forecasting Equations   53
4.4. Summary   54

5. Economic Lot-Size Determinations   55

5.1. Introduction   55
5.2. Economic Lot-Size Determinations When Replenishment is
      Instantaneous   55
5.3. Economic Lot-Size Determinations When Replenishment Occurs
      Over a Finite Period of Time   58
5.4. Differences between Instantaneous Replenishment and
      Replenishment over a Finite Period of Time   61
5.5. Change in Time Periods   62
5.6. Evaluation of the Effects of Changes in the Cost Elements   62
5.7. Minimum-Cost Determinations for More than One Product   62
5.8. Order Tables and Order Charts   66
5.9. Summary   69

6. Inventory and Inventory Functions   70

6.1. Introduction   70
6.2. The Function of Inventories   71
6.3. Types of Inventories   72
6.4. Two Basic Types of Inventory Systems   73
6.5. Safety Stock   76
6.6. Inventory Control Systems When Demand is not Level   80
6.7. A Variation of the Fixed-Order-Interval Inventory-Control
      System   85
6.8. Summary   87

7. Production Planning   88

7.1. Introduction   88
7.2. The Production Plan   88
7.3. A Production Plan for Example 1   89
7.4. A Production Plan For Example 1 with Safety Stocks   95
7.5. A Production Plan for Several Products   98
7.6. Summary   102

8. Adjusting the Production Plan   103

8.1. Introduction   103
8.2. Methods of Adjusting the Production Plan   104
8.3. Leveling Applied to Example 1   104
8.4. Reconciliation of the Adjusted Production Plan with Available
     Hours   111
8.5. The Effect of the Number of Periods Used in the Leveling
     Procedure   112
8.6. Summary   113

9. Scheduling Production   114

9.1. Introduction   114
9.2. Sequencing the Operations for One Product   115
9.3. The Assignment of Orders to Machines   122
9.4. The Use of Charts in Scheduling   125
9.5. The Schedule with Lead Times   125
9.6. Scheduling Several Products   127
9.7. Summary   129

10. Linear Programming Applied to Scheduling and
      Distribution   130

10.1. Introduction   130
10.2. Setting up the Problem   130
10.3. Solving the Problem   131
10.4. More Than One Optimum Solution   137
10.5. The Degenerate Case   138
10.6. The Dummy Plant or Dummy Warehouse   141
10.7. Unequal Production Costs   142
10.8. The Modi Method Applied to the Assignment of Orders to
      Machines   144
10.9. Summary   148

11. Where Today and Where Tomorrow?   149

    11.1. Where Does Production and Inventory Control Stand Today?   149
    11.2. What Should Be Expected in the Future   155

12. An Illustrative Case: The Paint and Allied Products
     Industry   156

    12.1. Introduction   156
    12.2. Forecasting   157
    12.3. Control Charts on the Monthly Forecast   166
    12.4. Economic Lot-Size Determination   166
    12.5. Production Planning   170
    12.6. Production Scheduling   177
    12.7. Summary   178

Problems   179

    Problem Group 1   179
    Problem Group 2   186
    Problem Group 3   194
    Problem Group 4   202
    Problem Group 5   209
    Problem Group 6   217

Bibliography   221

Index   223

1. The Nature of Production Control

1.1. Introduction

As a student of production control, it is necessary to have a knowledge of the nature of production control and its place in the manufacturing organization to better understand the reasons for and the areas of application of certain of the techniques to be presented in the remainder of this volume. The discussions that follow assume that the production control function is operating in a very broad sense. In many companies, its operation is far more restricted.

A very general statement of the objective of production control is to plan and control the flow of materials into, through, and out of the plant in such a manner that the optimum profit position is achieved within the framework of the company's goals. Thus, production control must establish a means of continued evaluation of customer demand, capital position, productive capacity, manpower, etc. This evaluation must consider not only the present status of these factors but must project them into the future. The time intervals to be included in these projections are dependent upon many factors which will be discussed later.

1

1.2. Functions of Production Control

The functions of production control are (1) to forecast the product demand, expressing quantity as a function of time (Chapter 3); (2) to monitor actual demand, compare with forecast demand, and revise forecasts if necessary (Chapter 4); (3) to establish economic lot sizes for purchased and for manufactured items (Chapter 5); (4) to determine the production requirements and inventory levels at specific points in time (Chapter 7); (5) to monitor inventory levels, compare with planned inventory, and revise production plans if necessary (Chapter 8); (6) to make detailed production schedules (Chapter 9); and (7) to plan the distribution of product (Chapter 10).

The diversity of the responsibilities of production control departments is illustrated by a recent survey made by *Factory* magazine in cooperation with the American Production and Inventory Control Society (APICS). The following is from the survey results:

Scheduling Production within the Plant and Maintaining Inventories are the Hard Core of P & IC. Other Responsibilities, Such as Make-Or-Buy Decisions and Customer Service, are Shared.

[Table 1.1] shows how widespread are the responsibilities of some production and inventory control departments. Basic to most are: setting inventory levels, scheduling production of material through the plant, dispatching production orders, and some control over raw materials. Responsibilities break into specifics beyond these general areas.

In many cases, they overlap with other departments. Take the general area of production planning. In no case did more than 50% of the P & IC departments assume responsibility for sales forecasting, plant capacity studies, or release of new products. Only 18% authorized tooling for new products. The biggest responsibility (77%) in production planning was determining the levels of production.

Customer service is another shared area, this time with the sales manager or a separate customer service department. Yet one of the surprising findings of this survey is that marketing-oriented responsibilities are claimed by almost half of the P & IC groups.

Routing of purchased goods and plant shipments is usually regarded as in the traffic department's bailiwick, or in purchasing's. But 25% of the plants assign it to P & IC. Even make-or-buy decisions are claimed by 37% of P & IC departments as their primary responsibility.

In what might appear to be a prime function of this group — control of raw material inventory — 30% of the P & IC groups disclaim responsibility. In inventory control of operating supplies — usually assigned to purchasing — 47% claim no responsibility. Control of operating supplies is split between purchasing, plant manager, department foremen, and chief storekeeper.

This confused picture on inventory responsibilities may stem from

27% not having a separate inventory control department. In these plants, responsibility for inventory control is spread from the controller's office to department foremen.

Not all plants are organized in the same way, either. In 60%, a P & IC manager reports to a plant manager. In 25%, production and materials control supervisors report to a production manager. Remaining 11% split responsibilities.*

Table 1.1. What Are Major Responsibilities of P & IC?*

Activity	Responsible (%)	Others also responsible (%)	
Production planning			
Levels of production	77	Production manager	8
Plant capacity studies	50	Chief industrial engineer	15
Release new products for production	50	Chief product engineer	24
Participate in sales forecast	35	Sales manager	36
Authorize new product tooling	18	Chief industrial engineer	24
Levels of inventories for:			
Work in process	88	Plant manager	3
Production materials	81	Procurement	5
Finished goods	70	Sales manager	9
Decide to manufacture new products	25	Top management	11
Customer service			
Delivery schedules	76	Sales manager	10
Delivery promises	76	Sales manager	11
Answers for customer follow-ups	48	Sales manager	28
Order records	46	Sales manager	26
Instructions to ship	44	Sales manager	28
Shipping department			
Control of physical quantities of finished goods	65	Shipping foreman	5
Traffic			
Routing shipments	27	Traffic department	36
Routing purchased goods	23	Procurement	32
		Traffic	26
Production control			
Product routing	55	Chief industrial engineer	9
Make-or-buy decisions	37	Chief product engineer	11

*"Exclusive Survey of Production and Inventory Control," *Factory* magazine, McGraw-Hill Publishing Co., Inc., April 1961. This survey was done in cooperation with the American Production and Inventory Control Society. Used by permission.

Table 1.1 (cont.)   What Are Major Responsibilities of P & IC?

Activity	Responsible (%)	Others also responsible (%)	
Production orders			
Preparation and issue	91	Production manager	1
Order frequency (no. of runs)	90	Plant manager	1
Quantity determination	90	Sales manager	2
Scheduling product through factory	87	Plant manager	2
Estimating manufacturing lead time	87	Production manager	2
Machine loading scheduled products	77	Production manager	3
Scrap allowances	68	Chief product engineer	3
Dispatching			
Schedules and instructions	91	Production manager	2
Follow-up reporting	87	Production manager	2
Expediting in plant	87	Production manager	2
Control quantity of work-in-process	82	Plant manager	5
Intra-plant traffic	66	Plant manager	3
Controlling raw material inventories			
Control quantity of production material	78	Procurement director	7
Placing purchase requisition	77	Procurement director	11
Record keeping	75	Procurement director	9
Determine item inventory level	75	Procurement director	9
Determine order frequency	73	Procurement director	14
Determine inventory reserves	71	Procurement director	10
Determine order quantity	70	Procurement director	16
Control operating supplies inventory	53	Procurement director	10
Control operating supplies quantities	48	Procurement director	11
Determine purchase lead time	36	Procurement director	51

The above survey very vividly points out the variations in the assignments of the production control department. The assignment of responsibilities to production control and to other departments is a function of higher management. It is important that these functions and responsibilities be specifically assigned to a particular organization with the full authority for accomplishment of the assigned tasks.

1.3. The Manufacturing Process

The manufacturing process can be depicted as an input-output situation as in Fig. 1.1. The input is the raw material used in the product; the operation encompasses the conversion of the raw material (by employing equipment, time, skills, money, management, etc.) to the finished product, which is the output. Production control is concerned with forecasting or predicting the required output, determining the necessary input, and planning and scheduling the processing of the material through the necessary conversion or manufacturing sequences.

The conversion process may be a very simple one, or it may be very complex. The product may flow continuously through the plant in con-

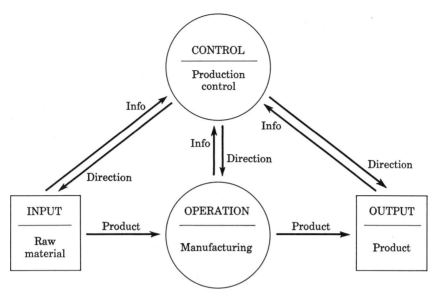

Fig. 1.1. Manufacturing as an input-output process.

tinuous or discrete units. The end result may be made up of many smaller items obtained from diverse sources. There are many combinations of things that may happen while the material flows through the plant. However, one thing is certain: there must be some form of control over the process, and this is where production control enters the picture.

1.4. Illustration of Production Control Problems

To illustrate some of the above concepts, let us assume that you are the production-control manager for a large concrete-block manufacturing company. You are currently engaged in planning for the next year's operation. Your first task will be to forecast the number of blocks your company can expect to sell. This forecast, or prediction, can be accomplished by a number of methods, some of which will be discussed later. For the time being, assume that the forecast has been made. In order to do your planning, you must have the forecast of the quantity of blocks expected to be sold during each planning period (day, week, month, etc.). From this information, you must determine the economic order quantities (those order quantities which give the minimum total annual cost) for each of the constituents you will need. There are other questions to be answered. Is it more economical to purchase the cement by the carload, by the truck load, or by the train load? Should the cement be purchased in bags or in bulk? Should you plan to maintain a minimum inventory of 100 tons, 500 tons, 1000 tons, or some other quantity of cement to meet unexpected fluctuations in customer demand and unexpected delays in the delivery of your orders? Is there adequate storage space to store cement in large quantities? If there is insufficient storage space at present, can you afford to pay demurrage charges, should you build or rent more storage space, or should you buy in smaller quantities? Can you produce the required number of blocks with your present capacity, or should you expand? Will one shift operation be adequate, or must you operate two or three shifts? Usually second- and third-shift operations require a premium wage; is this economical? Would the use of overtime, at a premium cost, help? Is it more profitable to refuse some orders than to pay overtime or shift premiums? Is it more profitable to establish several distribution points, or can you operate from one point? Must the blocks be produced in time to allow one day for delivery? Two days? More? Must the blocks be ready for delivery immediately, or is the customer willing to accept a "reasonable" delay for the processing of his order? What does the customer consider to be a "reasonable" delay?

These queries illustrate some typical questions for a specific product, but the principles of production control apply in far broader sense. Questions of the same general nature can be asked in all types of industry. Basic principles·can be applied regardless of the industry. The method of application of those principles will differ, however, for different types of industry and different types of manufacturing.

1.5. The Varying Nature of the Production Control Problem

The important problems of production control are somewhat dependent upon the industry and the company under consideration. The types of data available, the types of data necessary, the characteristics of the processing or manufacturing operation, the service demanded by the customer, the characteristics of the product, etc. will vary from one situation to another.

In the processing industries there are instances where raw materials cannot be stored but the finished product is capable of almost indefinite storage. An example is the canning of vegetables and fruit. In other situations the raw materials are capable of relatively long-term storage but the finished product is not. An example of this situation is the ready-mix concrete plant. Still other cases present a problem of limited procurement periods; foodstuffs, spices, etc. are examples. In the mining of coal and some metallic ores, both the raw materials and the finished products are capable of long-term storage.

Similar situations are present in the manufacturing and service industries. The grocery store is an example of a service industry where goods with both long and short storage lives can be purchased.

These factors determine where the major emphasis on production control must be placed. Examination of the production-control requirements in a continuous manufacturing operation reveals that the emphasis should be placed on the availability of the correct kind and quantity of raw materials at the appropriate times, the prevention of bottlenecks in the production line, and the removal of the finished product from the line and its distribution to the point of storage or sale. Much of the control is built into the production line. On the conveyer-controlled assembly line, the product moves at a predetermined rate, and the line will produce at that rate so long as the raw materials are available and are fed into the line, there are no equipment or personnel stoppages, and there is no limiting backlog of finished goods at the end of the line.

In intermittent manufacturing, other problems arise. In such an activity, there is no predetermined manufacturing process. Usually, a new and different process is required for each order. Stoppages or shortages at a limited number of points do not stop the entire flow of production. Since each item is built to a specific order, the finished product is usually shipped directly to the customer. In this type of manufacturing, the responsibility for balancing the production operations falls to the production-control group. In continuous manufacturing this responsibility lies with the engineering group that designs the manufacturing process; once established, it remains the same until major product changes or equipment replacements occur.

1.6. Summary

In a specific manufacturing, processing, or service operation, the production-control function may appear to have a very unique nature. This uniqueness has its origin in the demands of the customer, the design of the product, the raw materials, and the conversion process. The basic production-control problems exist in nearly all such operations. The emphasis, detail, method of resolution, etc. varies.

In the production-line, or continuous type of manufacturing, a part of the total production-control function is accomplished by the original process design, whereas in the intermittent type of manufacturing, the processing equipment must be of general-purpose types and little or no part of the control can be built in.

2. Functions and Documents in the Manufacturing Enterprise

2.1. Introduction

After examining the general nature of manufacturing in Chapter 1, it now seems advisable that we examine some of the functions or "jobs" that exist in a manufacturing enterprise. After this has been done, we should examine the interrelationships that exist between the various functions or jobs and particularly look at how the production-control function is related to the other functions. This appears best accomplished by examining the various pieces of paper, or, as they will be called, documents, that might be originated or used by the production-control function.

It is *not* intended that the functions or documents discussed in the remainder of this chapter shall include *all* functions or *all* documents that do or might exist in any plant. The general groupings of functions are only a matter of convenience for this discussion. However, the functions included are the more important items of concern in the area of production planning and inventory control.

2.2. Manufacturing Functions

In this group we shall include only those functions directly related to the manufacturing or movement of the product. These functions are
1. Receiving.
2. Warehousing.
3. Transportation.
4. Production.
5. Shipping.

The main purposes of these activities can be described as follows:
1. Receiving has the responsibility for getting raw materials into the plant. It accepts the material from the carrier and presents it to receiving inspection for evaluation. It also has the responsibility for establishing that the proper quantity of material has been received, but it generally has no responsibility for the quality of the material received, other than shipping damage.
2. Warehousing has the responsibility for storing raw materials until needed for production and for storing finished goods until ready to be shipped to the customer.
3. Transportation has the responsibility for moving all types of material within the plant area and perhaps from the terminal of the carrier or supplier.
4. Production has the responsibility for transforming the raw material into an *acceptable, economical* finished product.
5. Shipping has the responsibility for packing and starting the finished goods on their way to the customer.

Therefore, it may be said that the manufacturing functions have the responsibility for the handling and physical transformation of the raw materials into finished products.

2.3. Engineering Functions

In this group of functions we shall include those concerned with the engineering aspects of a manufacturing operation. These functions are
1. Product design.
2. Process design.
3. Tool design.
4. Plant engineering.
5. Cost estimating.
6. Methods and standards engineering.

The main purposes of each of these activities are
1. Product design has the responsibility for the development of new and salable products and for the interpretation of these new and

salable product designs into product descriptions, product drawings, and product specifications. Also, it controls all major changes to existing products.

2. Process design has the responsibility for the development of efficient processes for the manufacture of the products developed by the product design function.

3. Tool design has the responsibility for translating the requirements of the product and the capabilities of the machines into tooling for the manufacture of acceptable product in an *efficient* manner.

4. Plant engineering has the responsibility for the physical location of equipment and the design and installation of new facilities and buildings. It must see that work spaces are adequately lighted, well heated, etc. to aid in the efficient manufacture of acceptable product.

5. Cost estimating is concerned with the probable costs involved in product manufacture. This function is useful in estimating costs for purposes of quotation to customers, as well as for estimating costs of items that will definitely be produced.

6. Methods and standards engineering has the responsibility of establishing the detailed job methods and standards for the operations required in the manufacture of goods.

2.4. Control Functions

In this group of functions we shall include those functions concerned with the controlling of production, cost, and quality. The functions included are

1. Production control.
2. Quality control.
3. Cost control.
4. Procedures control.
5. Inspection.

The main purposes of each of the above-listed control functions are

1. Production control has the responsibility for establishing forecasts, production plans, production schedules, job assignments, product routing, inventory levels, economic purchased lot sizes, and product distribution.

2. Quality control is responsible for establishing and maintaining the necessary control of quality for raw materials, in-process materials, and finished goods. It is responsible for examining the finished product for conformance to specifications and for quality of performance in use.

3. Cost control shall be responsible for determining and reporting the cost of manufacture and comparing that cost with the amounts allocated in the budgets. Further, it determines and reports the costs of all operations within the company.
4. Procedures control establishes "standard operating procedures" in the company. It also establishes and coordinates all forms to be used.
5. Inspection examines raw materials, in-process goods, and finished products. The results are reported to the manufacturing function, the engineering function, the control function, and the support function. Further, it has the authority to hold raw material from acceptance, in-process material from further processing, and finished goods from shipment to the customer until the appropriate actions are taken by the engineering, quality-control, and/or purchasing and sales functions. These actions *must* result in the acceptance or rejection of questionable materials. Frequently, the inspection and quality control functions are combined.

2.5. Support Functions

In this group of functions we shall include those that support the activities of the previously mentioned functions in their mission of producing an acceptable, salable product. The functions included are
1. Procurement or purchasing.
2. Sales.
3. Plant maintenance.
4. Personnel.
The main purposes of each of the support functions are as follows:
1. Procurement or purchasing is to buy the necessary materials of the proper quality at the most favorable price and to secure deliveries on the time schedules established. This function will maintain a record of supplier performance to assist in the proper placement of future orders.
2. Sales is responsible for the sale of the company's product and for liaison after material has been delivered.
3. Plant maintenance is responsible for the routine maintenance of equipment and facilities, for the installation of new equipment and facilities, and for the repair of existing facilities and equipment.
4. Personnel is responsible for hiring, training, and termination of employees. It must see that employees with the proper skills are available in the necessary numbers at the required times.
These functions certainly do not encompass all of the functions of a

manufacturing concern. Further, they may appear under different titles and have different job descriptions in almost any and every company. However, they are some of the more important functions in a manufacturing operation and must be considered in the study of production control.

Having looked at the functions in a manufacturing enterprise, we shall next look at the "documents" necessary for the description and specification of product and for the control of manufacture. Again, as with the functions, only certain selected documents are included.

2.6. Documents

The documents of concern are
1. Sales forecast — an estimate of the sales volume for some future period of time.
2. Production program — a long-range plan, usually for the development and introduction of new products.
3. Production plan — the plan, usually by specific products, that will control production for some intermediate period of time. This is usually revised at intervals to correct errors in forecasts or inabilities to meet planned production, or to adjust inventories.
4. Production schedule — an expansion of the production plan to control the production of products and their components. Usually for a relatively short period of time.
5. Job order — authorizes the production department to perform a specific task. States what is to be done and when a job is to be done. Depending upon the type of scheduling used, it may specify the exact machine or equipment.
6. Completion report — the production supervisor's report of the completion of a job order. It may be combined with the job order.
7. Inventory record — a record of the item count of specific products, piece-parts, subassemblies, etc. that are in inventory. Inventory may occur as stored items or as in-process items.
8. Product descriptions — a statement of the physical or other characteristics of an item, similar to a catalog description.
9. Product drawings — completely define all products and all parts that are used in the manufacture or assembly of products.
10. Product specification — states what the product is capable of doing and under what conditions it must function. It may also describe the tests to be used in determining the acceptability of the product.
11. Process description — describes the detailed process to be used in the manufacture of the product and its component parts.
12. Cost estimate — a formal estimate of manufacturing costs under a

specified schedule. It may be a part of the information used in submitting quotations or in establishing budgets.

13. Job standard — the standard time required to perform a specified job under normal conditions.

14. Sales order — an official statement of the product sold and the conditions of sale. In intermittent manufacturing, it provides information for the production control department to authorize manufacture of an item.

15. Purchase requisition — the request from production control to purchasing to procure specific items to a given schedule.

16. Purchase order — the contract with a supplier to provide the item or items specified thereon at a specific price and under an established schedule. Essentially a sales order in reverse.

17. Receiving report — the official acknowledgement of the receipt of materials to the description and in the quantity specified on the purchase order. *It does not acknowledge the acceptability of the quality of the material.*

18. Receiving inspection report — contains the result of the inspection of material received after that material has been examined for conformance to specifications.

19. In-process inspection report — contains the result of the inspections performed on product during manufacture.

20. Final inspection report — contains the result of the inspections performed on the finished product prior to delivery.

21. Shipping report — a statement of the quantity of material shipped against a sales order including date and to whom shipped.

2.7. Interrelationship of Functions and Documents

It must be noted that documents are of no value unless they aid the functions in their contributions towards the goal.

The information shown in Table 2.1 is intended to show the logical use of documents to provide and control information flow in a manufacturing organization. It cannot be and is not all inclusive, nor is it a must that the exact pattern illustrated in Table 2.1 exist in all manufacturing operations. It should, however, be noted that every document listed in Table 2.1 is either originated or used in the production control department.

2.8. Summary

There are certain functions that must exist in all manufacturing organizations. One of the functions is production planning and inventory

Table 2.1. Interrelationship of Functions Shown by Usage of Documents

	Manufacturing	Engineering	Production Control	Quality Control	Cost Control	Inspection	Purchasing	Sales	Other Support Functions
Sales forecast	I	I	U					O	
Production program	U	U	O				I	I	
Production plan	U	I	O	U	U		I	I	I
Production schedule	U		O	U	U	U	I	I	
Job order	U		O	I	U	I			
Completion report	O		U	I	U	I			
Inventory record			O					U	
Product description	U	O	I					U	
Product drawings	U	O	U	U		U	U	U	
Product specification	U	O	I	U		U			
Process description	U	O	U	U		U			
Cost estimate	I	O	I		U			U	
Job standard	U	O	U		U				
Sales order			U		U			O	
Purchase requisition			O				U		
Purchase order	U		U	U	U	U	O		
Receiving report	O		U		U	I	U		
Receiving insp. report	I	I	U		U	O	U		
In-process insp. report	U	I	U		U	O			
Final inspection report	U	I	U		U	O		U	
Shipping report	O		U		U			U	

Code: I = For Information Purposes
U = For Use of Information Thereon
O = Originated By

control. It controls the manufacturing operation. It has responsibilities to other functions, and the other functions have responsibilities to production control.

In the same manner, it is reasoned that there are certain pieces of information that do exist and must exist in a successful enterprise. These pieces of information should be recorded on documents so that the information may be properly disseminated to the organizations concerned. The information contained on such documents may be only to keep people informed, or it may be used as a basis of action. The interrelationship of documents and functions is shown in Table 2.1.

3. Forecasting*

3.1. Introduction

A forecast is an estimate of the level of demand for a product or for several products for some period of time in the future. Therefore, a forecast is basically a guess, but by the use of certain techniques it can be more than just a guess. It can be said that a forecast is an educated guess; certainly, it should contain as little error as is humanly possible. To make a forecast most meaningful, it should be in terms of the units to be planned or scheduled, and it should cover a time period at least as long as the period of time required to make a decision and to put that decision into effect. There is little value, in fact, no value, in making a forecast for such a short time interval that effective action cannot be taken.

If a forecast is not exact, then why make a forecast at all? The answer is very simple — any and all decisions about the future are based on a forecast of sorts. Any time a decision is made about the future, there is at least an implied forecast underlying that decision. It can be stated with assurance that planned forecasts are more valuable and more accurate than intuitive forecasts. The primary concern in this chapter will be with the statistical methods which appear to assure a reasonable degree of accuracy and, therefore, which would be of value in modern production-control operations.

*This material adapted from John E. Biegel, "Statistics in Forecasting," *Management International*, 1961/6, November–December 1961, pages 162–189. Used by permission.

3.2. Sales Characteristics Affecting Forecasts

The nature of the product and its demand pattern affect the type of forecast to be made and the time period which must be covered or spanned.

If the product is of a nature such that the demand can be expected to be nearly constant from one period to the next, the time span of the forecast may be relatively short. Future planning can be based on the implicit assumption that demand will continue at the same level. In such cases, current capacity can generally handle most of the demand volume. Thus, there is little need for an extended forecast.

If the product is one that has cyclic variations in demand, alternate highs and lows, the forecast (production planning forecast) must cover at least one cycle. The preferable forecast covers from peak to peak. This gives a better opportunity to plan both production and inventory to meet the peak demand. If cyclic variations in demand exist, it may be necessary to depend upon overtime, and/or inventory, to meet demand.

If demand is expected to have a long-term upward trend, it is necessary to forecast for a time interval that will enable the intelligent planning of any necessary facilities expansion or equipment procurement. This time interval may vary from a few months to several years. For the downward trend or decline in demand, the forecast period must be of sufficient length to permit wise planning for contraction of the operation, for the introduction of new products, etc.

The demand forecast must be of a type and cover a time span consistent with the pattern of sales or demand, if it is to have its greatest value in planning. Its use in planning manufacturing activities is one of the primary functions of the demand forecast. In the remainder of this book the discussion will refer to sales forecasts, but generally the comments and techniques are also applicable to service demand forecasts.

3.3. Uses of Forecasts

When forecasts are made (and it should be a foregone conclusion that they will be), there must be a use for them. They must serve a purpose, and this purpose may affect the nature of the forecast. There are three major purposes:

1. To determine the necessity for and the size of plant expansions.
2. To determine the intermediate planning for existing products to be manufactured with existing facilities.
3. To determine the short-range scheduling of existing products to be manufactured on existing equipment.

There is one requirement that each of the above forecasts must meet; it must cover an expanse of time as long as that required to make a decision plus the time to make that decision effective. Forecasts to fulfill the first purpose above can be considered long-range forecasts. The forecast for plant expansion purposes we shall call the facilities forecast. The production planning forecast and the product forecast will be the terms applied to the forecasts fulfilling the second and third purposes above.

The nature of the forecast and perhaps its method of generation will be determined by its intended use. Certainly, the degree of detail in the forecast depends upon its use. For example, a product forecast in dollar volume by class or group of products is not as meaningful for scheduling purposes as a forecast of the number of units of each product. Likewise, a forecast of the number of units of each product is probably not necessary in the facilities forecast; instead, a forecast of dollar volume will suffice. As the forecast period is lengthened, the detail should be reduced. In such cases, the accuracy of the detailed forecast is probably poor, whereas the accuracy of a total volume forecast may be good.

3.4. Types of Forecasts

The discussion on the different uses for forecasts has suggested one method of classifying forecasts: according to use. Another possible classification is the time span covered. However, time span and use are nearly synonomous in this instance, since the use will be determined by the time span, and vice versa. The preceding statement is predicated on the fact that the degree of detail and the degree of accuracy possible are inversely related to the time span. This relationship is shown in Table 3.1.

Table 3.1. Types of Forecasts by Use

Type of Forecast by Use	Type of Forecast by Detail	Time Span of Forecast
Facilities Forecast	Maximum Expected Output (Dollar Volume)	Facilities planning time and construction time plus time between facilities expansions
Production Planning Forecast	Volume of Product by Similar Types	Several manufacturing cycles or at least one demand cycle where sales are seasonal
Product Forecast	Product Units to be Sold	Lead time plus at least one manufacturing cycle

Forecasts can be categorized in other ways. Another classification is based on the method of generation of the forecast. It can be (1) based on the subjective opinions of people working in the sales and marketing field, (2) based on an index of business activity, (3) based on an averaging of past sales data, (4) based on a statistical analysis of past sales data, or (5) based on a combination of methods.

3.4.1. The Subjective Opinion Forecast

The subjective opinion forecast is one where some or all of the marketing and sales people express their considered opinion of the volume of sales expected in the future. These opinions are then collected and evaluated. The evaluation results in a forecast for an interval of time in the future. This type of forecasting has the advantage that the people directly involved with selling have the responsibility for the forecast. They are in the best position to "sense" the probable future trends in the market. They have experience in selling the product under various marketing conditions and, therefore, should be the best qualified to express an opinion about the future. However, there are some disadvantages to such a method of developing the forecast. First, the salesmen may be very optimistic if sales in the immediate past have been good. On the other hand, they may be overly pessimistic if sales in the immediate past have been low. In other words, the opinions used in a subjective-type forecast may be too dependent upon sales experience in the immediate past. Second, there may be some strong individuals involved in establishing the forecast, and the result may not be an expression of a considered opinion of all the people involved, but a weighted opinion of these strong individuals. If these strong individuals are as correct or more correct than the entire group, there is no harm. On the other hand, if their opinions are biased, this bias must necessarily be reflected in the forecast. The subjective opinion forecast can be good or bad. Unfortunately, if it is bad, this method of forecasting is not amenable to an evaluation of its errors.

3.4.2. Forecasts Based on an Index

The forecast based on an index is as good or as bad as the index that serves as its foundation and the degree of correlation between the actual demand and the forecast based on the index. This type of forecast can be illustrated by some examples: (1) a building supply manufacturer might base his forecast of sales on the number of building permits issued in the area or on a national index of construction volume; (2) an appliance manufacturer might base his sales forecast on the gross national income, etc. A high degree of accuracy in a forecast of this type requires that the correlation between sales and the index should be high. The extent of the relationship between the index and the forecast is approximately the square of the coefficient of correlation. Therefore, a coefficient of correlation of 0.80 shows that only about 64 per cent of the sales volume can be attributed to the cause system that generated the index. From the above, it appears that a coefficient of correlation of nearly 0.95 is necessary before the forecast made from an index can be considered to have the required degree of accuracy. Also, it should be remembered that there are many false and sometimes ridiculous correlations, those in which there is no valid causal relationship between the "correlated" phenomena.

3.4.3. Forecasts Based on Averages

The forecast based on the averaging of past sales data represents the implied assumption that past demand is indicative of future demand. The validity of this assumption can be tested by the use of control charts. There is a variety of methods and variations of averaging that can be used for forecasting. The arithmetic average or mean is one possibility. It is an average of all past sales data.

When the data from only the more recent sales periods are used, we have a moving average. The number of pieces of data used in the moving average determines how it reacts to any given cause system. It will tend to lag a trend, to be out-of-phase (lagging), to depress the peaks and to raise the valleys of a cyclic demand pattern. The extent of the lag, the out-of-phase condition, and the smoothing is a function of the number of demand periods used in the moving average.

In some instances, one can justify a stronger emphasis on the immediate past demand in determining an estimate of future demand. This emphasis can be accomplished by the use of weighted averages. Again, by choice of the weighting factor, you can achieve a certain degree of smoothing, a certain amount of lag, and certain out-of-phase relationships. When applied to a cyclic pattern of demand without additional adjustment, the weighted average never forecasts the highest peaks or the lowest valleys.

With proper application and certain adjustments, the averaging of past demand data may give a satisfactory estimate of future sales volume, provided the cause system does not change. However, there are better and more reliable statistical techniques which can be used. When only averages are used, there is no estimate of the error of the forecast value. An estimate of the error is necessary for effective inventory planning. A more detailed discussion of the use of averages is given in the examples to follow.

3.4.4. The Statistical Forecast

The forecast based on a statistical analysis of past demand offers possibilities of being the most accurate method, provided there is a relationship between the past and the future. In fact, the past offers the best basis for decisions on future actions. However, one must modify the predictions from past data if he knows that certain events will or will probably happen in the future. Such events that might tend to increase sales are the expansion of sales area covered, the advent of an advertising or sales campaign, the withdrawal of a competitor from the field, etc. Some occurrences that might tend to decrease the sales volume are the entry of new competitors into the market, the product's becoming outdated, the entry of a new and competitive line by your company which will attract part of your own market for the old product, etc. Such considerations as the above should be reflected in the new forecasts.

The greater accuracy attainable by the statistical methods may introduce higher costs, but, even so, these higher costs should be overshadowed by the better planning and control of the production process and inventories, better customer service, etc. that is possible with a more accurate system. There are many statistical methods which can be used. Their application should be done by someone who is reasonably well versed in the methods of statistical analysis and in the interpretation of the results of such analyses.

The use of computers should greatly aid in the introduction and use of these techniques. However, the mechanized data-handling and data-processing techniques are recommended only in those instances where they can profitably serve the intended purpose. To say that you are not up to date if you do not have such equipment is not necessarily true. But to use manual techniques when you can profitably use a computer is an uneconomical situation which should be remedied.

3.4.5. Combination Methods

It is possible and perhaps desirable to combine some or all of the above types of forecasting and, perhaps, to add other methods. The assurance of the required degree of accuracy may come from close agreement of the forecasts made by several methods.

3.4.6. Market Research

Another forecasting problem arises when it is necessary to make decisions about the introduction of new products. A considerable amount of research is necessary to determine the sales potential of a product. This type of forecasting is generally called market research and will not be explored further. It is, however, an excellent field for the use of statistical techniques. In fact, a good market survey requires a thorough statistical analysis.

3.5. Forecast Accuracy Is Essential

An accurate forecast, no matter how obtained, is essential to good control of manufacturing. Business decisions are either directly or indirectly based on forecasts. Therefore, inaccuracies and errors in forecasts may result in unprofitable decisions. In a highly competitive market, success or failure may be dependent upon the degree of control possible through good forecasts.

3.6. Example 1: Level Demand with Random Variations

The easiest case to analyze and predict is when demand is level or constant with random variations. Such a case is illustrated by the data of Table 3.2. The best estimate of future demand for such a sales pattern is the arithmetic average or mean.

Table 3.2. Level Demand with Random Variations

Period	Month	Demand	Period	Month	Demand
1	Jan.	109	13	Jan.	131
2	Feb.	118	14	Feb.	134
3	Mar.	108	15	Mar.	147
4	Apr.	145	16	Apr.	125
5	May	110	17	May	130
6	June	126	18	June	128
7	July	117	19	July	127
8	Aug.	132	20	Aug.	109
9	Sept.	125	21	Sept.	135
10	Oct.	128	22	Oct.	130
11	Nov.	143	23	Nov.	120
12	Dec.	110	24	Dec.	110

3.6.1. The Forecast Based on the Arithmetic Average

The data of Example 1 is shown graphically in Fig. 3.1. The pattern shows the random variation about the central line.

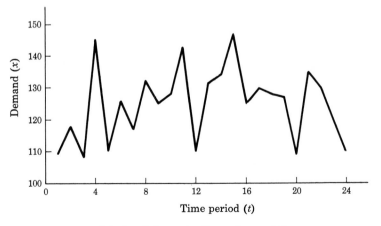

Fig. 3.1. Level demand with random variations.

Since the arithmetic average or mean is defined as

$$\bar{x} = \frac{\Sigma x}{n} \tag{3.1}$$

the mean of the data in Table 3.2 is

$$\bar{x} = \frac{109 + 118 + 108 + \cdots + 120 + 110}{24} = 125$$

Thus, the forecast for January of next year (period 25) would be 125 units. In fact, as long as the same cause system continues to generate the demand, the forecast for any and all months in the future would be 125 units. If so desired, from this knowledge, we can arrive at a forecast of 1500 units for the next year.

How accurate is the mean of a sample in predicting the mean of the population or universe? The accuracy with which the sample mean predicts the true mean is a function of the reciprocal of the square root of the sample size. To decrease the possible error between the true mean and your estimate of the true mean (the arithmetic average of the sample) by a factor of $\frac{1}{2}$ requires that four times as many items of data be used in calculating the sample mean. Such an increase in sample size may not be warranted, because many things can happen to change the underlying cause system. Such changes can be readily detected by control charts. The construction and use of one suitable type of control chart will be illustrated later.

When examining Fig. 3.1, we might wonder if we could predict the ups and downs in demand. The answer is no! However, we can predict the range of expected variations with certain probabilities. Such an estimate of error would be of considerable help in our later planning.

3.6.2. The Estimate of Error in the Forecast

The best estimate of the probable error in the forecast given above is the standard deviation. The standard deviation is defined as the square root of the sum of the squares of the deviations of the individual values from the mean divided by the number of values used minus one. This is expressed mathematically as

$$s_x = \sqrt{\frac{\Sigma (x - \bar{x})^2}{n - 1}} \tag{3.2}$$

For our example,

$$s_x = \sqrt{\frac{(109 - 125)^2 + (118 - 125)^2 + \cdots + (110 - 125)^2}{24 - 1}}$$

or 12 units.

The standard deviation needs to be calculated only when the first forecast is being established by the above method and again when there has been a definite change in demand. As long as the same cause system controls demand, the same forecast and estimate of error should be used.

Having found an estimate of the error in the forecast, how do we use it? The first decision that must be made is as follows: how often do we want to be correct when we say that the actual demand will fall within a specified number of units from the forecast value. Suppose we want to be able to say that the actual demand will fall within a certain pair of limits approximately 95 times out of 100. In that case, our upper limit for demand is $125 + 2(12)$ or 149, and our lower limit is $125 - 2(12)$ or 101. Note that the upper limit is $\bar{x} + 2s_x$ and the lower limit is $\bar{x} - 2s_x$. If we want to establish limits for expected demand that will be correct more than 95 times out of 100, we must use greater multiples of s_x, which mean wider limits. For example, limits of $\bar{x} + 3s_x$ and $\bar{x} - 3s_x$ should include the actual demand in 997 out of 1000 periods.

It is possible to reverse the above procedure and set limits on demand and then determine the approximate probability. For example, we want to know the probability that the demand in Example 1 falls between 110 and 140 units. First, we subtract 125, the mean, from 140 and 110 and divide the results by 12, (s_x). Second, using a table of normal probabilities, we find the probability of the demand falling in the range of 110 to 140. The normal deviates, $(140 - 125)/12$ and $(110 - 125)/12$, are $+1.25$ and -1.25 respectively. The probability is 0.79. The demand should not be less than 110 nor more than 140 in more than 21 out of 100 periods.

Keep in mind, however, that there are some assumptions that must be recognized in the interpretation of these statistical results. First, we have assumed that our sample is truly representative of the demand for the product. Second, in using the standard deviation and the average, we have assumed that the system of causes which gave us certain demands in the past will continue to generate the demand in the future.

3.6.3. Summary of the Forecast for Example 1

The forecast for demand from the data presented as Example 1 is
1. The average expected demand is 125 units.
2. The standard deviation in expected demand is 12 units.
3. In 95 out of 100 months the actual demand should fall between 101 and 149 units inclusive.

This gives the best information available for future planning.

3.7. Example 2: An Upward Trend with Random Variations

Although a statistical forecast for the data of Example 2 (See Table 3.3)

Table 3.3. An Upward Trend with Random Variations

Period	Month	Demand	Period	Month	Demand
1	Jan.	68	13	Jan.	74
2	Feb.	55	14	Feb.	80
3	Mar.	63	15	Mar.	96
4	Apr.	82	16	Apr.	74
5	May	87	17	May	71
6	June	63	18	June	71
7	July	77	19	July	66
8	Aug.	78	20	Aug.	86
9	Sept.	62	21	Sept.	85
10	Oct.	78	22	Oct.	89
11	Nov.	74	23	Nov.	91
12	Dec.	62	24	Dec.	103

is not as simple as for the data of Example 1, it can still be done without excessive work. Remember, these calculations need to be done only when these methods are used the first time, and when there are changes in the basic causes from which this demand arises.

3.7.1. Establishing the Trend Line

If the demand appears to follow a steady upward or downward trend with random variations about the trend line (see Fig. 3.2), the regression line will be the best estimate of future demand, if we want to minimize the

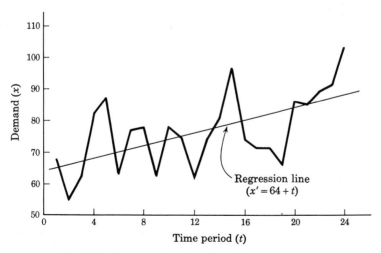

Fig. 3.2. An upward trend with random variations.

square of the deviations from the trend line. The regression line is defined as:

$$x' = a + bt \qquad (3.3)$$

where $b = \dfrac{n \Sigma\, xt - (\Sigma\, x)(\Sigma\, t)}{n \Sigma\, t^2 - (\Sigma\, t)^2}$

$\quad a = \bar{x} - b\bar{t}.$

For the data of Example 2, the regression line is

$$x' = 64 + t$$

where x' is the forecast demand and t is the number of the period for which the forecast is being made. So, for the twenty-fifth period, the forecast is 89 units; for the thirty-sixth period, it is 100 units. The total forecast for the next year is $89 + 90 + 91 + \cdots + 99 + 100 = 1134$. This can also be done as follows: $12(88) + 12(13)/2$. This latter calculation is based on the relationship that the sum of n consecutive numbers starting with 1 is $n(n + 1)/2$. Another useful relationship is that the sum of the squares of the first n consecutive numbers is $n(n + 1)(2n + 1)/6$.

3.7.1.1 Simplified Calculations for the Regression Line.* The calculations for the trend line can be simplified by choosing arbitrary origins and intervals for both the demand and the time. If we do this, the arithmetic may be considerably simplified. In Table 3.4, the regression line is computed by use of a simplified method. The results will be the same if the calculations are done correctly.

Another approach that is simpler when a relatively small quantity of data are used is to compute an average and a correction value. The two values to be determined are

1. $\qquad \bar{x} = \dfrac{\Sigma\, x}{n} \quad$ and

2. $\qquad m = (n - 1)x_t + (n - 3)x_{t-1} + (n - 5)x_{t-2} + \cdots$
$$\qquad\qquad\qquad + (n - (2n - 1))x_{t-n+1}$$

Then,

$$x' = \bar{x} + \frac{3m}{n(n + 1)} + (t - t_0)\frac{6m}{(n - 1)n(n + 1)}$$

*The material in Section 3.7.1.1 was adapted from Brown, Robert G., *Statistical Forecasting for Inventory Control*, McGraw-Hill Book Company, Inc., New York, 1959, pages 36–38. Used by permission.

Table 3.4. Simplied Calculations for Regression Line

Month	Period (t)	Demand (x)	t−12 (h)	x−76 (k)	(h)²	(hk)	(k)²
Jan.	1	68	−11	−8	121	88	64
Feb.	2	55	−10	−21	100	210	441
Mar.	3	63	−9	−13	81	117	169
Apr.	4	82	−8	6	64	−48	36
May	5	87	−7	11	49	−77	121
June	6	63	−6	−13	36	78	169
July	7	77	−5	1	25	−5	1
Aug.	8	78	−4	2	16	−8	4
Sept.	9	62	−3	−14	9	42	196
Oct.	10	78	−2	2	4	−4	4
Nov.	11	74	−1	−2	1	2	4
Dec.	12	62	0	−14	0	0	196
Jan.	13	74	1	−2	1	−2	4
Feb.	14	80	2	4	4	8	16
Mar.	15	96	3	20	9	60	400
Apr.	16	74	4	−2	16	−8	4
May	17	71	5	−5	25	−25	25
June	18	71	6	−5	36	−30	25
July	19	66	7	−10	49	−70	100
Aug.	20	86	8	10	64	80	100
Sept.	21	85	9	9	81	81	81
Oct.	22	89	10	13	100	130	169
Nov.	23	91	11	15	121	165	225
Dec.	24	103	12	27	144	324	729
Totals			12	11	1156	1108	3283

$$b = \frac{24(1108) - (12)(11)}{24(1156) - (12)^2} = 0.959, \quad a = 76 + \frac{11}{24} - (0.959)\left(12 + \frac{12}{24}\right) \quad a = 64.47$$

$$x' = 64 + t$$

To see how this method works, let us first calculate the regression line for the last six periods of Table 3.3. For these six periods:

$$\Sigma x = 520$$

$$\Sigma xt = 11{,}282$$

$$\Sigma t = 129$$

$$\Sigma t^2 = 2791$$

$$b = \frac{6(11{,}282) - 520(129)}{6(2791) - (129)^2} = 5.8286$$

$$a = \frac{520}{6} - 5.8286\left(\frac{129}{6}\right) = -38.6482$$

$$x' = -38.6482 + 5.8286t$$

By using the other method, we obtain:

$$\bar{x} = \frac{520}{6} = 86.6667$$

$$m = 5(103) + 3(91) + 1(89) + (-1)(85) + (-3)(86) + (-5)(66)$$
$$= 204$$

$$x' = 86.6667 + \frac{3(204)}{6(7)} + (t - t_0)\frac{6(204)}{5(6)(7)}$$

$$x' = 101.2381 + 5.8286(t - t_0)$$

where t_0 number of the last period used in the sums (in this case, t_0 is 24). Since t_0 is 24, we can reduce the last equation to

$$x' = -38.6483 + 5.8286t$$

Except for errors due to rounding, the result is the same. For computational purposes, it is probably easier to use the form with the factor $t - t_0$.

3.7.2. The Estimate of Error in the Forecast

The standard deviation of the variations about the regression line, designated as s_{xt}, can be determined from

$$s_{xt} = \sqrt{1 - r_{xt}^2}\, s_x \qquad (3.4)$$

where

$$r_{xt} = b\sqrt{\frac{n\,\Sigma\,t^2 - (\Sigma\,t)^2}{n\,\Sigma\,x^2 - (\Sigma\,x)^2}} \qquad (3.5)$$

For Example 2,

$$r_{xt} = 0.568$$
$$s_x = 11.94$$
$$s_{xt} = 9.8$$

For practical purposes, s_{xt} may be considered to be 10 units. The use and interpretation of s_{xt} in Example 2 is similar to the use and interpretation of s_x in Example 1, except that the limits now apply about the value of x' rather than of $\bar{x}$. When the above is used, the actual demand should be within + or $-2s_{xt}$ units of the forecast (x') in 95 out of 100 months.

3.7.3. Summary of the Forecast for Example 2

The forecast for the demand expected from the data presented as Example 2 is
1. The expected demand is $x' = 64 + t$.
2. The standard error of estimate, s_{xt}, is 10 units.

3. In 95 out of 100 months the actual demand should fall within the limits of $x' + 20$ and $x' - 20$ units inclusive.

For the case where a trend exists, the above method gives the best information available for forecasting the future, provided there is no change in the cause system underlying the demand for the product.

3.8. Example 3: Cyclic Demand with Random Variations

When demand follows a cyclic pattern, as illustrated by the data of Table 3.5 and as shown graphically in Fig. 3.3, one approach is to use a combination of regression lines.

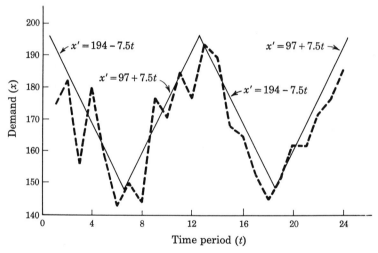

Fig. 3.3. Cyclic demand with random variations.

Table 3.5. Cyclic Demand with Random Variations

Period	Month	Demand	Period	Month	Demand
1	Jan.	175	13	Jan.	194
2	Feb.	182	14	Feb.	190
3	Mar.	156	15	Mar.	168
4	Apr.	180	16	Apr.	165
5	May	158	17	May	153
6	June	143	18	June	145
7	July	150	19	July	152
8	Aug.	144	20	Aug.	162
9	Sept.	177	21	Sept.	162
10	Oct.	171	22	Oct.	172
11	Nov.	185	23	Nov.	177
12	Dec.	177	24	Dec.	186

3.8.1. Establishing the Regression Lines

Examination of Fig. 3.3 reveals that there is a probable downward trend from January through June and an upward trend from July through December. If we assume this to be true, a regression line can be determined for the data for January through June of both years combined and another regression line for July through December of both years. The two lines will be adjusted to give a smooth pattern. These calculations are shown in Table 3.6.

Table 3.6. Computations for Regression Lines with Cyclic Demand

Month	Period (t)	Demand (x)	t−3.5 (h)	x−168 (k)	(h)²	(hk)	(k)²
Jan.	1	175	−2.5	7	6.25	−17.5	49
Feb.	2	182	−1.5	14	2.25	−21.0	196
Mar.	3	156	−0.5	−12	0.25	6.0	144
Apr.	4	180	0.5	12	0.25	6.0	144
May	5	158	1.5	−10	2.25	−15.0	100
June	6	143	2.5	−25	6.25	−62.5	625
Jan.	1	194	−2.5	26	6.25	−65.0	676
Feb.	2	190	−1.5	22	2.25	−33.0	484
Mar.	3	168	−0.5	0	0.25	0.0	0
Apr.	4	165	0.5	−3	0.25	−1.5	9
May	5	153	1.5	−15	2.25	−22.5	225
June	6	145	2.5	−23	6.25	−57.5	529
	Total		0.0	−7	35.00	−283.5	3181
July	7	150	−2.5*	−18	6.25	45.0	324
Aug.	8	144	−1.5	−24	2.25	36.0	576
Sept.	9	177	−0.5	9	0.25	−4.5	81
Oct.	10	171	0.5	3	0.25	1.5	9
Nov.	11	185	1.5	17	2.25	25.5	289
Dec.	12	177	2.5	9	6.25	22.5	81
July	7	152	−2.5	−16	6.25	40.0	256
Aug.	8	162	−1.5	−6	2.25	9.0	36
Sept.	9	162	−0.5	−6	0.25	3.0	36
Oct.	10	172	0.5	4	0.25	2.0	16
Nov.	11	177	1.5	9	2.25	13.5	81
Dec.	12	186	2.5	18	6.25	45.0	324
	Total		0.0	−1	35.00	238.5	2109

*Values are $t − 9.5$.

There are two regression lines in this case:
1. When $t = 1, 2, \ldots, 6$, $x' = 194 − 7.5t$
2. When $t = 7, 8, \ldots, 12$, $x' = 97 + 7.5t$

where the period numbers repeat the series 1 through 12 for each year. These lines are shown in Fig. 3.3.

The above calculations can also be done by the shorter method presented in Section 3.7.1.1. The results are

$$\bar{x}_1 = 167.42$$

$$m_1 = -\frac{567}{2} = -283.5$$

$$x_1' = 195.77 - 8.10t$$

$$\bar{x}_2 = 167.92$$

$$m_2 = \frac{477}{2} = 238.5$$

$$x_2' = 103.12 + 6.82t$$

$$b = \frac{(8.1 + 6.8)}{2} = 7.5$$

$$x' = 167.42 + 3.5(7.5) - 7.5t, \quad t = 1, 2, \ldots, 6$$

$$x' = 167.92 - 9.5(7.5) + 7.5t, \quad t = 7, 8, \ldots, 12$$

The above can be reduced to:

$$x' = 194 - 7.5t, \quad t = 1, 2, \ldots, 6$$

$$x' = 97 + 7.5t, \quad t = 7, 8, \ldots, 12$$

Thus, we have established a forecasting method for cyclic demand by a statistical approach to the problem.

3.8.2. The Estimate of Error in the Forecast

Again, the standard deviations of the variations about the regression lines can be computed in a manner similar to that of Section 3.7.2. By combining the results, a reasonable value for s_{xt} is 7. This value is used in the same manner as before.

3.8.3. Summary of the Forecast for Example 3

The forecast for demand from the data presented as Example 3 is
1. The expected demand is $x' = 194 - 7.5t$, when $t = 1, 2, \ldots, 6$ (January through June), and $x' = 97 + 7.5t$, when $t = 7, 8, \ldots, 12$ (July through December).
2. The standard error of the estimate, s_{xt}, is 7 units.
3. In 95 out of 100 months, the actual demand should fall within limits of $x' + 14$ and $x' - 14$ units inclusive.

3.9. Example 4: Cyclic Demand Following an Upward Trend with Random Variations Superimposed.

A variation of Examples 2 and 3 might occur if demand is cyclic but also following an upward trend. Such a demand pattern is present in the data of Table 3.7. The data is shown graphically in Fig. 3.4, and a trend appears

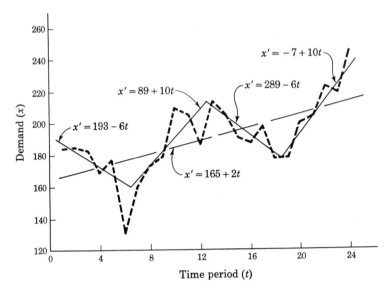

Fig. 3.4. Cyclic demand following an upward trend with random variations superimposed.

Table 3.7. Cyclic Demand Following an Upward Trend with Random Variations Superimposed

Period	Month	Demand	Period	Month	Demand
1	Jan.	184	13	Jan.	214
2	Feb.	185	14	Feb.	206
3	Mar.	183	15	Mar.	191
4	Apr.	169	16	Apr.	188
5	May	177	17	May	198
6	June	131	18	June	178
7	July	160	19	July	178
8	Aug.	173	20	Aug.	200
9	Sept.	179	21	Sept.	205
10	Oct.	210	22	Oct.	223
11	Nov.	206	23	Nov.	219
12	Dec.	187	24	Dec.	245

to exist throughout the total time as well as cyclic variations around that trend. Again, regression lines are useful in forecasting for this type of demand pattern.

3.9.1. Establishing the Regression Lines

The regression lines are established in three steps:
1. Find the regression line for all of the data.
2. Find regression lines for the cycle about the regression line found in step (1).
3. Combine the results.

The regression line for all of the data is

$$x' = 165 + 2t$$

The regression lines to be used for forecasting are

$$x' = 385 - 6t, \text{ when } t = 25, 26, \ldots, 30$$
$$x' = -103 + 10t, \text{ when } t = 31, 32, \ldots, 36$$

These lines are determined approximately and do not completely minimize the sum of squares of the x deviations about the regression lines. The four regression lines shown in Fig. 3.4 are

$$x' = 193 - 6t, \text{ when } t = 1, 2, \ldots, 6$$
$$x' = 89 + 10t, \text{ when } t = 7, 8, \ldots, 12$$
$$x' = 289 - 6t, \text{ when } t = 13, 14, \ldots, 18$$
$$x' = -7 + 10t, \text{ when } t = 19, 20, \ldots, 24$$

Based on the above, your forecast for next January is $385 - 6(25) = 235$; for next December it is $-103 + 10(36) = 257$. The slope of the regression line stays the same, but the intercept changes from year to year. For periods 37 through 42, the intercept is $385 + 96$, or 481. For periods 43 through 48, the intercept is $-103 - 96$, or -199. Note that the intercepts change by 96 units each year.

3.9.2. The Estimate of Error in the Forecast

The estimate of error in this case is the standard deviation of the variations about the regression lines. Perhaps the easiest and most straightforward method of computing this parameter is to calculate the regression line values for each of the 24 periods using the regression lines from Section 3.9.1. After doing this, find the differences between the regression line values and the corresponding actual demands; square these values; sum; divide by 23; and take the square root.

The standard error of the estimate for the forecasting method for Example 4 is 10.4, or 10. Again, the previous interpretations of this parameter apply. (Since the regression line is approximate, the value of s_{xt} is also approximate.)

3.9.3. Summary of the Forecast for Example 4

The forecast for the data of Example 4 can be summarized as follows:
1. The expected demand is
    a. $x' = 385 - 6t$, when $t = 25, 26, \ldots, 30$ (January through June of the third year).
    b. $x' = -103 + 10t$, when $t = 31, 32, \ldots, 36$ (July through December of the third year).
2. The standard error of the estimate, s_{xt}, is 10 units.
3. In 95 out of 100 months, the actual demand should fall within the range $x' + 20$ and $x' - 20$ units inclusive.

3.10. The Moving Average as a Forecast Method

The moving average can be used as a forecasting method. In certain cases, it may be advantageous, whereas in others it may give rather inaccurate results. The moving average uses only a certain predetermined number of past demands. The moving average is the sum of the demands for the desired number of past periods divided by the number of demands included in the sum. Each period, a new moving average is computed by dropping the demand for the most prior period and adding the demand for the most recent period.

To see how the moving average works, suppose that we choose to use the last seven periods in each of the four previous examples. Our forecasts are
1. Example 1: 123 units $[(128 + 127 + \cdots + 110)/7]$.
2. Example 2: 84 units.
3. Example 3: 165 units.
4. Example 4: 207 units.

The forecasts by the statistical methods previously discussed are
1. Example 1: 125 units.
2. Example 2: 89 units.
3. Example 3: 186.5 units.
4. Example 4: 235 units.

From the above, we can see that as the demand pattern departs from a constant or level demand, the moving average gives results which may vary widely from the statistical results based on the regression lines. It is possible to use moving averages with correction factors, but even then, we may find rather large discrepancies between the methods.

It is characteristic of the moving averages that:
1. They lag a trend; i.e., they give lower values than the regression line for an upward trend and higher values than the regression line for a downward trend. If correction factors are used, the moving averages should vary randomly about the regression lines.

2. They are out of phase (lagging) when the data is cyclic. The amount of lag is dependent on the number of periods used in the moving average.
3. The maximum forecast by a moving average will be less than the maximum demand in a cyclic pattern, whereas the minimum forecast will exceed the minimum actual demand of a cyclic pattern.

The underlying assumptions when the moving averages are used are the same as for the statistical methods presented in Sections 3.6 through 3.9, inclusive.

We can obtain an estimate of the error in a moving-average forecast by the same methods as were previously used. To be correct, it should be computed each time a new forecast is made (period by period).

The moving-average forecast is logically for only one month (period) in the future. It can be extended for longer periods of time if you take into consideration the cycles, etc., that may occur. In most instances, you should expect a moving-average forecast to be less accurate than a forecast by the more precise statistical methods previously discussed.

3.11. The Weighted-Average Forecast

The weighted-average forecast places more emphasis on the more recent demands than on the prior demands. Mathematically, the weighted average is defined as

$$f_0 = (1 - w)d_{-1} + (1 - w)wd_{-2} + (1 - w)w^2 d_{-3} + \cdots \\ + (1 - w)w^{k-1}d_{-k} + \cdots \qquad (3.6)$$

where f_0 is the forecast for the next period.

w is the weighting factor, $(0 < w < 1)$.

d_{-k} is the demand experienced in the kth period prior to the present.

The forecasts for the data previously used by the weighted average method with $w = 0.2$ are

1. Example 1: 112.3 units $[(0.8)(110) + (0.8)(0.2)(120) + (0.8)(0.2)^2 (130) + (0.8)(0.2)^3(135) + (0.8)(0.2)^4(109)]$.
2. Example 2: 100.4 units.
3. Example 3: 183.8 units.
4. Example 4: 239.6 units.

These values differ from those previously computed. Also, a different choice of weighting factor will give you different forecasts.

There are certain characteristics of the weighted-average forecast that should be recognized. Some of the important characteristics are shown in Table 3.8.

Table 3.8. Effect of Choice of Weighting Factor on the Forecast
Under Several Demand Patterns

Type of Demand Pattern	Value of Weighting Factor	
	$w \to 0$	$w \to 1$
Constant (no variation)	Forecast equals demand.	Forecast equals demand.
Varying about an average value	Forecast approaches demand but lags by about one period.	Forecast approaches the average.
An upward trend	Forecast approaches demand but lags by about one period. (Forecast is lower.)	Forecast has an upward slope and lags demand by several periods. (Forecast is lower.)
A downward trend	Forecast approaches demand but lags by about one period. (Forecast is higher.)	Forecast has a downward trend but a lesser slope. (Forecast is higher.)
Cyclic	Forecast approaches demand but lags by about one period. (Maximum forecast is less than maximum demand and minimum forecast is greater than minimum demand.)	Forecast approaches the average. (Any cyclic pattern in the forecast lags the cyclic pattern in demand by several periods.)

Once the first forecast has been established by a weighted average, the following forecasts are obtained by:

$$f_0 = (1 - w)d_{-1} + wf_{-1} \qquad (3.7)$$

where f_{-1} is the last prior forecast.

The weighted-average method is a modification of the arithmetic average and moving average methods. It is difficult to arrive at an estimate of the error in a forecast made by this method.

3.12. Other Statistical Techniques

In the previous discussions, we have assumed the relationship between demand and time to be either random (Example 1) or linear and random (Examples 2, 3, and 4). With that assumption, we were correct in using forms of linear regression for the discussions of Sections 3.7, 3.8, and 3.9. In those discussions, we have considered that a time series may be comprised of three components:

1. Random variations.

2. Trends.

3. Cycles or oscillations (but only linear variations).

However, both the trend and the cycles may be nonlinear. When the last two components exist, we also assume that there is a definite cause system from which they were generated.*

Random variations are those variations which have no pattern and are thus unpredictable. We can, however, predict the range of variation under certain conditions and with certain probabilities.

Trends are predictable, persistent, unidirectional patterns in the data. Trends may be linear or curvilinear. For purposes of demand forecasting, they should be expected to persist.

Cycles or oscillations are persistent, alternate ups and downs in the data. They are also predictable. These variations may be linear or curvilinear, too. In demand, the usual period of a cycle is expected to be one year or less, although this is not a requirement.

In demand forecasting, the trend and the cycle may be important even though the data is rather limited. This statement is predicated on the fact that demand for a product is a dynamic thing and thus is probably changing. In a time series, time is long or short depending on the nature of the data involved. For example, in geologic time, years are microscopic, whereas in the life of some elementary particles, microseconds are long.

The nature of business presents two facts which must be recognized:

1. It is doubtful that reliable and relevant data is available for more than four or five years.

2. Most detailed production planning periods will not exceed one year because of the uncertainty of the more distant future.

Time series can be represented in a number of ways. Two additional representations we will examine are

1. An algebraic series in t.

2. A trigonometric function in t.

The algebraic series in t can be expressed as

$$x' = b_0 + b_1 t + b_2 t^2 + \cdots + b_q t^q \tag{3.8}$$

The trigonometric representation is

$$x' = b_0 + b_1 t + b_2 \sin \frac{\pi(c_1 t + c_2)}{b_4} + b_3 \cos \frac{\pi(c_3 t + c_4)}{b_5} \tag{3.9}$$

If the only constants that exist are b_0 and b_1, we have the linear regression line of Eq. (3.3). If more constants exist, we have either a higher-order

---

*For an interesting and more extended discussion, see, M. G. Kendall, *The Advanced Theory of Statistics*, Volume 2, London: Charles Griffin and Company, Limited, 1946, pages 369–371.

equation in t or a trigonometric pattern superimposed on an average value [if $b_1 = 0$ in (3.9)] or on a regression line [if $b_1 \neq 0$ in (3.9)].

The desirability of extending a series beyond a quadratic or cubic is questionable unless

1. The pattern has persisted for a long period of time with only small random variations (the implication being that it will continue to follow the same pattern).

2. The product is very expensive, has a limited storage life, yet is highly competitive.

In regression analysis the usual assumption is that the line or curve which minimizes the sum of the squares of the deviations from the regression line is the line of best fit. Thus, it is necessary to decide how good a fit is desirable. In demand forecasting, we know there are random variations, and the polynomial that fits every point may give a very poor forecast. Such a procedure may involve a considerable amount of unnecessary computation.

3.12.1 Curvilinear Regression

When we assume the data to have a curvilinear form, we run into a more extensive problem in computation. The best approach is to start with $q = 1$, and to determine the regression line and the sum of squares of the deviations from that line. Then proceed to do the same things for $q = 2$, $q = 3$, etc. until you are satisfied with the fit or until you find that the next higher value of q gives a poorer fit.

In regression, the function to be minimized is

$$E = \Sigma \, (x - b_0 - b_1 t - b_2 t^2 - \cdots - b_q t^q)^2 \tag{3.10}$$

If (3.10) is differentiated with respect to b_j and set equal to zero, we get one equation for each value of j. In all, there are j equations, whose solution can be put in the form of the determinant:

$$\begin{vmatrix} x' & 1 & t & t^2 & \ldots & t^q \\ u_{01} & u_0 & u_1 & u_2 & \ldots & u_q \\ u_{11} & u_1 & u_2 & u_3 & \ldots & u_{q+1} \\ \cdot & \cdot & \cdot & \cdot & \ldots & \cdot \\ \cdot & \cdot & \cdot & \cdot & \ldots & \cdot \\ \cdot & \cdot & \cdot & \cdot & \ldots & \cdot \\ u_{q1} & u_q & u_{q+1} & u_{q+2} & \ldots & u_{2q} \end{vmatrix} = 0 \tag{3.11}$$

where $u_j =$ the jth moment of t.

$u_{j1} =$ the bivariate moment, $\Sigma \, (t^j x)$.

The solution of the determinant of (3.11) gives the regression curve to the qth power of t.

3.12.1.1. *Curvilinear Regression Applied to Example 2.* Although the data of Example 2 appear to follow a linear trend, it is possible that a quadratic equation might fit better. In order to make such a computation (using h and k as in Table 3.4, instead of t and x), we need additional sums. These are the $\Sigma\ h^2k/n$, $\Sigma\ h^3/n$, and $\Sigma\ h^4/n$. For the case where $q = 2$, Eq. (3.11) takes the form:

$$\begin{vmatrix} k & 1 & h & h^2 \\ u_{01} & u_0 & u_1 & u_2 \\ u_{11} & u_1 & u_2 & u_3 \\ u_{21} & u_2 & u_3 & u_4 \end{vmatrix} = 0$$

where $u_{01} = \Sigma\ k/n = 11/24 = 0.4583$

$u_{11} = \Sigma\ hk/n = 1108/24 = 46.1667$

$u_{21} = \Sigma\ h^2k/n = 4010/24 = 167.0833$

$u_0 = 1$

$u_1 = \Sigma\ h/n = 12/24 = 0.5000$

$u_2 = \Sigma\ h^2/n = 1156/24 = 48.1667$

$u_3 = \Sigma\ h^3/n = 10{,}440/24 = 870.0000$

$u_4 = \Sigma\ h^4/n = 100{,}684/24 = 4195.1667$

From this the quadratic regression curve is

$$x' = 86.90 - 1.28t + 0.05t^2$$

and a more exact regression line is

$$x' = 64.47 + 0.96t$$

The sum of squares of the deviations from the quadratic curve is 4005, compared to the sum of squares of the deviations about the regression line, which is 2254 (these are the results of rounding the x' values to the nearest whole number). In this example, the linear regression line gives a better fit than the quadratic curve.

There is no way of telling beforehand if a second-degree or third-degree equation will give a better fit than a line. It is a matter of evaluation after computation.

Another possible method of determining the regression curves is the use of orthogonal polynomials. These techniques will not be discussed here, but the interested reader is referred to Kendall.*

*M. G. Kendall, *The Advanced Theory of Statistics*, pages 146–149.

3.12.2. The Trigonometric Form Applied to Example 4

The data of Example 4 appear to have a trigonometric form super-imposed on an upward trend. Therefore, it may be more reasonable to use a form of Eq. (3.9) rather than a series of regression lines.

In Example 4, the regression lines cross the over-all trend at $t = 3.5$, 9.5, 15.5, and 21.5. From this fact, we can assume the period of the cycle to be 12 time units and the appropriate angles to be described by

$$\frac{\pi}{12}(2t - 1)$$

(The angles are 15 deg, 45 deg, 75 deg, ...) Furthermore, since the data start at an apparent maximum, we will assume that $b_2 = 0$ in Eq. (3.9). (The desired forecasting equation then becomes a function of t and

$$\cos\frac{\pi}{12}(2t - 1)$$

At this point, we have established values for the following parameters:

$$b_2 = 0$$
$$c_3 = 2$$
$$c_4 = -1$$
$$b_5 = 12$$

Also, we have reduced Eq. (3.9) to

$$x' = b_0 + b_1 t + b_3 \cos \pi(2t - 1)/12$$

The next step is to use the least squares approach to find the forecasting function with the best fit.

The function to be minimized is

$$E = \Sigma \left(x - b_0 - b_1 t - b_3 \cos \frac{\pi(2t - 1)}{12} \right)^2 \qquad (3.12)$$

The least squares solution of Eq. (3.12) is

$$\begin{vmatrix} x' & 1 & t & \cos A \\ \Sigma x & n & \Sigma t & \Sigma \cos A \\ \Sigma xt & \Sigma t & \Sigma t^2 & \Sigma t \cos A \\ \Sigma x \cos A & \Sigma \cos A & \Sigma t \cos A & \Sigma \cos^2 A \end{vmatrix} = 0 \qquad (3.13)$$

where $A = \dfrac{\pi(2t - 1)}{12}$.

When the data of Example 4 are used, the solution of Eq. (3.13) is

$$x' = 165 + 2t + 20 \cos \frac{\pi(2t - 1)}{12} \qquad (3.14)$$

This has a slightly larger sum of squares than the best linear regression lines. However, the use of the trigonometric function has one computational advantage: regardless of its form, it assumes the continuity of time. The linear regression lines previously used have required a recursion in the time scale or a change in the line intercept.

3.13. Determination of the Periodicity of Demand Data

In Section 3.12.2, we more or less arbitrarily assumed a certain periodicity for the data. It is possible to approach this problem from a statistical standpoint. Such techniques are in the realm of autocorrelation and autoregression.*

In general, we can usually determine the periodicity of such data from observation. Most demand patterns that have seasonal patterns will have maximums and minimums that are functions of the product and time (season) of the year. The autocorrelation techniques become useful when the seasonality is not obvious.

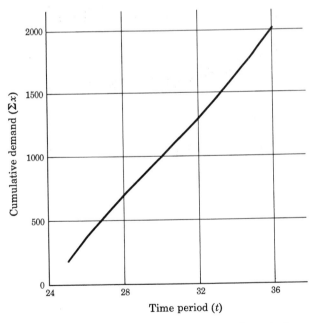

Fig. 3.5. Cumulative forecast demand for Example 3.

*For the formulation and a discussion of these techniques, the reader is referred to Maurice G. Kendall, "*The Advanced Theory of Statistics,*" Chapter 30.

Table 3.9. Cumulative Demand for Examples 1, 2, 3, and 4

Period	Month	Demand							
		Example 1		Example 2		Example 3		Example 4	
		Monthly	Cumulative	Monthly	Cumulative	Monthly	Cumulative	Monthly	Cumulative
25	Jan.	125	125	89	89	187	187	235	235
26	Feb.	125	250	90	179	179	366	229	464
27	Mar.	125	375	91	270	172	538	223	687
28	Apr.	125	500	92	362	164	702	217	904
29	May	125	625	93	455	157	859	211	1115
30	June	125	750	94	549	149	1008	205	1320
31	July	125	875	95	644	149	1157	207	1527
32	Aug.	125	1000	96	740	157	1314	217	1744
33	Sept.	125	1125	97	837	164	1478	227	1971
34	Oct.	125	1250	98	935	172	1650	237	2208
35	Nov.	125	1375	99	1034	179	1829	247	2455
36	Dec.	125	1500	100	1134	187	2016	257	2712

3.14. The Total-Demand Forecast

The total-demand forecast is the accumulated expected demand over a number of forecast periods. In production planning it may be desirable to have this information.

The accumulated demands for the data given in Examples 1, 2, 3, and 4 are given in Table 3.9. The cumulative demand for Example 3 is shown in Fig. 3.5.

The expected error in a forecast of this type is approximately $s_x\sqrt{n}$ or $s_{xt}\sqrt{n}$, where n is the number of periods accumulated. For example, for Fig. 3.5, the expected range of the cumulated demand through the thirty-third period is $\pm 2(7)\sqrt{9}$ or ± 42 units.

3.15. Summary

This chapter has discussed some of the subjective and some of the objective methods of demand forecasting. The best candidates for accurate forecasting methods are the statistical techniques based on an analysis of past demand data with adjustments for predictable events of the future.

One of the essential requirements of an effective production and inventory planning and control system is an accurate and reliable forecast. Since we cannot predict the future exactly, we must also estimate the error that may exist in our prediction. The most reliable techniques for this are statistical procedures.

An advantage of the techniques discussed in this chapter is that they are designed to be useful for predicting not for just one, but for several periods into the future. We must realize that the accuracy of the forecast decreases with an increase in the length of the forecast period. The forecast should be revised only when there has been a change in the underlying cause system. The methods presented in this chapter can be refined, or more elaborate and refined methods may be used. We must not confuse preciseness with accuracy. To be precise with erroneous data or an improper method only leads to a false sense of accomplishment.

4. Controlling the Forecast*

4.1. Introduction

Once the forecast has been made, we cannot ignore it until it is time to make the next forecast. To do a good job of forecasting requires that we continually compare the forecast against actual demand and take action to revise the forecast when there is a statistically significant change in demand. Also, we must determine the cause or causes of such changes in demand. The time to do this is immediately after the change occurs, not next year or five years later.

There are many devices that can be used to detect any changes in demand. However, many require a considerable quantity of data and this amount of data may not be available. The simplest forms of control devices are the statistical control charts used in quality control. One such chart that can be used where there is a minimum quantity of data available is the moving-range chart.

4.2. The Moving-Range Chart

The moving-range chart compares the changes in demand from one

*This material adapted from John E. Biegel, "Statistics in Forecasting," *Management International*, 1961/6, November–December 1961, pages 162–189.

period to the next with the expected random variations in demand. The moving range (MR) is the absolute value of the difference between demand in successive periods. For example, the moving range for January–February of Table 3.2 is $|109 - 118| = 9$, and the moving range for February–March is $|118 - 108| = 10$.

The moving range-chart is constructed as follows:

1. Determine the difference between actual demand and the values determined from the forecasting equations.
2. Determine the moving-range.
3. Compute the average moving-range $(M\bar{R})$.
4. Compute the control limits $(UCL = +2.66M\bar{R}, LCL = -2.66M\bar{R})$.
5. Plot the control chart (plot the values found in step 1 and the control limits found in step 4).

There should be at least 10 and preferably 20 MR values used in determining the control limits. These limits are set so that only three points in 1000 would be expected to fall outside the limits due to chance alone. Thus, if a point is outside the control limits, we should make a preliminary investigation to see if there has been any obvious change in the underlying cause system. Also, it serves as a warning that we should watch this product very closely. If another point goes outside the control limits, a detailed investigation should be made of the cause for such an occurrence.

If all of the points plotted fall within the control limits, it is generally safe to assume that we have the right forecasting equations. If points fall outside the limits, we apparently do not have the correct forecasting equations, and they should be revised accordingly. We can use the control chart to tell us where the change occurred and can determine a forecasting equation from the data appropriate to the present demand cause system.

4.2.1. The Moving-Range Chart for Example 1

The computations for the moving-range chart for Example 1 are shown in Table 4.1. The moving-range chart is plotted in Fig. 4.1. All of the points fall within the limits.

Since the demand for periods 1 through 24 is in control, the best forecast for the future is the average of past demand of 125 units of product per month. We should also watch for runs or trends, as well as points outside the control limits, on the control chart. If a sizable number of points begin to appear on one side of the center line of the chart, there has probably been a significant shift in demand.

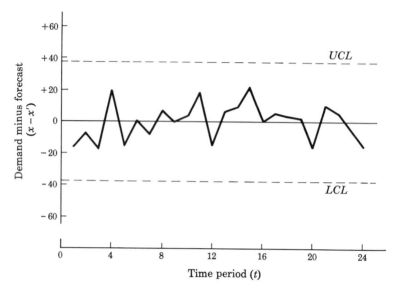

Fig. 4.1. Moving-range chart for Example 1.

4.2.2. The Moving-Range Chart for Example 2

The computations for the moving-range chart for Example 2 are shown in Table 4.2, and the moving-range chart is shown in Fig. 4.2.

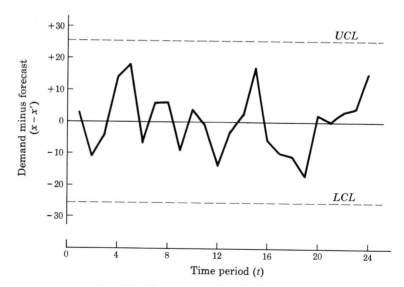

Fig. 4.2. Moving-range chart for Example 2.

Table 4.1. Computations for the Moving-Range Chart for Example 1

Month	Period	Demand	Moving-Range	Demand Minus Forecast Equation Value ($x' = 125$)
Jan.	1	109		−16
			9	
Feb.	2	118		−7
			10	
Mar.	3	108		−17
			37	
Apr.	4	145		20
			35	
May	5	110		−15
			16	
June	6	126		1
			9	
July	7	117		−8
			15	
Aug.	8	132		7
			7	
Sept.	9	125		0
			3	
Oct.	10	128		3
			15	
Nov.	11	143		18
			33	
Dec.	12	110		−15
			21	
Jan.	13	131		6
			3	
Feb.	14	134		9
			13	
Mar.	15	147		22
			22	
Apr.	16	125		0
			5	
May	17	130		5
			2	
June	18	128		3
			1	
July	19	127		2
			18	
Aug.	20	109		−16
			26	
Sept.	21	135		10
			5	
Oct.	22	130		5
			10	
Nov.	23	120		−5
			10	
Dec.	24	110		−15
			325	

$M\bar{R} = 325/23 = 14.1, \; UCL = +2.66M\bar{R} = 37.5, \; LCL = -2.66M\bar{R} = -37.5$

Table 4.2. Moving-Range Chart Computations for Example 2

Month	Period	Demand	Forecasting Equation Value	Difference	Moving Range
Jan.	1	68	65	3	
					14
Feb.	2	55	66	−11	
					7
Mar.	3	63	67	−4	
					18
Apr.	4	82	68	14	
					4
May	5	87	69	18	
					25
June	6	63	70	−7	
					13
July	7	77	71	6	
					0
Aug.	8	78	72	6	
					17
Sept.	9	62	73	−11	
					15
Oct.	10	78	74	4	
					5
Nov.	11	74	75	−1	
					13
Dec.	12	62	76	−14	
					11
Jan.	13	74	77	−3	
					5
Feb.	14	80	78	2	
					15
Mar.	15	96	79	17	
					23
Apr.	16	74	80	−6	
					4
May	17	71	81	−10	
					1
June	18	71	82	−11	
					6
July	19	66	83	−17	
					19
Aug.	20	86	84	2	
					2
Sept.	21	85	85	0	
					3
Oct.	22	89	86	3	
					1
Nov.	23	91	87	4	
					11
Dec.	24	103	88	15	—
					232

$M\overline{R} = 232/23 = 10.1, UCL = 2.66(10.1) = +26.9, LCL = -2.66(10.1) = -26.9$

Like the moving-range chart for Example 1, this chart shows control. Again, assuming that the same cause system for demand will continue, we have arrived at the best forecasting equations based on the least squares criterion.

4.2.3. The Moving-Range Chart for Example 3

The computations for the moving-range chart for Example 3 are shown in Table 4.3, and the chart is plotted in Fig. 4.3. In this example, we used the cyclic type of forecasting equations.

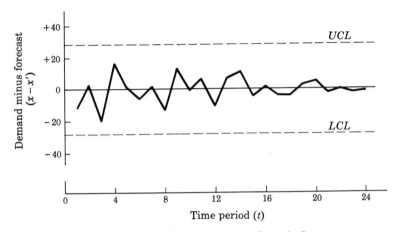

Fig. 4.3. Moving-range chart for Example 3.

4.2.4. The Moving-Range Chart for Example 4

The moving-range chart computations for Example 4 are shown in Table 4.4. The moving-range chart is shown in Fig. 4.4. By constructing

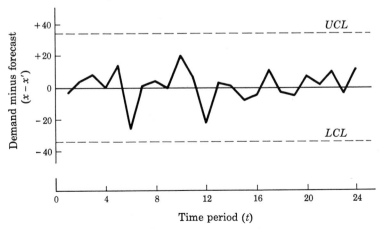

Fig. 4.4. Moving-range chart for Example 4.

Table 4.3. Moving-Range Chart Calculations for Example 3

Month	Period	Demand	Forecasting Equation Value	Difference	Moving Range
Jan.	1	175	187	-12	
					15
Feb.	2	182	179	3	
					19
Mar.	3	156	172	-16	
					32
Apr.	4	180	164	16	
					15
May	5	158	157	1	
					7
June	6	143	149	-6	
					7
July	7	150	149	1	
					14
Aug.	8	144	157	-13	
					26
Sept.	9	177	164	13	
					14
Oct.	10	171	172	-1	
					7
Nov.	11	185	179	6	
					16
Dec.	12	177	187	-10	
					17
Jan.	13	194	187	7	
					4
Feb.	14	190	179	11	
					15
Mar.	15	168	172	-4	
					5
Apr.	16	165	164	1	
					5
May	17	153	157	-4	
					0
June	18	145	149	-4	
					7
July	19	152	149	3	
					2
Aug.	20	162	157	5	
					7
Sept.	21	162	164	-2	
					2
Oct.	22	172	172	0	
					2
Nov.	23	177	179	-2	
					1
Dec.	24	186	187	-1	
					239

$M\bar{R} = 239/23 = 10.4$, $UCL = 2.66(10.4) = 27.7$, $LCL = -2.66(10.4) = -27.7$

Table 4.4. Moving-Range Chart Calculations for Example 4

Month	Period	Demand	Forecasting Equation Value	Difference	Moving Range
Jan.	1	184	187	−3	
					7
Feb.	2	185	181	4	
					4
Mar.	3	183	175	8	
					8
Apr.	4	169	169	0	
					14
May	5	177	163	14	
					40
June	6	131	157	−26	
					27
July	7	160	159	1	
					3
Aug.	8	173	169	4	
					4
Sept.	9	179	179	0	
					21
Oct.	10	210	189	21	
					14
Nov.	11	206	199	7	
					29
Dec.	12	187	209	−22	
					25
Jan.	13	214	211	3	
					2
Feb.	14	206	205	1	
					9
Mar.	15	191	199	−8	
					3
Apr.	16	188	193	−5	
					16
May	17	198	187	11	
					14
June	18	178	181	−3	
					2
July	19	178	183	−5	
					12
Aug.	20	200	193	7	
					5
Sept.	21	205	203	2	
					8
Oct.	22	223	213	10	
					14
Nov.	23	219	223	−4	
					16
Dec.	24	245	233	12	
					———
					297

$M\bar{R} = 297/23 = 12.9,\ UCL = 2.66(12.9) = 34.3,\ LCL = -2.66(12.9) = -34.3$

Table 4.5. Comparison of Forecast Demand and Actual Demand for Examples 1, 2, 3, and 4

Month	Period	Example 1			Example 2			Example 3			Example 4		
		Forecast	Demand	D − F	Forecast	Demand	D − F	Forecast	Demand	D − F	Forecast	Demand	D − F
Jan.	25	125	125	0	89	78	−11	187	199	12	235	240	5
Feb.	26	125	124	−1	90	71	−19	179	185	6	229	241	12
Mar.	27	125	111	−14	91	89	−2	172	165	−7	223	224	1
Apr.	28	125	137	12	92	100	8	164	168	4	217	200	−17
May	29	125	120	−5	93	107	14	157	145	−12	211	197	−14
June	30	125	114	−11	94	100	6	149	141	−8	205	189	−16
July	31	125	104	−21	95	86	−9	149	154	5	207	201	−6
Aug.	32	125	95	−30	96	94	−2	157	165	8	217	205	−12
Sept.	33	125	118	−7	97	85	−12	164	189	25	227	225	−2
Oct.	34	125	124	−1	98	110	12	172	171	−1	237	241	4
Nov.	35	125	120	−5	99	120	21	179	167	−12	247	232	−15
Dec.	36	125	117	−8	100	94	−6	187	199	12	257	275	18
Total		1500	1409	−91	1134	1134	0	2016	2048	32	2712	2670	−42

the charts in this manner, the cyclic variations and trends are removed, because the forecasting equations follow these trends and cycles.

4.3. Use of the Moving-Range Chart to Determine the Appropriateness of the Forecasting Equations

In the previous sections, we have examined the moving-range chart as a device to determine the correctness of the use of our forecasting equations for predicting the future demand from the past demand. The charts have verified that the past-demand data was from the same cause system. Now we want to examine the use of the moving-range chart to see if the future demand is created by the cause system that was operative in the past. To do this, we need to know the future demand.

Assume that the data given for the examples was more than one year ago and that the forecasting equations and control charts have been used during the past year. The demands for the past year are given in Table 4.5, along with the forecasts we had made, and the differences between the forecast and the actual demand have been computed.

The data for Example 1 show that the demand during that year was less than forecast in the last 8 months. Also, it has been less than forecast in 10 out of the last 12 months. This is a significant change, and the new forecast should be the arithmetic average of those past 8 periods. This average is 114 units, so our forecast for the next period is 114 units. Since we have revised the forecast, we must also revise the control chart. A new chart should be constructed with new limits based on the last 8 periods.

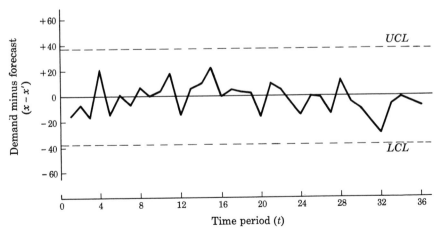

Fig. 4.5. Moving-range chart for Example 1 extended through the 36th period.

These limits should be considered temporary and should be occasionally revised until about 20 periods are included in the average moving-range. The new control limits are $+2.66(\frac{61}{7}) = +23.2$ and $-2.66(\frac{61}{7}) = -23.2$. So we have a change in demand and a possible decrease in variability. The moving-range control chart for Example 1 has been extended through the thirty-sixth period in Fig. 4.5.

To use the moving-range chart for controlling forecast, we should plot the difference between forecast and actual demand for each sales period as soon as the data is available. The point plotted on the control chart should be compared with the control limits. Also, we should check to see if trends from our forecasting equations are appearing. As long as the chart stays in control, we can assume that we have found a satisfactory forecasting method.

4.4. Summary

One procedure for evaluating a statistical forecasting method is the moving-range chart. It has the advantages of being an objective procedure as well as offering simplicity of construction and maintenance.

The control chart really tells three important things about a demand pattern:

1. It tells if the past demand is statistically stable.
2. It tells if the present demand is following the past pattern.
3. If the present demand is not following the past demand pattern, the control chart tells how to revise the forecasting method.

Thus, we accomplish several things with one very simple tool.

5. Economic Lot-Size Determinations

5.1. Introduction

In the purchase or in the manufacture of a product, there are certain cost elements which in combination should be minimized. Certainly, in an efficient manufacturing operation, the individual cost elements will be adjusted to assure that the over-all cost of the operation is at a minimum. The problem for consideration at this point is to control the quantities (units) of material manufactured or procured as a lot so that the over-all costs associated with the manufacture or the purchase are at a minimum. After a study of inventory systems, further comments will be made on the effect of the inventory system on the economic lot size.

5.2. Economic Lot-Size Determinations When Replenishment Is Instantaneous

The general solution of the economic lot-size problem is dependent on the nature of the replenishment of stock. Replenishment of stock can be instantaneous, or it can occur over a finite period of time. The problem where replenishment can be considered instantaneous will be considered first.

If the company selling the product of Example 1 were to buy a component of that product, certain costs would be involved. Those costs are the following:

1. The cost of procurement (order costs).

2. The cost of the material (item costs).

3. The cost of the storage of the material until it is used (storage costs).

The first of the above costs, order costs, arise from the internal and external costs associated with a purchase order. Such costs are exclusive of the second and third costs above (item costs and storage costs). Included in order costs are such items as the cost of the forms used, the cost of making a purchase requisition and processing it for approvals, the cost of obtaining quotations, the cost of processing a purchase order, the cost of following up and expediting the purchase order, the cost of transporting the goods, etc. In general, order costs include any cost whose size or amount is affected by the number of orders processed.

The second of the above costs, item costs, arise from the price of the material items. An element which must always be considered is the quantity discount which may be available. If the price break (change from one unit cost to a different unit cost which is lower) occurs in the region of the economic lot size at the higher price, it is well to check the total cost at the economic lot size at the higher unit price and the lot size at the price break and select that lot size which gives the minimum total cost for a period of time (usually a year).

The third of the above costs arises from the elements of cost that vary with the amount of material stored, or even with the fact that material is stored at all. Into this category go such items as taxes, insurance, handling, cost of using or for the rental of storage space, the cost of the money invested in the stock, costs due to the risk of spoilage or obsolescence, etc. If material is not stored, there will be no taxes or insurance to be paid, there will be no handling into or out of the storage area, there will be no space to provide or, if space is already available, it can be used for other profitable purposes. If no money is invested in stock, that money can be used to make money in other ways. If no inventory or stock exists, there is no risk of obsolescence or deterioration in quality.

The economic lot-size determination involves the consideration of two major factors, cost and quantity. In general terms, the problem of the economic lot-size determination or the minimum-cost lot size involves the minimization of total annual cost, which can be expressed as

$$C = \frac{As}{q_0} + sc + \frac{iq_0}{2} \tag{5.1}$$

where C = the total annual cost.

A = the order cost.

s = annual usage or annual demand.

q_0 = the quantity to be purchased in one lot.

c = the cost of a unit of purchased product.

i = the annual cost of storing one item.

In Eq. (5.1), the three cost elements are shown by the three expressions. The annual ordering cost is As/q_0. This can be easily seen if one considers that s/q_0 (annual usage divided by the quantity per order) is the number of orders per year. When this is multiplied by A (order cost per order), the result is the annual cost of placing orders. The annual material cost is sc, where s is the quantity to be purchased during the year, and c is the cost of each item purchased. The annual cost of storing material is the average quantity stored during the year, which is $q_0/2$, multiplied by the cost of storing an item, which is i dollars per unit. This can be expressed as follows:

> The total annual cost of purchasing material equals the cost of ordering the material plus the cost of the material plus the cost of storing the average amount of material in stock during the year.

If we differentiate Eq. (5.1) with respect to q_0 and solve for q_0, we obtain an expression for the minimum-cost order quantity or the economic lot size. This expression is

$$q_0 = \sqrt{\frac{2As}{i}} \tag{5.2}$$

Notice that the cost of each item, c, from Eq. (5.1) does not enter into the minimum-cost order quantity, q_0, obtained in Eq. (5.2). Therefore, we can arrive at the conclusion, which holds in general for all production-control problems, that any cost element that is not affected by the plan does not affect the solution.

5.2.1. Economic Lot-Size Determinations for Example 1

If we assume that we will purchase a component of the product in Example 1, there are certain costs associated with its purchase. For purposes of illustration, the following costs are appropriate:

A (order cost) = \$8.33

s (annual usage) = 1500 units

i (annual storage cost) = 0.10/unit/year

$$q_0 = \sqrt{\frac{2 \times 8.33 \times 1500}{0.10}} = 500 \text{ units}$$

Therefore, the minimum total annual cost would be realized if 500 units were ordered as needed. This means that $\frac{1500}{500}$, or 3, orders would be placed each year. Since the demand is essentially constant throughout the year, an order would be placed every $\frac{250}{3}$ days, or about every 83 days. (This assumes 250 working days in a year.) The quantity ordered and the spacing of orders will vary, depending on the inventory control system in use. This will be discussed at a later point. The reader should not concern himself about a decimal portion of an order presumably to be purchased in any given year, because, besides the inventory control system, the ordering interval may be affected by a departure of demand from forecast; also, if the material is not used in the year it is purchased, it will probably be used during the following year.

The above problem can also be solved graphically, as in Fig. 5.1. The

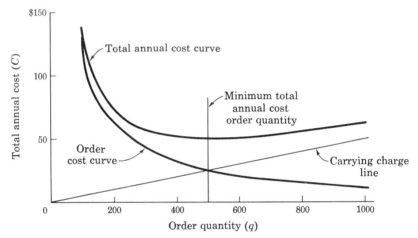

Fig. 5.1. Graphical economic purchased lot-size determination for Example 1.

order costs and the inventory carrying costs are plotted against order quantity. From these two the total cost is obtained. The order quantity with the minimum total cost is obtained from the minimum point of the total cost curve.

From Fig. 5.1 it can be seen that the minimum-cost order quantity occurs in a region of the total cost curve that is relatively flat. Actually, the total variable annual cost at 400 units per order is \$51.25; at 500 units per order it is \$50.00; at 600 units per order it is \$50.83; and at 700 units per order it is \$52.86. (These solutions neglect the unit costs.) From this it is seen that an increase of 40 per cent above the minimum total annual cost order quantity results in a very slight increase in the total cost (5.72 per cent).

5.3. Economic Lot-Size Determinations when Replenishment Occurs over a Finite Period of Time

If in the previous section we had assumed ideal conditions, i.e., a constant rate of usage, zero inventory at each replenishment point, and instantaneous replenishment, we would have an inventory pattern like that shown in Fig. 5.2.

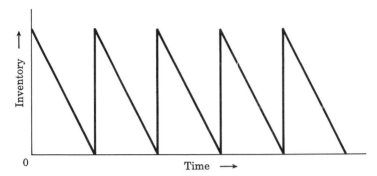

Fig. 5.2. Inventory under constant usage and instantaneous replenishment.

On the other hand, if we again assume the above conditions, except that we replace the instantaneous replenishment condition with the replenishment over a finite period of time, we get a situation similar to that portrayed by Fig. 5.3.

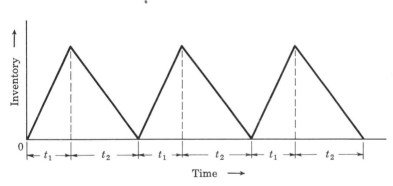

Fig. 5.3. Inventory under constant usage and replenishment over a finite period of time.

In this instance, replenishment of the inventory occurs over the time period t_1 of each cycle, and usage is occurring during $t_1 + t_2$, or the entire cycle. This has the effect of increasing the economic lot size, since the average quantity in inventory is no longer q_0, but something less than q_0.

If we add further definitions to those given for the economic lot size with instantaneous replenishment, we can arrive at an expression for the economic lot size with replenishment over a finite period of time. The required definitions are

$$p = \text{annual production rate}$$

$$q_m = \text{economic manufactured lot size}$$

With reference to Fig. 5.3, the inventory is increasing during t_1 at the daily rate of $(p - s)/250$. (This assumes that t_1 is in days.) The maximum inventory will be $(t_1)(p - s)/250$, and the average inventory will be $(t_1/2)$ $(p - s)/250$. But t_1 is equal to the economic lot size q_m, divided by the production rate p. Thus $t_1 = 250q_m/p$. Substituting this value of t_1 in the above, we obtain a value for the average inventory of

$$\left(\frac{250q_m}{2p}\right)\frac{(p - s)}{250} = \frac{q_m\left(1 - \dfrac{s}{p}\right)}{2}$$

By the same reasoning that was used to obtain Eq. (5.1), we obtain Eq. (5.3):

$$C = \frac{As}{q_m} + sc + \frac{iq_m\left(1 - \dfrac{s}{p}\right)}{2} \tag{5.3}$$

and through the use of calculus we can obtain an expression for q_m (economic manufactured lot size). This expression is

$$q_m = \sqrt{\frac{2As}{i\left(1 - \dfrac{s}{p}\right)}} \tag{5.4}$$

5.3.1. Determination of the Economic Manufactured Lot Size for Example 1

If the component of Example 1 were manufactured in our own plant with a setup cost of \$8.33, an annual usage of 1500 units, an annual storage cost of \$0.10/unit, and an annual production rate of 12,000 units, we could obtain the economic lot size. Note that these values are the same that were used previously except for the addition of the annual production rate. The economic manufactured lot size is

$$q_m = \sqrt{\frac{2(\$8.33)(1500)}{\$0.10\left(1 - \dfrac{1500}{12,000}\right)}} = 535 \text{ units}$$

The fact that inventory is built over a period of time instead of instantaneously results in a larger economic lot size.

5.4. Differences between Instantaneous Replenishment and Replenishment over a Finite Period of Time

We will further examine the above examples. We would place three orders per year if we were operating under conditions of instantaneous replenishment. Likewise, there would be $\frac{1500}{535}$, or 2.8, orders in the year if replenishment were from a source producing at the rate of 12,000 units per year. The condition of instantaneous replenishment occurs if the material is purchased in lots or if the production rate is sufficiently higher than the sales rate for the factor s/p to tend to zero. The production rate at a supplier's plant is of no concern in the determination of economic lot sizes unless it is such that the material is not delivered in lots as large as the economic purchased lot size. Under instantaneous replenishment, the maximum inventory is 500 units, and the average inventory is 250 units. Under replenishment from a source producing at 12,000 units per year, the maximum inventory is

$$535\left(1 - \frac{1500}{12,000}\right)$$

or 468, units, and the average inventory is 234 units. Therefore, even with a larger lot size, the average inventory is less under replenishment over a finite period of time.

The maximum inventory with instantaneous replenishment is q_0, and the average inventory is $q_0/2$. If inventory replenishment is from production over a finite period of time, the maximum inventory is $q_m\left(1 - \frac{s}{p}\right)$ and the average inventory is $\dfrac{q_m\left(1 - \dfrac{s}{p}\right)}{2}$.

The number of orders per year, n, is $\dfrac{s}{q}$ or $\sqrt{\dfrac{si}{2A}}$ with instantaneous replenishment of inventory and $\sqrt{\dfrac{si\left(1 - \dfrac{s}{p}\right)}{2A}}$ if inventory replenishment occurs over a finite period of time.

If we look at Eq. (5.4), we see that as s approaches p, lot size becomes very large. This seems natural since, if the amount produced is only slightly larger than the amount used, inventory will build very slowly. On the other hand, if p becomes very large compared to s, Eq. (5.4) approaches Eq. (5.2). Consequently, it can be said that if the production rate is very large compared to the sales or demand rate, the economic lot size becomes the same as for instantaneous replenishment. Also, if the production rate equals the sales rate, the most economic production level is continuous production.

5.5. Change in Time Periods

In the examples just given using Eq. (5.3) and (5.4), the time period used was one year. This restriction is not necessary so long as we have s and i for the same time period when Eq. (5.2) is used. This same condition applies to Eq. (5.4), but in Eq. (5.4) it is also necessary that the values of s and p used in the ratio s/p are for the same time period; however, they do not need to be for the same time period as the s and i above. This variation in time intervals can be illustrated from the previous examples. When we used Eq. (5.2), we could have used s and i for a month instead of a year. Then, s would have been $\frac{1500}{12}$, or 125, and i would have been $\$0.10/12$, or $\$0.00833$, per month. When these values are used,

$$q_0 = \sqrt{\frac{2(8.33)125}{0.00833}}$$

or 500 units. If we use these values of s and i and use s and p as units per day in the ratio s/p, we get

$$q_m = \sqrt{\frac{2(8.33)(125)}{0.00833\left(1 - \dfrac{6}{48}\right)}}$$

or 535 units.

5.6. Evaluation of the Effects of Changes in the Cost Elements

In (5.2), a change in A affects the minimum total annual cost order quantity by $\sqrt{A_1/A_0}$, where A_1 is the new order cost, and A_0 is the original order cost. The same type of relationship exists for changes in s. If there is a change in i, the change in the order quantity is inverse to the change in i, and the magnitude of the change in q_0 is $\sqrt{i_0/i_1}$. From this, we can arrive at the general conclusions given in Table 5.1.

5.7. Minimum-Cost Determinations for More Than One Product

When several products must be produced on the same equipment or production line, it may not be possible to schedule the minimum total annual cost order quantity of each product without extensive complications or excessive inventories. Such a situation can and does arise when the minimum total annual cost order quantities of the several products are expected to

Table 5.1. Effect of Changes in Cost Elements on the Minimum Total Annual Cost Order Quantity

	Factor	Direction of Change	Magnitude of Change in q	Direction of Change in q
$q_0 = \sqrt{\dfrac{2As}{i}}$	s	$+$	$\sqrt{\dfrac{s_1}{s_0}}$	$+$
	s	$-$		$-$
	A	$+$	$\sqrt{\dfrac{A_1}{A_0}}$	$+$
	A	$-$		$-$
	i	$+$	$\sqrt{\dfrac{i_0}{i_1}}$	$-$
	i	$-$		$+$
$q_m = \sqrt{\dfrac{2As}{i\left(1-\dfrac{s}{p}\right)}}$	s	$+$	$\sqrt{\dfrac{s_1\left(1-\dfrac{s_0}{p}\right)}{s_0\left(1-\dfrac{s_1}{p}\right)}}$	$+$
	s	$-$		$-$
	A	$+$	$\sqrt{\dfrac{A_1}{A_0}}$	$+$
	A	$-$		$-$
	i	$+$	$\sqrt{\dfrac{i_0}{i_1}}$	$-$
	i	$-$		$+$
	p	$+$	$\sqrt{\dfrac{1-\dfrac{s}{p_0}}{1-\dfrac{s}{p_1}}}$	$-$
	p	$-$		$+$

meet demand for an unequal number of days. The solution to such problems is only an extension of that when considering the production of only one product. With a slight modification, we arrive at an expression for the fraction of the yearly demand of each product rather than the quantity of each product to be produced.

The appropriate expression for the fraction of the yearly demand to be produced as a lot is:

$$f_s = \sqrt{\frac{2\,\Sigma\,A_k}{\Sigma\,s_k i_k\left(1 - \dfrac{s_k}{p_k}\right)}} \tag{5.5}$$

In Eq. (5.5), the definitions for A, s, i, and p are the same as those used in Section 5.3 and the subscript refers to the kth product. The conversion from the fraction of the yearly demand to the quantity to be produced as a lot is readily accomplished and is equal to s/f_s.

The best method for the solution of Eq. (5.5) is to use a tabular form as in Table 5.2. The fraction of yearly demand, f_s, from Table 5.2 is 0.0557. The

Table 5.2. Determination of Minimum Total Annual Cost Quantities of Several Products

Example	Sales Rate (Units/Year) s_k	Production Rate (Units/Year) p_k	Inventory Cost (Dollars/Unit/Year) i_k	Setup Cost (Dollars) A_k	$\left(1 - \dfrac{s_k}{p_k}\right)$	$s_k i_k \left(1 - \dfrac{s_k}{p_k}\right)$
1	1500	12,000	$ 5.00	$ 9.00	0.8750	6,562.50
2	1134	5,000	10.80	21.00	0.7732	9,469.54
3	2016	6,667	7.50	16.50	0.6976	10,547.71
4	2716	8,000	6.75	13.50	0.6605	12,108.95
				$60.00		38,688.70

conversions to quantities are made in Table 5.3. The number of production days per cycle are also shown in Table 5.3. These values are obtained by

Table 5.3. Units per Cycle and Days per Cycle
for Each of Several Products

Example	Units per Cycle	Days per Cycle
1	84	1.74
2	63	3.16
3	112	4.21
4	151	4.73
		13.84

multiplying the units per cycle by the production days per year and dividing that product by the units that can be produced in a year.

If a solution is attempted by the use of the economic lot size of each individual product, we obtain the results shown in Table 5.4.

Table 5.4. Individual Economic Lot Sizes for Several Products

Example	Economic Lot Size	Production Days per Lot	Sales Days per Lot	Lots per Year
1	78.6	1.64	13.1	19.1
2	75.5	3.78	16.6	15.1
3	112.8	4.23	14.0	17.9
4	128.3	4.01	11.8	21.2
		13.66		

A look at the column headed "Sales Days per Lot" in Table 5.4 shows that to schedule the four products requires a compromise. Note that an economic lot of the product of Example 4 will last only 11.8 days, whereas an economic lot of the product of Example 2 will last 16.6 days.

The total annual cost under the combined solution exceeds that under the individual solutions by a very small amount. Therefore, for a very small saving, we avoid the problem of trying to schedule each product at its own economic lot size. Further, it is probably impossible to schedule the production in economic lot sizes such that more than a small portion of this difference will be realized. In fact, such scheduling may actually result in a higher annual cost because of added planning and possibly added inventory.

There are two further comments to be made regarding the above method of solving the economic number of runs for several products: first, the farther the number of lots per year for each product departs from the number of lots per year under the combined solution, the greater the added cost;

second, in some cases, it may be possible to schedule an unequal number of lots of some of the products to reduce the total cost if there is a wide difference between the number of lots under the combined solution and the number of lots under the individual economic lot size solutions. For example, if product x has an economic manufactured lot size that is about twice that of products u, v, and w, then we should schedule two lots of u, v, and w for every lot of product x. Such an arrangement will probably prove the most economical.

5.8. Order Tables and Order Charts

It is possible to establish order tables and order charts (alignment charts) to use for determining economic lot sizes. These tables and charts can be constructed in a number of different forms depending on how you choose to use them.

Examination of Eq. (5.2) shows that q_0 is dependent on three other factors: A, s, and i. These factors may vary from product to product. However, the table can accommodate only two variables and one fixed factor. We can make a set of tables to cover the range of values we expect to see for A, s, and i. We will have the minimum number of tables if we choose the factor with the least number of different values as the fixed item for constructing the tables.

5.8.1. The Purchase-Lot-Size Order Table for Variable A and s with Fixed i

For purposes of illustration, an order table for $i = \$1.00$ is presented as Table 5.5. In Table 5.5, the order cost, A, varies from \$2.00 to \$8.00 in

Table 5.5. Order Table for $i = \$1.00$

A	s						$\sqrt{2A/i}$
	1200	2400	3600	4800	6000	7200	
2	69	98	120	139	155	170	2.000
3	85	120	147	170	190	208	2.449
4	98	139	170	196	219	240	2.828
5	110	155	190	219	245	268	3.162
6	120	170	208	240	268	294	3.464
7	130	183	225	259	290	318	3.742
8	138	196	240	277	310	339	4.000
$\sqrt{s}$	34.64	48.99	60.00	69.28	77.46	84.85	

one-dollar increments. The annual usage (demand), s, varies from 1200 units to 7200 units in 1200-unit increments. The same order sizes hold if both i and s are for one year, one month, etc. The multiplying factors used to construct the table are shown as the bottom row and the right-hand column. For instance, the economic purchased lot size when $A = \$5.00$, $s = 4800$ units, and $i = \$1.00$ is 219 units. This value, 219, equals the product of 3.162 and 69.28, the row and column multiplying factors respectively. To use the table, we select the row for the given value of A and the column for the given value of s and read the economic purchased lot size at the intersection of the chosen row and column.

5.8.2. The Manufactured-Lot-Size Order Table for Variable A and s with Fixed p and i

If we want an order table for manufactured lot sizes, we must consider the production rate. Now, to have complete coverage of all possibilities, we need to have a set of tables for different values of i and also for different values of p. This means that we would need a set of tables that, in number, equals the product of the number of values of i times the number of values of p. In Table 5.6, we have an order table for $i = \$1.00$, $p = 12,000$ units,

Table 5.6. Order Table for $i = \$1.00$ and $p = 12,000$ units per year

A	\multicolumn{6}{c}{s}	$\sqrt{2A/i}$
	1200	2400	3600	4800	6000	7200	$\sqrt{2A/i}$
20	231	346	454	566	693	849	6.324
30	283	424	555	693	848	1039	7.746
40	327	490	641	800	980	1200	8.944
50	365	548	717	894	1095	1342	10.000
60	400	600	786	980	1200	1470	10.954
70	432	648	849	1058	1296	1588	11.832
80	462	693	907	1131	1386	1697	12.649
$\sqrt{\dfrac{ps}{p-s}}$	36.52	54.77	71.71	89.44	109.54	134.16	

A takes on values in the range from \$20.00 to \$80.00 in ten dollar increments, and s varies from 1200 units to 7200 units in 1200-unit increments. The multiplying factor in the bottom row takes into account the production rate and is used in the same way as in Table 5.5.

5.8.3. The Purchase-Lot-Size Order Chart for Variable A and s with Fixed i

An order chart for Table 5.5 is shown in Fig. 5.4. To use Fig. 5.4, lay a straightedge across the chart connecting the desired value of A and s and read q_0 from the q_0 scale where the straightedge crosses. The dotted line in Fig. 5.4 shows $q_0 = 219$ for $A = \$5.00$ and $s = 4800$ units. Note that the scales in Fig. 5.4 are logarithmic.

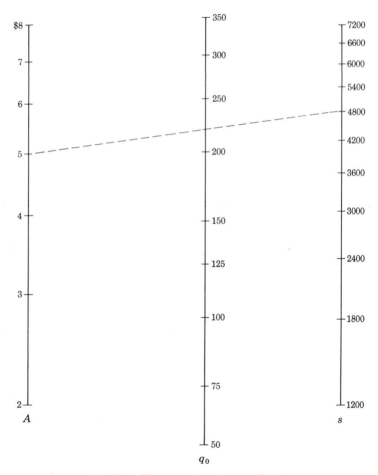

Fig. 5.4. Alignment chart for i = $1.00.

5.8.4. The Purchase-Lot-Size Order Chart for Variable A, s, and i

The order chart is more versatile than the order table. One can make a single chart to cover a range of values for several variables. In Fig. 5.5, the order chart covers a broad range of values for A, s, and i. As the range of values is increased, the accuracy of determining the lot size is necessarily decreased, unless the physical size of the chart is increased proportionately. However, the flat portion of the total cost curve near the economic lot size tends to reduce the monetary error if we are slightly off from the exact economic order size.

It is possible to make an order chart for manufactured lot sizes for ranges of the variables A, s, i, and p. Such a chart will be more complex than Fig.

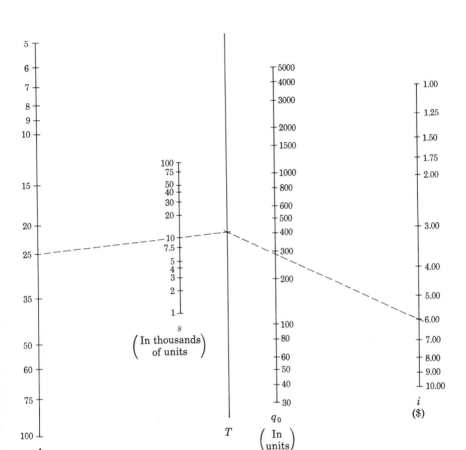

Fig. 5.5. Alignment chart for variables **A**, **s**, and **i**.

5.5 but if it is used frequently, it will soon pay for itself. Instead of computing an economic lot size for each product, we construct the chart, which will reduce the computation costs in the long run.

5.9. Summary

The costs to be used in determining the minimum total annual cost order quantity must be those costs directly affected by the plan. These costs include the costs associated with money invested in inventory.

The economic lot size is an important consideration in purchasing and manufacturing. Since the economic lot size occurs where the total cost curve is relatively flat, the error introduced by slightly inexact costs and approximate economic lot sizes may not be too serious.

6. Inventory and Inventory Functions

6.1. Introduction

Inventory may be defined as material held in storage for later use or sale. Inventory may take the form of raw materials held for processing, goods in the process of manufacture, and finished goods held for sale. Inventories are essential for the proper functioning of a manufacturing enterprise.

The raw-material inventories are held for later conversion to semi-finished or finished goods. Raw-material inventories must exist because generally it is not economically feasible either to purchase or to schedule the delivery of raw materials as they are needed in the manufacturing process.

Since manufacturing or processing always takes time, there are always inventories comprised of goods in the process of manufacture. In some industries materials must be processed in lots or batches. In other industries the flow of material may be steady with the product existing simultaneously in several stages of completion. In still other types of manufacturing it is desirable, from economic considerations, to process or schedule material in lots.

The nature of the product, the nature of the customer demand, and the nature of the manufacturing process determine, to a considerable extent, the need for finished-goods inventory. If the customer is willing to wait for the product to be manufactured (including the procurement of the raw materials), there is no need for finished-goods inventories. The customer may be willing to wait for some types of products to be manufactured, but he may also expect other types of products to be available immediately upon demand.

Sometimes the nature of the product prohibits extensive finished-goods inventories (in terms of the time the goods in inventory will supply customer demand). Fresh fruits, vegetables, and some other foods usually have a limited storage life so that extensive inventories of these products are not desirable. If the material must be processed in batches or lots, finished-goods inventories will usually exist.

In most manufacturing there are other inventories that do not directly go into the product. These inventories exist in the form of tools, supplies, equipment, etc.

Since inventories can take many forms, the holding of inventories creates many problems. The objective of production and inventory planning and control is to find the solutions to such problems. In this way, production control is involved with the planning of production operations, the movement and the storage of goods. Such planning should be done in a manner that will insure a maximum return on the investment in materials, labor, etc. Because of the direct relationship between inventory levels, production schedules, and customer demand, the planning and control of inventories must be integrated with the forecast of demand, the planning of production, and the control of production.

6.2. The Functions of Inventories

Inventories serve to isolate the supplier, the producer and the consumer. Inventories also permit the procurement of raw materials in economic lot sizes as well as the processing of these raw materials into finished goods in the most economical quantities. Raw-material inventories isolate the supplier of the raw materials from the user of these raw materials. Finished-goods inventories isolate the customer from the producer of the goods. In-process inventories isolate the departments within the plant. In a plant where materials are processed in lots, there is a need to have some inventories of semifinished goods existing between departments. For example, material processed in Department A is further processed in Department B. The output from Department B is transferred to Department C for additional processing. Now, suppose a production delay occurs in Department B. If there are no inventories between departments, the output of Department C is directly affected by the production delay in Department B. In a similar manner, any production delay in Department A directly affects the output of Departments B and C unless there are some inventories between departments. Conversely, when inventories exist between departments, limited delays in one department will not immediately affect other departments in the plant. A delay in Department A will not affect the output of Department C until all of the inventories between Department A and Department C have been exhausted.

The preceding discussion might imply that very large inventories should exist between departments in a plant, between the supplier and the producer, and between the producer and the consumer. From the standpoint of economics, there is an optimum size of inventory. These inventories should be economic lot sizes plus a "buffer" or safety stock. The material used in the normal course of business will be that which is produced in economic lot sizes. This is frequently called *cycle stock*. The material that is not expected to be used in the normal course of business is the safety stock. Safety stock is held for use when demand exceeds forecast, when production is less than planned, or when lead times are longer than normal.

6.3. Types of Inventories

Between the supplier and the manufacturer, inventories exist for (1) the movement of material, (2) the isolation of the supplier and the manufacturer, and (3) the purchase and manufacture of goods in economic quantities.

Inventories of finished goods are generally held for three reasons: (1) to enable the manufacture of goods in economic quantities (generally considered as lot-size inventories), (2) to provide for future sales or demand (anticipation stocks), and (3) to serve as a cushion against fluctuations in actual demand from forecast demand (fluctuation or safety stock).

Movement inventories arise because of the lead time between successive operations, the lead time to buy material, or the lead time to get material from the point of manufacture to the point of distribution. In themselves, they create no great problem, provided the lead time is known. If a company can obtain raw materials in exactly two weeks, then its orders will always be two weeks ahead of the time the raw material is needed in the plant. On the other hand, if the time to procure varies randomly from one week to three weeks, then more than two weeks lead time must be allowed on each order. This means that, dependent on the actual time allowed to procure, more raw material than was previously necessary under constant lead time should be in inventory at the plant, or the company risks a shutdown due to lack of raw materials. Therefore, as was previously stated, the lead time to procure materials creates no problems if the lead time is known exactly.

Anticipation stocks are held to meet known forecast demand. Anticipation stocks may be built up to meet the forecast demand of an accelerated sales campaign or a peak season, or to tide the company over a vacation period. Since both the amount and the timing of the demand are presumably known, anticipation stocks generally do not create serious planning problems.

Safety stocks are held to meet unpredictable variations in demand. They fulfill a need arising from the variation in the actual demand from the forecast demand, the variation of actual production from planned production and the variations in lead times.

6.4. Two Basic Types of Inventory Systems

There are two basic inventory systems; all others are variations. The first of these systems to be discussed is the fixed-order-size inventory system. The second is the fixed-order-interval system. It is important that the above distinction be made when inventory systems are discussed. In the first case, a fixed quantity is ordered at equal or varying intervals. In the second case, a variable quantity is ordered at fixed intervals.

In the ideal situation, the fixed-order-size system works as follows: a fixed quantity of material is ordered whenever the stock on hand reaches zero. With instantaneous replenishment and zero lead time, the order is received at the same time it is placed. The order quantity (inventory) is used up at a constant rate, and when it again reaches zero another order is placed. In fact, under these conditions the two basic systems are identical. The operation under ideal conditions is portrayed graphically in Fig. 6.1.

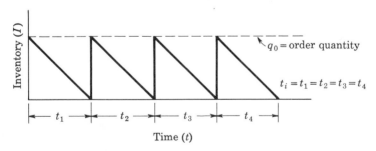

Fig. 6.1. Basic inventory systems under ideal conditions.

By now, it should be self-evident that the order quantity, q_0, is also the economic purchased lot size. In fact, the economic purchased or manufactured lot size should be the basis for determining either the order size or the order interval.

Departures from ideal conditions result in the two basic inventory systems. A very simple variation of the fixed-order-size inventory-control system is commonly referred to as the "two-bin" system.

6.4.1. The Fixed-Order-Size Inventory System Applied to Example 1

To illustrate the two basic systems, we shall use the illustration previously presented for Example 1 (see Section 5.2.1). We determined the economic purchased lot to be 500 units. Further, the forecast demand was 1500 units per year. Let us assume the lead time to be one month. Therefore, if there are 250 days in a year, the expected daily usage is $\frac{1500}{250}$ or 6 units per day. Then 500 units would last $\frac{500}{6}$ or 83.3 days. Further, let us assume that there is some safety stock available. (The manner of computing the safety stock will be illustrated later in this chapter.) With a lead time of one month ($21\frac{5}{6}$ days), we need to reorder when there are 6(21.83) or 131 units in stock (above the safety stock). This value is called the reorder point.

Under the fixed-order-size inventory system, we would operate in the following manner: assume that we start with 500 units plus our safety stock on January 1. We keep a count of inventory, and when stock has been reduced to 131 units more than our safety stock, we place an order for 500 units. Under constant usage, this order should arrive when our stock on hand reaches the level of the safety stock. When we have replenished our stock, we again have 500 units plus safety stock. The cycle repeats itself. This is illustrated in Fig. 6.2.

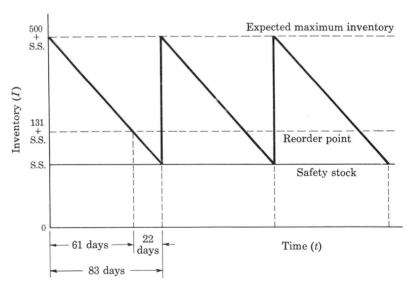

Fig. 6.2. Operation of the fixed-order-size inventory system for a component of the product of Example 1.

6.4.2. The Fixed-Order-Interval Inventory System Applied to Example 1

To illustrate the differences between the two systems, we will examine the fixed-order-interval inventory system when we reorder every 83 days. In 83 days, the expected usage is 83(6) or 498 units. We will reorder 22 days prior to the time the inventory is expected to reach the safety stock level, or 61 days after an order has been received. The quantity ordered will be the difference between 500 plus the safety stock and the amount on hand at the reorder point plus an amount to last through the lead time [500 + Safety Stock − On Hand + 6(22)]. In this case, the order quantities will vary, but the time between orders will be constant. If we assume that we have 500 units plus safety stock on hand on January 1, we can illustrate the

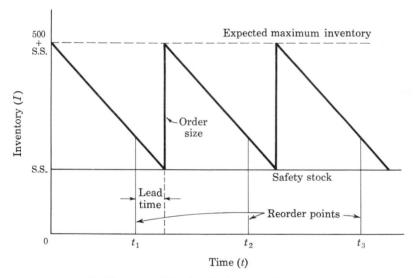

Fig. 6.3. Operation of the fixed-order-interval inventory system for a component of the product of Example 1.

fixed-order-interval inventory system by Fig. 6.3. In Fig. 6.3, $t_2 - t_1 = t_3 - t_2$, but the maximum inventory will vary depending upon usage. Also, the order size will vary according to the amount used in any particular order interval.

6.4.3. Reorder Rules

The reorder rules can be expressed as follows:
1. *Fixed-Order-Size Reorder Rule.* Reorder a fixed quantity whenever the inventory reaches a point such that the quantity on hand plus orders

placed but not received equals the expected usage during the lead time plus the safety stock.

2. *Fixed-Order-Interval Reorder Rule.* Reorder a quantity equal to the difference between the amount on hand and the desired maximum inventory plus the expected usage during the lead time minus the orders placed but not received at the fixed-order dates.

The fixed-order-size inventory-control system requires that the amount of stock or inventory on hand is known at all times. It further requires that the person or persons responsible for the inventory know the reorder point for each stock-keeping item. The fixed-order-interval inventory-control system requires that the amount of stock or inventory is known at the fixed-order points. It further requires that the person or persons responsible for the inventory know the desired maximum inventory and the expected usage during the lead time.

6.5. Safety Stock

Safety stocks or fluctuation stocks are held to meet variations of actual demand from forecast demand, of actual production from planned production, and of actual lead times from expected lead times. Safety stock levels should be set to provide economic protection against being out of stock. Thus, it is necessary to know the desired level of customer service, the distribution of demand variations, the distribution of production variations and the distribution of lead-time variations.

The level of customer service is difficult to determine. It can be expressed in many ways; such as, the number of times we are out of stock, the number of units back-ordered, the number of customer orders delayed, etc. For the above-mentioned measures of customer service to be of value, they must be expressed as functions of time. An appropriate level of customer service might be to permit back-ordering once in a year.

The distribution of variations of actual demand from forecast demand can be made from sales records. Production records can provide the necessary information for the distribution of the variations of actual production from planned production. There is also data available from company records to construct the distribution of lead-time variations. We will use only one of the distributions, variations of demand, in the following discussions on safety stock.

6.5.1. Safety Stock in the Fixed-Order-Size Inventory System

The amount of safety stock required is dependent not only on the level of service but also on the type of inventory system. In the fixed-order-size inventory system, the safety stock needs to protect over the lead time only, whereas in the fixed-order-interval inventory system, the safety stock must protect against run-out over a cycle plus the lead time. This is illustrated in Figs. 6.4 and 6.5.

In Fig. 6.4, under normal, expected conditions, we order a fixed quantity of material when our inventory reaches A. If usage is normal during the

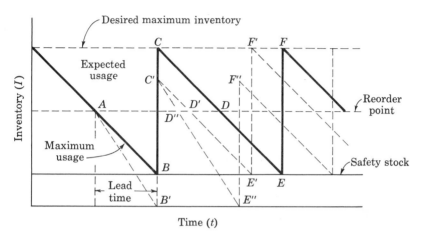

Fig. 6.4. Safety stock in fixed-order-size inventory system.

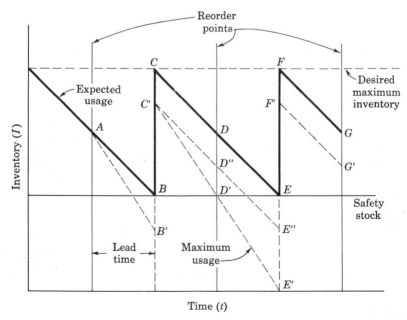

Fig. 6.5. Safety stock in the fixed-order-interval inventory system.

lead time and continues to be normal, the inventory pattern will follow the solid line (A, B, C, D, E, and F). However, if usage is at its expected maximum from point A, our inventory pattern will follow the line A, B', C', D'', E'' and F'''. Note that under maximum-usage conditions, we order more frequently, but the safety stock needs to protect for maximum usage only during the lead time. This can be seen by following the pattern A, B', C', D', E', and F'. In that case maximum usage occurs only during AB', and after one more cycle we are restored to our original inventory position. In the fixed-order-size inventory control system, the safety stock is determined by the difference between the maximum usage and the expected usage over the lead time.*

6.5.2. Safety Stock in the Fixed-Order-Interval Inventory System

In Fig. 6.5, the normal inventory pattern is shown by A, B, C, D, E, F, and G. At points A, D, and G an order is placed. The amount ordered is the desired maximum inventory minus the inventory on hand plus the expected usage during the lead time. If maximum usage should occur for an extended period of time (A to E'), the inventory pattern is A, B', C', D', E', F', and G'. Because the order interval is fixed, the safety stock must cover the lead time (AB') plus the cycle time ($C'D'E'$). If maximum usage occurs only during a lead time, the pattern is $AB'C'D''E''FG$. Therefore, the safety stock under a fixed-order-interval system will be greater than under a fixed-order-size inventory system.

6.5.3. Determination of Safety Stock Quantities

By using statistical methods, it is possible to establish safety stock levels to give the desired probabilities of being out of stock during any extended period of time. Such probabilities are correct only over large numbers of exposures and short-run experiences may depart widely from the long-run probabilities.

For the determination of safety stock under the fixed-order-size inventory control system, the following cost equation must be minimized:

$$C = \frac{As}{q} + cs + \frac{iq}{2} + iz_p s_x \sqrt{t} \qquad (6.1)$$

where z_p = the standard normal deviate to give the desired probability of being out of stock each time the inventory reaches a minimum

s_x = the standard deviation of demand variations

t = the lead time.

*Maximum usage is the demand at the chosen level of customer service.

In the fixed-order-interval inventory system, the lead time, t, in Eq. (6.1) is replaced by the lead time plus the order interval, and

$$C = \frac{As}{q} + cs + \frac{iq}{2} + iz_p s_z \sqrt{t + r} \qquad (6.2)$$

where r = the order interval.

It is not a simple matter to minimize either Eq. (6.1) or Eq. (6.2) because z_p is functionally related to the order quantity. As the order quantity increases, the number of orders per year decreases and the safety stock level will also be decreased as long as the probability of being out of stock is to remain the same for the year. We can determine the economic level of safety stock and the economic order quantity by choosing lot sizes or order intervals and computing the total cost of our choices according to Eq. (6.1) or Eq. (6.2).

We can obtain an approximate economical solution when using the fixed-order-size inventory system by finding the economic lot size without safety stocks and setting a safety stock level based on that order quantity. In the fixed-order-interval inventory system, the approximate level of safety stock is based on the order interval determined without consideration of safety stock.

6.5.3.1. *Approximate Solution for Safety Stock for Example 1 Under the Fixed-Order-Size Inventory System.* In Example 1, the annual usage is 1500 units, the economic lot size is 500 units, and the standard deviation demand is 11 units. If the lead time is ten days, the level of customer service is to be one period during the year in which we are out of stock, and if we assume there are 240 days in a year, the safety stock is four units. This is obtained as follows:

$$\text{Safety Stock} = (0.43)\left(\frac{11}{\sqrt{20}}\right)\sqrt{10}$$

The 0.43 is the standard normal deviate to give a one third probability of being out of stock just prior to each replenishment point, the $\sqrt{20}$ converts the standard deviation of monthly demand to the standard deviation of daily demand, and the $\sqrt{10}$ is the square root of the lead time. This approximate solution has a total variable annual cost of $50.40. The exact solution will decrease this cost by a very small amount.

6.5.3.2. *Approximate Solution for Safety Stock for Example 1 Under the Fixed-Order-Interval Inventory System.* In Section 6.5.3.1., we established certain conditions pertaining to Example 1. If we use these conditions, the safety stock under the fixed-order-interval inventory system is ten units. The square root of the lead time is changed to the square root of the lead time plus the order interval. In this case, the order interval is 80 days. The total variable annual cost of this solution is $51.00 since we must carry more safety stock.

It should be remembered that the above-mentioned methods of computing safety stock are based on several assumptions: (1) the level of demand is relatively stable and constant from sales period to sales period, (2) the distribution of demand is known and approximates a normal distribution, (3) the costs involved are known and will stay relatively constant, and (4) the lead time is known and is constant.

If the lead time varies, it adds another element to the safety stock. We need to allow for long lead times as well as heavy demand. However, lead time in itself does not create serious problems so long as it is known.

6.6. Inventory Control Systems When Demand Is not Level

If the demand is not essentially level, the choice of inventory-control system must reflect this fact. If demand is following an upward trend, the fixed-order-size system is probably preferable. However, the safety stock either should gradually increase with an increase in demand, or it can be computed to give satisfactory protection at the higher demands and over-protection at the lower levels of demand. If the fixed-order-size system is used, the orders become more frequent as the rate of demand becomes higher, and the usage during the lead time is also higher. On the basis of this latter fact, the need for more safety stock becomes evident.

When the fixed-order-interval inventory system is used under conditions where demand is following an upward trend, the orders become progressive-

Table 6.1. Demand for Example 5

Month	Monthly Demand	Daily Demand
1	100	5
2	120	6
3	140	7
4	160	8
5	180	9
6	200	10
7	220	11
8	240	12
9	260	13
10	280	14
11	300	15
12	320	16
	2520	

ly larger, and at the same time the safety stock becomes sizable. Unless there are other strong and compelling reasons for using the fixed-order-interval system, the facts favor the fixed-order-size inventory control system under those conditions where a trend exists in the sales data.

The operation of the two types of inventory-control systems under a trend in demand can be illustrated by the following hypothetical example (Example 5). The demand data are given in Table 6.1 under the assumption of 20 days in each month and 240 days in the year. Further, we make the assumption that the daily demand during any month is constant. This demand pattern is shown in Figs. 6.6 and 6.7.

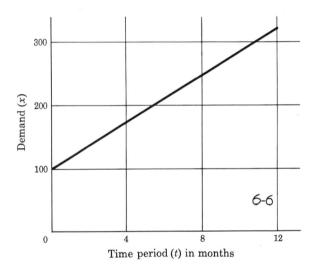

Fig. 6.6. Monthly demand for Example 5.

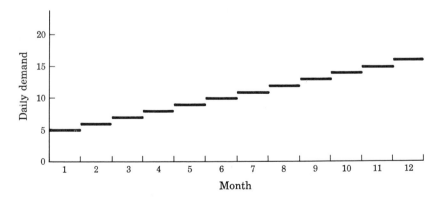

Fig. 6.7. Daily demand for Example 5.

At this point, it is necessary to determine the economic lot size. The following data are assumed to be applicable:

Order cost = \$17.50

Carrying cost = \$2.00

Annual usage = 2520

Then

$$q_0 = \sqrt{\frac{2(17.50)(2520)}{2}} = 210 \text{ units}$$

Table 6.2 is constructed from the data in Table 6.1 under the assumptions

Table 6.2. Stock Levels for Example 5 under the Fixed-Order-Size Inventory System

Day			Inventory Level	
Reorder Point	Replenishment Point	At Reorder Point	Before Replenishment	After Replenishment
				410
30		250		
	36		220	430
61		252		
	67		212	422
87		247		
	93		202	412
109		250		
	115		200	410
129		251		
	135		196	406
148		244		
	154		184	394
165		245		
	171		180	390
181		246		
	187		176	386
196		246		
	202		175	385
210		250		
	216		175	385
224		246		
	230		166	376
237		248		
	243		166	376

used in the construction of Fig. 6.7 and the assumption that an order is placed at the end of the day in which the inventory reaches or drops below the reorder point. All orders are placed in stock on the morning of the day following the receipt of the orders. If we assume that our safety stock is 200 units and our lead time is 5 days, we can determine the maximum expected inventory, the reorder points, and the replenishment points.

$$\text{Maximum expected inventory} = 200 + 210 = 410$$

$$\text{Expected average daily usage} = \frac{2520}{240} = 10.5$$

$$\text{Reorder point} = 200 + (10.5)(5) = 255$$

The operation of the fixed-order-interval system is shown in Table 6.3.

Table 6.3. Stock Levels for Example 5 under the Fixed-Order-Interval Inventory System

Day		Order Size	Inventory Level		
Reorder Point	Replenishment Point		At Reorder Point	Before Replenishment	After Replenishment
					410
15		130	335		
	21			310	440
35		115	350		
	41			320	435
55		135	330		
	61			295	430
75		155	310		
	81			270	425
95		175	290		
	101			245	420
115		195	270		
	121			220	415
135		215	250		
	141			195	410
155		235	230		
	161			170	405
175		255	210		
	181			145	400
195		275	190		
	201			120	395
215		295	170		
	221			95	390
235		315	150		
	241			70	385

The same conditions apply, but we need to establish the order interval rather than the order size. Since the economic lot size is 210 units and the most appropriate order interval is $240/n$ or $240q_0/s$, which is $(240)(210)/2520 = 20$ days. Therefore, our first reorder point is at the end of the fifteenth day, and the other reorder points occur every twentieth day thereafter.

The two patterns of inventory under the two systems are shown graphically in Figs. 6.8 and 6.9. Note that the minimum stock level varies more
under the fixed-order-interval system. Also, under the fixed-order-interval
system, there is a wide variation in the order size and the maximum inventory. These variations result in added carrying costs. Under the fixed-

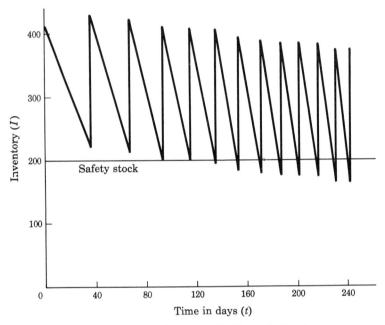

Fig. 6.8. Pattern of inventory for Example 5 under
fixed-order-size inventory system.

order-size system, the minimum inventory level varied from 166 to 220,
whereas under the fixed-order-interval system, the minimum inventory
level varied from 70 to 320 units. This means that about 34 units of safety
stock would have been adequate under the fixed-order-size inventory system, whereas about 130 units of safety stock would have been necessary
under the fixed-order-interval system.

If we compute the annual carrying costs (for cycle stock and safety stock)
for both inventory systems, we can see the effect of the inventory system
when the demand follows an upward trend. The average inventory carrying
cost for the fixed-order-size system is $588.17, and for the fixed-order-
interval system it is $619.17. This is not much difference, but if we reduce
the safety stock to a minimum, we find the carrying costs for the fixed-
order-size system to be $256.17, compared to $479.17 for the fixed-order-

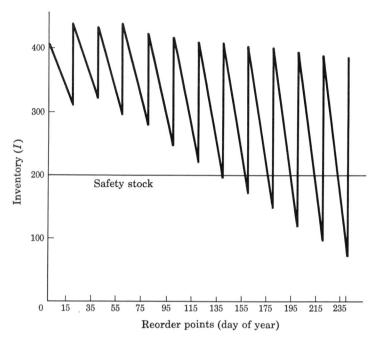

Fig. 6.9. Pattern of inventory for Example 5 under
fixed-order-interval inventory system.

interval system.   Therefore, the carrying costs in this instance with minimum safety stock are almost twice as much under the fixed-order-size
system.   The variations in the necessary amount of safety stock and in the
carrying cost of cycle stock plus safety stock illustrate the effect of the
fixed-order-size system's having to protect only during the lead time and
the fixed-order-interval system's having to protect during the lead time
plus the cycle time.

The same type of comparisons can be made for situations in which the
demand is cyclic.   Again, the fixed-order-size inventory-control system will
more closely approach the expected maximum and minimum inventories.

6.7. A Variation of the Fixed-Order-Interval Inventory-Control System

A variation of the fixed-order-interval system is to establish an intermediate value of inventory (I_i) such that if the stock on hand at a review
period is between I_i and the maximum expected inventory, no order will be
placed.   This can also be stated as follows: orders are placed only when the
inventory on hand is less than or equal to I_i.   The expected result of such a

system is to reduce the number of very small orders, but as a result of such a system some rather large orders will be placed. However, the incremental costs of the large orders are probably not as great as those of small orders. To illustrate this fact, recall the total cost curve in the economic-lot-size determination. The absolute value of the slope of the total cost curve is greater for order-size increments below the economic order size than it is for the same size increments above the economic order size. Therefore, for any distribution of demand variation about some average value, it is possible to select that expected distribution of order sizes so that the total annual cost will be a minimum. Such a system is characterized by the three parameters:

$$I_m = \text{maximum desired inventory}$$
$$I_i = \text{maximum inventory at reorder}$$
$$t = \text{length of the review period}$$

The operation of such an inventory-control system is shown in Fig. 6.10. Note that there was no order placed at the end of the second period because the inventory on hand exceeded the maximum inventory to call for an

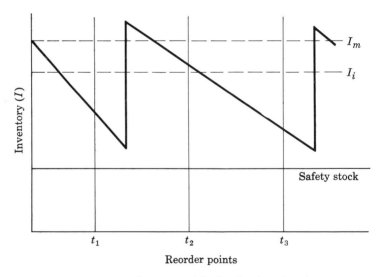

Fig. 6.10. Operation of the fixed-order-interval inventory system with minimum order size.

order. This type of inventory-control system has been discussed by Arrow, Harris, and Marschak.*

*K. Arrow, T. Harris, and J. Marschak, "Optimal Inventory Policy," *Econometrica*, **Vol. 19,** No. 3 (July, 1951).

6.8. Summary

There are two basic inventory-control systems. Each has its advantages and disadvantages. Further, it is possible to have a system tailor-made for any particular company.

In establishing inventory levels, it is necessary to consider unexpected random variations in demand as well as known demands. This inventory is called safety stock. When inventory is held to meet a known demand, it is called anticipation stock.

7. Production Planning

7.1. Introduction

After the expected demand for the future is known, a production plan for that period should be established. The time span will vary with conditions, much as the time span of the production planning forecast should vary with conditions. It may cover a period of a few weeks up to a year or more. Since certain decisions about the future will be based on the production plan, its time span must be sufficient to establish the plan, to make the necessary decisions based on the plan, and to put them into effect.

7.2. The Production Plan

The production plan must provide the required quantities of product at the proper time and at a minimum total cost consistent with quality requirements. The production plan should be the basis for the establishment of many of the operating budgets. It should establish manpower requirements and hours to be worked, both regular time and overtime. Further, the production plan establishes the equipment requirements and the level of the anticipation inventories.

In setting up the production plan, we must keep in mind that if demand must be met when it occurs, there are three sources that can be used:

1. Current production.
2. Inventory on hand.
3. Current production and inventory.

If back orders are permissible, the current demand may be deferred to some time in the near future. When material can be back-ordered, we have a situation comparable to something between a continuous manufacturing operation and an intermittent manufacturing operation. It does provide flexibility, but it should not be relied upon to avoid the problem of meeting demand when it occurs.

7.2.1. Stability of the Work Force

One factor that should always be considered in production planning is the stability of the work force. The more highly skilled the employees, the more important a stable work force becomes. There are certain industries that are seasonal and are accepted as such. One excellent example of such an industry is the growing and processing of fruits and vegetables in the colder climates. There is one crop each year which must be processed in a few weeks. The remainder of the year there is no activity. This fact is generally accepted by the workers, many of whom are itinerant laborers. However, when skills are involved, there may be serious effects from abnormal variations in work force. These effects may show up in the unavailability of better employees, in the necessity for higher wages, in poor community relations, and in high costs for the operation of the personnel department to accomplish the necessary hiring, layoff, training, etc.

When demand is nearly constant throughout the year, the necessity for a stable work force creates no serious problem. If demand is cyclic, one must either vary the size of the work force or use inventories to meet demand. The use of inventories and a level work force to meet a cyclic demand has one direct financial advantage — there is a lower investment in plant and equipment. If demand is on an upward trend, an expansion in the size of the work force, increasing efficiency, or some other means of reducing the number of hours per unit or increasing the number of hours available is called for. A downward trend in demand usually requires a reduction in the size of the work force if efficiency is to be maintained. Thus, planning under these various conditions must be consistent with demand, company policies, and economic production.

7.3. A Production Plan for Example 1

In Table 3.9, the monthly and cumulative demand forecast is given for Example 1. This forecast is in terms of units of product, and we have the choice of converting units of product to man-hours represented or to convert production man-hours to units of product. In the following examples, all units will be converted to man-hours, and the man-hour values will be used in the solutions.

If the product of Example 1 requires 10 man-hours, we get the demand forecasts shown in Table 7.1. The product unit values are also given for comparative purposes. From Table 7.1, we see that 15,000 man-hours are required during the coming year.

Table 7.1. Demand for Example 1 in Units and in Production Hours

Period	Monthly Forecast Units	Monthly Demand Hours	Cumulative Forecast Units	Cumulative Demand Hours
25	125	1250	125	1250
26	125	1250	250	2500
27	125	1250	375	3750
28	125	1250	500	5000
29	125	1250	625	6250
30	125	1250	750	7500
31	125	1250	875	8750
32	125	1250	1000	10,000
33	125	1250	1125	11,250
34	125	1250	1250	12,500
35	125	1250	1375	13,750
36	125	1250	1500	15,000

After determining the man-hours required, we should next consider the number of man-hours available during the year. In Table 7.2 is the num-

Table 7.2. Regular Time Line-Hours Available

Period	Month	Days	Monthly Line-Hours	Cumulative Line-Hours
25	Jan.	22	176	176
26	Feb.	19	152	328
27	Mar.	21	168	496
28	Apr.	22	176	672
29	May	22	176	848
30	June	20	160	1008
31	July	22	96*	1104
32	Aug.	22	176	1280
33	Sept.	20	160	1440
34	Oct.	23	184	1624
35	Nov.	19	152	1776
36	Dec.	21	168	1944
	Total	253	1944	

*80 line-hours vacation in July.

ber of working days in each month, the number of line-hours (or the number of hours for one man working full time), and the number of cumulative line-hours. There are 1944 line-hours available during the year. (*Note* The plant ceases all nonessential operations during two weeks in July. This is the plant vacation.)

Since we must have 15,000 man-hours available during the year, we need 15,000/1944 men, or 7.7 men. If we were going to make a production plan for this product alone, we would have to decide whether seven or eight men should be used (assuming that a level work force is required throughout the year). If we choose to use seven men, we must necessarily plan to work some overtime at premium pay. On the other hand, to use eight men means that we must pay for some production time that is not required. Without setting up the production plan, we cannot exactly determine the cost of each alternative, since we do not know, at this point, the amount of material to be carried in inventory under each alternative, nor do we know the distribution of the available man-hours compared to the required man-hours. However, we can determine the absolute minimum cost or lower bound values of both alternatives. If we use seven men, the minimum amount of overtime is $15,000 - 7(1944)$ or 1392 hours. If we use eight men, the minimum amount of regular time not used (which must be paid for) is $8(1944) - 15,000$ or 552 hours. If the cost of an hour of regular time is $2.00 and the overtime premium is $1.00 per hour, the lower bounds of the incremental costs are $1392.00 and $1104.00 for using seven and eight men, respectively. Thus, there is only a minor cost difference, and production plans using both seven and eight men should be compared.

One factor not considered above is absenteeism due to sickness or other reasons. If, from past records, we find that each man is present, on the average, 98 per cent of the time, we could divide the 1,5000 man-hours by 0.98 to obtain the number of man-hours to be planned; or we could multiply the time available in each month by 0.98. For Example 1, if there is any expected absenteeism, the preferable production plan would seem to call for eight men. Another factor not considered is the availability of inventory at the beginning of the year and the desired inventories during the year. These also affect the planning.

To facilitate the making of the production plan, we can use a table such as Table 7.3. Along the left-hand side we list the man-hours required in each month. Along the top is shown the month in which the product is to be manufactured. Below this is shown the number of regular time (R.T.) hours available in each month. (These values are based on the hours given in Table 7.2 and the use of seven men.) Also shown in the same row are the number of overtime hours available (at 25 per cent of the regular time hours). Under the assumptions that demand must be met when it occurs, that overtime costs a premium of $1.00 per hour, and that the inventory

Table 7.3. Minimum Cost Production Plan for Example 1

Month in Which Required	Man Hours Required		Jan. R.T.	Jan. O.T.	Feb. R.T.	Feb. O.T.	Mar. R.T.	Mar. O.T.	Apr. R.T.	Apr. O.T.	May R.T.	May O.T.
			1232	308	1064	266	1176	294	1232	308	1232	308
Jan.	1250	Available	1232	308								
		Cost	0	1.00								
		Planned	1232	18								
Feb.	1250	Available		290	1064	266						
		Cost		1.04	0	1.00						
		Planned		. . .	1064	186						
Mar.	1250	Available		290		80	1176	294				
		Cost		1.08		1.04	0	1.00				
		Planned		. . .		. . .	1176	74				
Apr.	1250	Available		290		80		220	1232	308		
		Cost		1.12		1.08		1.04	0	1.00		
		Planned		. . .		. . .		. . .	1232	18		
May	1250	Available		290		80		220		290	1232	308
		Cost		1.16		1.12		1.08		1.04	0	1.00
		Planned		. . .		. . .		. . .		. . .	1232	18
June	1250	Available		290		80		220		290		290
		Cost		1.20		1.16		1.12		1.08		1.04
		Planned		. . .		. . .		. . .		. . .		. . .
July	1250	Available		290		80		220		290		290
		Cost		1.24		1.20		1.16		1.12		1.08
		Planned		. . .		. . .		. . .		. . .		260
Aug.	1250	Available		290		80		220		290		30
		Cost		1.28		1.24		1.20		1.16		1.12
		Planned		. . .		. . .		. . .		. . .		. . .
Sept.	1250	Available		290		80		220		290		30
		Cost		1.32		1.28		1.24		1.20		1.16
		Planned		. . .		. . .		. . .		. . .		. . .
Oct.	1250	Available		290		80		220		290		30
		Cost		1.36		1.32		1.28		1.24		1.20
		Planned		. . .		. . .		. . .		. . .		. . .
Nov.	1250	Available		290		80		220		290		30
		Cost		1.40		1.36		1.32		1.28		1.24
		Planned		. . .		. . .		. . .		. . .		. . .
Dec.	1250	Available		290		80		220		290		30
		Cost		1.44		1.40		1.36		1.32		1.28
		Planned		. . .		. . .		. . .		. . .		. . .
Total Production Planned	R.T.		1232		1064		1176		1232		1232	
	O.T.			18		186		74		18		278

Using no Inventories and Seven Men

To Be Produced

June R.T.	June O.T.	July R.T.	July O.T.	Aug. R.T.	Aug. O.T.	Sept. R.T.	Sept. O.T.	Oct. R.T.	Oct. O.T.	Nov. R.T.	Nov. O.T.	Dec. R.T.	Dec. O.T.	Total Production Planned
1120	280	672	168	1232	308	1120	280	1288	322	1064	266	1176	294	Planned
														1250
														1250
														1250
														1250
														1250
1120 0 1120	280 1.00 130													1250
	150 1.04 150	672 0 672	168 1.00 168											1250
				1232 0 1232	308 1.00 18									1250
					290 1.04 ...	1120 0 1120	280 1.00 130							1250
					290 1.08 ...		150 1.04 ...	1288 0 1250	322 1.00 ...					1250
					290 1.12 ...		150 1.08 ...	38 .04 38	322 1.04 ...	1064 0 1064	266 1.00 148			1250
					290 1.16 ...		150 1.12 ...		322 1.08 ...		118 1.04 ...	1176 0 1176	294 1.00 74	1250
1120	280	672	168	1232	18	1120	130	1288	0	1064	148	1176	74	13608 1392

carrying charge of one man-hour of product is $0.04 per month, we get the plan shown in Table 7.3.

From the parts of Table 7.3 explained above, we can work out the most economical production plan for Example 1 under the given conditions. In January we require 1250 man hours. We have available 1232 man-hours regular time at zero incremental cost. (If we produce this product, our costs cannot be less than when we produce it on regular time in the month in which it is sold. This is why the cost for regular time in the same month is listed as zero.) After using all of the regular time in January, we still need 18 hours which can come only from overtime in January. So our incremental costs for January are 18 units at $1.00, or $18.00. In the month of February we have 1064 R.T. and 266 O.T. hours available. If necessary, we could use as many as 290 (308-18) O.T. hours from January to meet February requirements. If this were done, the incremental cost for all units produced on overtime in January to meet requirements in February would be $1.04. (One dollar is for the overtime premium, and the $0.04 is for carrying the product in inventory for one month.) We now make the production plan, using the hours which cost the least. To meet the 1250 man-hour requirement, we use 1064 R.T. hours plus 186 O.T. hours (1250 − 1064) in February. This is the lowest cost combination and gives an incremental cost of $186.00 for February. To meet March requirements, we have 1176 R.T. hours plus 294 O.T. hours in the month of March, 80 O.T. hours from the month of February and 290 O.T. hours from the month of January. The incremental costs are $0.00, $1.00, $1.04 and $1.08, respectively. (January production for March sale must be held 2 months at $0.04 per man-hour per month.)

The plan is summarized at the right and bottom of the table. The plan calls for 13,608 regular time hours plus 1392 overtime hours apportioned according to the column at the right and row at the bottom of the table.

The incremental costs can be summarized as follows:

1. Overtime costs $1392.00.
2. Inventory carrying costs   28.32.

The total incremental cost is $1420.32. This is $255.68 more than the cost of using eight men under the same conditions. (It is left as an exercise for the reader to show this cost differential.) The inventory costs for Table 7.3 are

$$260(\$0.08) + 150(\$0.04) + 38(\$0.04) = \$28.32$$

The production plan of Table 7.3 can also be summarized as in Table 7.4. The 410 units of inventory planned for the end of June include the 260 units produced in May for sale in July plus the 150 units produced in June for sale in July. The inventories established in Table 7.3 are *anticipation* stocks. They are to be used in meeting a forecast demand.

Table 7.4. Summary of the Production Plan of Table 7.3

Month	Forecast Demand (Hours)	Planned Production Regular Time (Hours)	Overtime (Hours)	Planned Ending Inventory (Hours)
Opening Stock				0
Jan.	1250	1232	18	0
Feb.	1250	1064	186	0
Mar.	1250	1176	74	0
Apr.	1250	1232	18	0
May	1250	1232	278	260
June	1250	1120	280	410
July	1250	672	168	0
Aug.	1250	1232	18	0
Sept.	1250	1120	130	0
Oct.	1250	1288	0	38
Nov.	1250	1064	148	0
Dec.	1250	1176	74	0

7.4. A Production Plan For Example 1 with Safety Stocks

No consideration was given to safety stocks in the previous illustration. If we had 85 units in inventory at the beginning of the year and planned to reduce this by five units per month during the year, we could no longer use the production requirements of Table 7.3. (Since we did not consider inventories in Table 7.3, the demand and production requirements were identical.) It is necessary first to determine the production requirements before a production plan is made when safety stocks are considered. This has been done in Table 7.5. The 85 units in safety stock represent 850 man-hours. The safety stock requirement is reduced by 50 man-hours per month. The new production requirements are shown in Table 7.5. The total production requirement for the year is reduced to 14,400 man-hours. (The inventories above are not exactly safety stocks in all respects. The 85 units may represent the desired safety stocks at the beginning of the year plus any excess inventory resulting from overproduction during the past. The overproduction may have been a result of exceeding the planned production or from overestimating demand. If we assume that the proper amount of safety stock is 25 units rather than 85 units, it might be better to reduce this inventory gradually rather than all in one month. This is what has been done in Table 7.5.)

A minimum-cost production plan under these conditions, employing

Table 7.6. Minimum Cost Production Plan for Example 1

Month in Which Required	Man Hours Required		Jan.		Feb.		Mar.		Apr.		May	
			R.T.	O.T.	R.T.	O.T.	R.T.	O.T.	R.T.	O.T.	R.T.	O.T.
			1232	308	1064	266	1176	294	1232	308	1232	308
Jan.	1200	Available	1232	308								
		Cost	0	1.00								
		Planned	1200	...								
Feb.	1200	Available	32	308	1064	266						
		Cost	.04	1.04	0	1.00						
		Planned	32	...	1064	104						
Mar.	1200	Available		308		162	1176	294				
		Cost		1.08		1.04	0	1.00				
		Planned		...		...	1176	24				
Apr.	1200	Available		308		162		270	1232	308		
		Cost		1.12		1.08		1.04	0	1.00		
		Planned		...		...		...	1200	...		
May	1200	Available		308		162		270	32	308	1232	308
		Cost		1.16		1.12		1.08	.04	1.04	0	1.00
		Planned		...		...		...	...	...	1200	...
June	1200	Available		308		162		270	32	308	32	308
		Cost		1.20		1.16		1.12	.08	1.08	.04	1.04
		Planned		...		...		...	32	...	32	...
July	1200	Available		308		162		270		308		308
		Cost		1.24		1.20		1.16		1.12		1.08
		Planned		...		...		...		...		96
Aug.	1200	Available		308		162		270		308		212
		Cost		1.28		1.24		1.20		1.16		1.12
		Planned		...		...		...		...		...
Sept.	1200	Available		308		162		270		308		212
		Cost		1.32		1.28		1.24		1.20		1.16
		Planned		...		...		...		...		...
Oct.	1200	Available		308		162		270		308		212
		Cost		1.36		1.32		1.28		1.24		1.20
		Planned		...		...		...		...		...
Nov.	1200	Available		308		162		270		308		212
		Cost		1.40		1.36		1.32		1.28		1.24
		Planned		...		...		...		...		...
Dec.	1200	Available		308		162		270		308		212
		Cost		1.44		1.40		1.36		1.32		1.28
		Planned		...		...		...		...		...
Total Production Planned	R.T.		1232		1064		1176		1232		1232	
	O.T.			...		104		24		...		96

Using Inventories and Seven Men

To Be Produced

June		July		Aug.		Sept.		Oct.		Nov.		Dec.		Total Production Planned
R.T.	O.T.	R.T.	O.T.	R.T.	O.T.	R.T.	O.T.	R.T.	O.T.	R.T.	O.T.	R.T.	O.T.	
1120	280	672	168	1232	308	1120	280	1288	322	1064	266	1176	294	
														1200
														1200
														1200
														1200
														1200
1120 0 1120	280 1.00 16													1200
	264 1.04 264	672 0 672	168 1.00 168											1200
				1232 0 1200	308 1.00 ...									1200
				32 .04 32	308 1.04 ...	1120 0 1120	280 1.00 48							1200
					308 1.08 ...		232 1.04 ...	1288 0 1200	322 1.00 ...					1200
					308 1.12 ...		232 1.08 ...	88 .04 88	322 1.04 ...	1064 0 1064	266 1.00 48			1200
					308 1.16 ...		232 1.12 ...		322 1.08 ...		218 1.04 ...	1176 0 1176	294 1.00 24	1200
1120	280	672	168	1232	...	1120	48	1288	...	1064	48	1176	24	13608 792

Table 7.5. Determination of Cumulative Production Requirements for
Example 1 When Safety Stocks Are Considered

Period	Month	Cumulative Demand (Hours)	Desired Ending Inventory (Hours)	Cumulative Production Requirements (Hours)
Opening Stock			850	
25	Jan.	1,250	800	1,200
26	Feb.	2,500	750	2,400
27	Mar.	3,750	700	3,600
28	Apr.	5,000	650	4,800
29	May	6,250	600	6,000
30	June	7,500	550	7,200
31	July	8,750	500	8,400
32	Aug.	10,000	450	9,600
33	Sept.	11,250	400	10,800
34	Oct.	12,500	350	12,000
35	Nov.	13,750	300	13,200
36	Dec.	15,000	250	14,400

seven men, is worked out in Table 7.6. The incremental costs of this plan
are $820.16. From Table 7.6, it can be seen that inventories will alter the
production plan. Thus, inventory levels, if minimum inventories (safety
stock) are to exist, must be established prior to making the production plan.
We cannot escape the fact that production and inventories are interrelated,
and all planning must consider both. Again, we have established the anticipation stocks in excess of the other inventories by the production plan.

7.5. A Production Plan for Several Products

The approach used in the previous sections is applicable to the planning
of several products. Again, using the forecasts of Table 3.9 and converting
units of product to man-hours of production, we can establish man-hour
demands. Table 7.7 shows these demands if the product of Example 1 requires 10 man-hours per unit, the product of Example 2 requires 24 man-
hours per unit, the product of Example 3 requires 18 man-hours per unit,
and the product of Example 4 requires 15 man-hours per unit. There are
119,184 man-hours required. At 1944 hours per man per year, there are
more than 61 men but fewer than 62 men necessary to manufacture the required product on regular time.

Since the method being used in this chapter assumes the number of
available man-hours to be known, we will establish the production plan
based on 60 men. It could be that 61 men or 62 men might be more
economical. To determine the most economical number of men requires

Table 7.7. Total Monthly and Cumulative Demand (Hours)
for Examples 1, 2, 3, and 4

Period	Month	Monthly Demand (Hours)	Cumulative Demand (Hours)
25	Jan.	10,277	10,277
26	Feb.	10,067	20,344
27	Mar.	9,875	30,219
28	Apr.	9,665	39,884
29	May	9,473	49,357
30	June	9,263	58,620
31	July	9,317	67,937
32	Aug.	9,635	77,572
33	Sept.	9,935	87,507
34	Oct.	10,253	97,760
35	Nov.	10,553	108,313
36	Dec.	10,871	119,184

construction of several plans, with varying manpower, until a minimum cost plan is found. The cost to be minimized is the incremental cost. This method of planning makes the implicit assumption that the number of men to be used can be any multiple of one. If there are limitations on the number of men that can be used, or if men must be added to the force or removed from the force in increments, then only the allowable work force sizes should be used. The man-hours available with 60 men are shown in Table 7.8. The total number of regular time hours available is 2544 less

Table 7.8. Regular Time Man-Hours Available
with Sixty Men

Period	Month	Regular Time Man-Hours Available	
		Monthly	Cumulative
25	Jan.	10,560	10,560
26	Feb.	9,120	19,680
27	Mar.	10,080	29,760
28	Apr.	10,560	40,320
29	May	10,560	50,880
30	June	9,600	60,480
31	July	5,760	66,240
32	Aug.	10,560	76,800
33	Sept.	9,600	86,400
34	Oct.	11,040	97,440
35	Nov.	9,120	106,560
36	Dec.	10,080	116,640
Total		116,640	

Table 7.9. Minimum Cost Production Plan for Several Products

Month in Which Required	Man Hours Required		Jan. R.T.	Jan. O.T.	Feb. R.T.	Feb. O.T.	Mar. R.T.	Mar. O.T.	Apr. R.T.	Apr. O.T.	May R.T.	May O.T.
			10560	2640	9120	2280	10080	2520	10560	2640	10560	2640
Jan.	10277	Available	10560	2640								
		Cost	0	1.00								
		Planned	10277	...								
Feb.	10067	Available	283	2640	9120	2280						
		Cost	.04	1.04	0	1.00						
		Planned	283	...	9120	664						
Mar.	9875	Available		2640		1616	10080	2520				
		Cost		1.08		1.04	0	1.00				
		Planned		...		...	9875	...				
Apr.	9665	Available		2640		1616	205	2520	10560	2640		
		Cost		1.12		1.08	.04	1.04	0	1.00		
		Planned		...		...	...	...	9665	...		
May	9473	Available		2640		1616	205	2520	895	2640	10560	2640
		Cost		1.16		1.12	.08	1.08	.04	1.04	0	1.00
		Planned		...		...	...	...	...	...	9473	...
June	9263	Available		2640		1616	205	2520	895	2640	1087	2640
		Cost		1.20		1.16	.12	1.12	.08	1.08	.04	1.04
		Planned		...		...	...	...	...	...	...	...
July	9317	Available		2640		1616	205	2520	895	2640	1087	2640
		Cost		1.24		1.20	.16	1.16	.12	1.12	.08	1.08
		Planned		...		...	205	...	895	...	1087	...
Aug.	9635	Available		2640		1616		2520		2640		2640
		Cost		1.28		1.24		1.20		1.16		1.12
		Planned		...		...		...		...		...
Sept.	9935	Available		2640		1616		2520		2640		2640
		Cost		1.32		1.28		1.24		1.20		1.16
		Planned		...		...		...		...		...
Oct.	10253	Available		2640		1616		2520		2640		2640
		Cost		1.36		1.32		1.28		1.24		1.20
		Planned		...		...		...		...		...
Nov.	10553	Available		2640		1616		2520		2640		2640
		Cost		1.40		1.36		1.32		1.28		1.24
		Planned		...		...		...		...		...
Dec.	10871	Available		2640		1616		2520		2640		2640
		Cost		1.44		1.40		1.36		1.32		1.28
		Planned		...		...		...		...		...
Total Production Planned	R.T.		10560		9120		10080		10560		10560	
	O.T.			...		664		...		...		...

To Be Produced														
June		July		Aug.		Sept.		Oct.		Nov.		Dec.		Total Production Planned
R.T.	O.T.	R.T.	O.T.	R.T.	O.T.	R.T.	O.T.	R.T.	O.T.	R.T.	O.T.	R.T.	O.T.	
9600	2400	5760	1440	10560	2640	9600	2400	11040	2760	9120	2280	10080	2520	Planned
														10277
														10067
														9875
														9665
														9473
9600 / 0 / 9263	2400 / 1.00 / ...													9263
337 / .04 / 337	2400 / 1.04 / ...	5760 / 0 / 5760	1440 / 1.00 / 1033											9317
	2400 / 1.08 / ...		407 / 1.04 / ...	10560 / 0 / 9635	2640 / 1.00 / ...									9635
	2400 / 1.12 / ...		407 / 1.08 / ...	925 / .04 / 335	2640 / 1.04 / ...	9600 / 0 / 9600	2400 / 1.00 / ...							9935
	2400 / 1.16 / ...		407 / 1.12 / ...	590 / .08 / ...	2640 / 1.08 / ...		2400 / 1.04 / ...	11040 / 0 / 10253	2760 / 1.00 / ...					10253
	2400 / 1.20 / ...		407 / 1.16 / ...	590 / .12 / 490	2640 / 1.12 / ...		2400 / 1.08 / ...	787 / .04 / 787	2760 / 1.04 / ...	9120 / 0 / 9120	2280 / 1.00 / 56			10553
	2400 / 1.24 / ...		407 / 1.20 / ...		2640 / 1.16 / ...		2400 / 1.12 / ...		2760 / 1.08 / ...		2224 / 1.04 / ...	10080 / 0 / 10080	2520 / 1.00 / 791	10871
9600	...	5760	1033	10560	...	9600	...	11040	...	9120	56	10080	791	116640 / 2544

than the total number of hours required. The lower bound of the incremental cost of this plan is $2544.00. It may be more, but it will not be less.

The minimum-cost production plan with 60 men is shown in Table 7.9. The total incremental cost is $2911.64. This could most likely be reduced by employing 61 men.

Now, it might be well to examine the planning problem in a different manner. Suppose we employed 62 men and were producing the four products for which we established the production plan in Table 7.9. If we utilized all of the regular time hours, we could have the production plan in Table 7.10. The production plan shows that we need eight hours of over-

Table 7.10. A Production Plan Using Cumulative Data

Month	Cumulative Forecast Demand (Hours)	Cumulative Planned Production (Hours)	Planned Inventory (Hours)
Jan.	10,277	10,912	635
Feb.	20,344	20,336	−8
Mar.	30,219	30,752	533
Apr.	39,884	41,664	1780
May	49,357	52,576	3219
June	58,620	62,496	3876
July	67,937	68,448	511
Aug.	77,572	79,360	1788
Sept.	87,507	89,280	1773
Oct.	97,760	100,688	2928
Nov.	108,313	110,112	1799
Dec.	119,184	120,528	1344

time during February; otherwise, we cannot meet our requirements. If we use eight hours of overtime in February and all available regular time, we would have 1352 man-hours of inventory at the end of the year. Although this approach is simpler, it still requires additional planning to obtain the minimum-cost production plan. The method cited previously is much better, because we get an answer directly.

7.6. Summary

Production planning can be accomplished by a methodical approach to the problem. The techniques are straightforward and understandable. They have one serious restriction, which probably cannot be easily overcome: the size of the work force must be assumed before the plan is made. However, more elaborate methods can be used to determine the most economical size of work force.

8. Adjusting the Production Plan

8.1. Introduction

Once the production plan has been established, there are two primary reasons for adjustment. They are

1. The actual demand may depart from the forecast demand that was used to establish the production plan.
2. The actual production may not equal the planned production.

As we indicated in the chapter on forecasting, the forecast and the actual demand will not always be equal; in fact, there will be a distribution of variations of actual demand from forecast demand. The variations cannot be predicted as to their point of occurrence in time, but the distribution of their magnitude can be fairly well established. The actual production may depart from the planned production for a number of reasons. There may be a breakdown in the production line, there may be sickness among some of the employees, there may be a shortage of parts, or actual production may exceed planned production due to operations being more efficient than they normally are. There are, therefore, a number of reasons for adjustment. Because of these reasons and the fact that in some cases departures of demand and production may, for an extended period of time, all go in the same direction, the inventories on hand may build up excessively or may become excessively low. It is the objective of any adjusting system to prevent excess inventories or deficiency in inventory.

8.2. Methods of Adjusting the Production Plan

Any number of methods could be used in adjusting a production plan. Two which appear to be quite different but yet are also quite close are the weighted-average method and the leveling method. The weighted-average method applies a weighting factor against the departure of actual inventory from planned inventory and applies this to the production plan for some future period of time. It operates in much the same manner as the weighted average method of forecasting. The leveling method in many respects is quite similar and also is in some ways simpler. In the method of leveling, the departure of actual inventory from planned inventory is leveled or spread over a number of periods as an adjustment to the planned production for those periods. The choice of the leveling factor makes a considerable difference in the variations experienced from the actual production plan. The choice of leveling factor also affects the variations in actual inventory from planned inventory. Another factor which must be considered in establishing an adjusting method is the amount of time required to make an adjustment effective. In the examples with which we have been dealing, where our forecast and our production plan are for a month's period at a time, we would not have sufficient information to make an adjustment until the end of a month. This would give little time — in fact, generally insufficient time — to make adjustments to the production plan in the month immediately following. A number of things must be done before an adjustment can be made effective. First, the new or the adjusted production plan must be established. From this adjusted production plan a production schedule must be established. Once the production schedule is established, the necessary procurement must be made and even though material is already on order, some adjustments in the orders or in the delivery dates may be necessary in order to accomplish the adjusted production plan. Perhaps the best means of illustrating the method of leveling is by example.

8.3. Leveling Applied to Example 1

By use of the forecast and demand data of Example 1 for periods 25 through 36, we can illustrate the use of the leveling method for adjusting the production plan (see Table 4.5). From these data and the data of Table 7.2, we established the production plan of Table 7.3 which was summarized in Table 7.4.

The application of the leveling technique can be illustrated by use of a tabular arrangement such as Table 8.1. As this illustration develops, the reader should consider that, in the actual situation, the adjustments are made on a period-by-period basis and cannot all be completed at the same

Table 8.1. Adjustment of the Production Plan for Example 1 by Leveling over One Period

Month	Demand			Production			Inventory		
	Actual	Forecast	Actual Minus Forecast	Planned	Adjustments	Adjusted Plan	Actual	Planned	Actual Minus Planned
Opening Stock							0	0	0
Jan.	1250	1250	0	1250		1250	0	0	0
Feb.	1240	1250	−10	1250		1250	10	0	+10
Mar.	1110	1250	−140	1250	0	1250	150	0	+150
Apr.	1370	1250	+120	1250	−10	1240	20	0	+20
May	1200	1250	−50	1510	−140	1370	190	260	−70
June	1140	1250	−110	1400	+120	1520	570	410	+160
July	1040	1250	−210	840	−50	790	320	0	+320
Aug.	950	1250	−300	1250	−110	1140	510	0	+510
Sept.	1180	1250	−70	1250	−210	1040	370	0	+370
Oct.	1240	1250	−10	1288	−300	988	118	38	+80
Nov.	1200	1250	−50	1212	−70	1142	60	0	+60
Dec.	1170	1250	−80	1250	−10	1240	130	0	+130

time. (In fact, time is an integral part of all production-control situations, but it must be condensed in any text discussion.)

Considering the situation as of the first of January, we have certain information available to us. We know the forecast demand for each of the months. This is shown in the "Demand—Forecast" column of Table 8.1. We know the opening stock shown in the "Inventory—Planned" and "Inventory—Actual" columns. From Table 7.4 we also know the desired or planned inventory for the end of each month. These values are entered in the "Inventory—Planned" column of Table 8.1. The production plan determined in Table 7.3 is entered in the "Production—Planned" column.

At the end of January, we know the actual demand for the month was 125 units (from Table 4.5) or 1250 hours, when the conversion is made. This value is entered in the "Demand—Actual" column. Since forecast demand and actual demand are equal, the entry in the "Demand—Actual Minus Forecast" column is zero. In this example, we are assuming that actual production will always equal the adjusted planned production. For January, no adjustment has been made, so we produced 1250 hours, sold 1250, and have zero inventory. This is shown in the "Inventory—Actual" column. The entry in the "Inventory—Actual Minus Planned" column will be zero.

The objective of the leveling procedure is to adjust the planned production to compensate for the departures of actual sales from forecast demand. Thus, we must adjust the planned production upward or downward a total of units equal to the departure of actual demand from forecast demand. We have numerous choices of the number of periods over which this adjustment should occur. The number of periods used for the leveling should be a function of the desired end result. This will be discussed further at a later point in this chapter. In this first example we will make the total adjustment in one month's production. It must be realized that usually it will not be possible to make an adjustment in the period immediately following. Any change in a production plan will result in changes in the shop schedules, in the purchasing schedules, etc. Such changes may involve not only the product under consideration, but other products may be affected. Thus, a certain amount of time is necessary to effect a change in the production plan. In this example, and in the others to follow, we shall use one month for the elapsed interval between when it is known that an adjustment is required and when it actually occurs.

Any departure of actual sales from forecast demand during January would show up as an adjustment to the planned production in March. Since January sales were equal to the January forecast, there is no adjustment to the planned production for March.

At the end of February, we see that actual sales were less than forecast demand by 10 hours, and the actual inventory becomes 10 hours

$(10 = 0 + 1250 - 1240)$. The new inventory is equal to the old inventory plus the production during the period minus the usage during the period. This can be expressed as

$$I_i = I_{i-1} + p_i - s_i \qquad (8.1)$$

where I_i = ending inventory.

  I_{i-1} = beginning inventory.

  p_i = production during the ith period.

  s_i = demand during the ith period.

The relationship expressed in Eq. (8.1) is a very important one, for it says that the inventory at any point in time sums up the production and demand of all past periods. The solution of many production and inventory planning and control problems will be simplified if this relationship is used.

The fact that sales in February were less than the forecast by 10 hours requires that an adjustment be made in April production. This is a -10 adjustment to April production, giving an adjusted planned production of 1240 hours.

The remainder of Table 8.1 is constructed in the same manner as for the months of January and February.

Examination of Table 8.1 reveals that the actual production, "Production —Adjusted Plan" varies from 790 to 1520 hours, or about 48 per cent. If we do not include July, the variation is about 35 per cent. Further, actual inventory departs from planned inventory within a total range of 580 hours (from a -70 to $+510$). We might wonder if such variations are practical. Further, what is the significance of the minus inventories? The minus departures of actual from planned inventories can have significance in two ways if the actual inventory is negative: (1) they can represent lost sales, in which case the actual inventory should be shown as zero and a compensating adjustment made to planned production, or (2) they can represent back orders (material to be delivered in the future), in which case they should be carried as minus inventories. The latter situation is assumed in this chapter.

To illustrate other applications of the leveling technique, Table 8.2 was constructed to show the same situation, except that the adjustment or leveling occurs over five periods instead of one period.

In Table 8.2, the -10 adjustment from February shows up as a -2 adjustment to the planned production in the months of April, May, June, July, and August. The -140 adjustment from March shows up as a -28 adjustment in the months of May, June, July, August, and September. Otherwise, the table is constructed in the same manner as Table 8.1.

The "Production—Adjusted Plan" column now shows smaller variations in production (from 824 to 1480), and the actual inventory varies

Table 8.2. Adjustment of the Production Plan for Example 1 by Leveling over Five Periods

Month	Demand			Production			Inventory		
	Actual	Forecast	Actual Minus Forecast	Planned	Adjustments	Adjusted Plan	Actual	Planned	Actual Minus Planned
Opening Stock							0	0	0
Jan.	1250	1250	0	1250	0	1250	0	0	0
Feb.	1240	1250	−10	1250	0	1250	10	0	+10
Mar.	1110	1250	−140	1250		1250	150	0	+150
Apr.	1370	1250	+120	1250	0 − 2	1248	28	0	+28
May	1200	1250	−50	1510	0 − 2 − 28	1480	308	260	+48
June	1140	1250	−110	1400	0 − 2 − 28 + 24	1394	562	410	+152
July	1040	1250	−210	840	0 − 2 − 28 + 24 − 10	824	346	0	+346
Aug.	950	1250	−300	1250	−2 − 28 + 24 − 10 − 22	1212	608	0	+608
Sept.	1180	1250	−70	1250	−28 + 24 − 10 − 22 − 42	1172	600	0	+600
Oct.	1240	1250	−10	1288	+24 − 10 − 22 − 42 − 60	1178	538	38	+500
Nov.	1200	1250	−50	1212	−10 − 22 − 42 − 60 − 14	1064	402	0	+402
Dec.	1170	1250	−80	1250	−22 − 42 − 60 − 14 − 2	1110	342	0	+342

Table 8.3. Adjustment of the Production Plan for Example 1 by Leveling over Ten Periods

Month	Demand			Production			Inventory		
	Actual	Forecast	Actual Minus Forecast	Planned	Adjustments	Adjusted Plan	Actual	Planned	Actual Minus Planned
Opening Stock							0	0	0
Jan.	1250	1250	0	1250		1250	0	0	0
Feb.	1240	1250	−10	1250		1250	10	0	+10
Mar.	1110	1250	−140	1250		1250	150	0	+150
Apr.	1370	1250	+120	1250	0 − 1	1249	29	0	+29
May	1200	1250	−50	1510	0 − 1 − 14	1495	324	260	+64
June	1140	1250	−110	1400	0 − 1 − 14 + 12	1397	581	410	+171
July	1040	1250	−210	840	0 − 1 − 14 + 12 − 5	832	373	0	+373
Aug.	950	1250	−300	1250	0 − 1 − 14 + 12 − 5 − 11	1231	654	0	+654
Sept.	1180	1250	−70	1250	0 − 1 − 14 + 12 − 5 − 11 − 21	1210	684	0	+684
Oct.	1240	1250	−10	1288	0 − 1 − 14 + 12 − 5 − 11 − 21 − 30	1218	662	38	+624
Nov.	1200	1250	−50	1212	0 − 1 − 14 + 12 − 5 − 11 − 21 − 30 − 7	1135	597	0	+597
Dec.	1170	1250	−80	1250	0 − 1 − 14 + 12 − 5 − 11 − 21 − 30 − 7 − 1	1172	599	0	+599

from 0 to +608. However, the average number of excess items in inventory (considering only plus values) is greater (266) than it is under the conditions of Table 8.1 (151). Thus, we have reduced variations in production on a month-by-month basis, but at the same time this reduction of production variation requires that we carry more inventory.

Leveling over ten periods of production is illustrated in Table 8.3. Using the same data, we obtain variations in production (from 832 to 1495). In this instance, we again show no negative inventories and our average excess inventory is 330 hours. (*Note* Had the inventory gone negative near the beginning of the year, leveling over ten periods rather than five, or one, gives a greater probability that it could have stayed negative for a long period of time.)

Figure 8.1 shows a graphical comparison of the manner in which the number of leveling periods affects the variation of actual production from

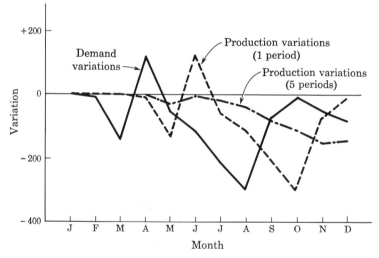

Fig. 8.1. Effect of the number of leveling periods on variations of actual production from planned production.

planned production. When adjustments are leveled over one period, the variation in actual production from planned production is merely displaced (out of phase) by the number of periods required to make the adjustment effective. When leveling is over five periods, there is a smaller departure of actual production from planned production.

In Fig. 8.2 we have a comparison of the variation of actual inventory from planned inventory by leveling over one period and five periods. As we previously stated, the average inventory is higher with the longer leveling period. If we plot the results of leveling over ten periods on Fig. 8.1 and 8.2, we shall find that they give lesser variations in production and greater variations in inventory.

From the above, we see that we must make a choice between increasing

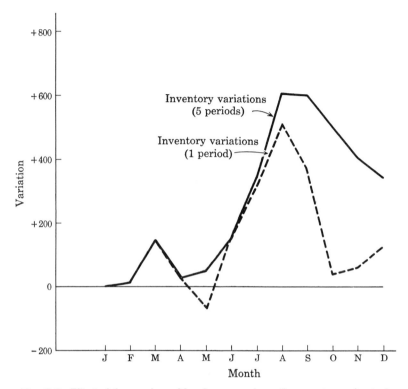

Fig. 8.2. Effect of the number of leveling periods on the variations of actual inventory from planned inventory.

the average amount of inventory and thus the cost of carrying inventory, thereby reducing production variations, or allowing wider production variations in return for less inventory.

8.4. Reconciliation of the Adjusted Production Plan with Available Hours

In Table 8.1, we should compare the adjusted planned production with the available hours from Table 7.3. For January through May, the available hours exceed the adjusted plan, but in June the adjusted plan requires 1520 hours, and there are only 1400 hours available. Thus, the adjusted planned production for June in Table 8.1 should be 1400 hours. The actual inventory for June would be 450 hours. This still exceeds the planned inventory. Now, we must decide what is to be done about the 120 hours planned for in June but not produced in June. There are two alternatives: (1) not to make any compensations for it, or (2) to add 120 hours to the adjusted planned production in the months immediately following. If we do not make any compensating changes, our total adjustments will be -120 hours from what they should have been. If we include it in the immediately following months, we can increase the adjusted planned production in July by 50 hours ($672 + 168 - 790$) and in August by 70 hours. (It is easy to see that at least half of this deficiency must be made up — the November inventory is 60 units. But in an actual situation, we cannot see the future as we can in an example.)

8.5. The Effect of the Number of Periods Used in the Leveling Procedure

When the leveling procedure is used for the adjustment of production plans, there is a very noticeable effect resulting from the number of periods over which any adjustment is made.

When all of the adjustment is made in one period, the variation in production follows the variation in demand but is out of phase with it by the number of periods required to make an adjustment. As the number of periods used in leveling is increased, the tendency is to smooth out the variations of actual production from the original planned production. Also, the differences become farther out of phase as the number of periods increase. Another effect, which has already been pointed out, is on the departure of actual inventory from planned inventory. If demand varies from forecast, then actual inventory is going to vary from planned inventory. The amount of variation is dependent upon the number of periods used for leveling. As more periods are used, the actual inventory departs further from the planned inventory. Therefore, in choosing the number of periods in which the adjustment will be made, it is necessary to make an economic decision between the cost of a variable production plan versus the cost of variable inventory levels. If it is desired to hold the production plan essentially constant, then we must be willing to accept rather wide departures of actual inventory from planned inventory. On the other hand, if it is more economical to hold actual inventory very close to planned inventory, we must accept rather wide variations of actual production from planned production.

In the determination of safety stock, we considered only the variations in demand. By now, it should be apparent that variations in production as well as variations in the method of adjusting production and, consequently, the adjustments in inventory will also affect the required amounts of safety stock. The entire planning and control operation is interrelated, and the effects of action at one point in the process are noticeable at many other points.

8.6. Summary

There are two primary reasons why adjustment of a production plan is necessary: one, departure of actual demand from forecast demand, and two, departure of actual production from planned production. There are a number of methods of adjusting the production plan. The one discussed in this chapter was termed "leveling;" when the "leveling method" is used, there are certain economic considerations which must be made in the choice of the leveling period or periods.

9. Scheduling Production

9.1. Introduction

Once a definite production plan has been established, the next step is to schedule the planned quantity of product through the manufacturing process. This function falls into the area most commonly known as production scheduling. The detail required in the schedule is a function of the type of manufacturing. If the manufacturing process is an assembly line involving very few products, it is possible to schedule the required number of units into the line. If the plant is a job-shop type of operation, it is probably economical to schedule the detailed operations, movements, etc. of each piece part, each subassembly, each major assembly, and each final assembly. In fact, the work may be assigned to individual machines or to individual classes of machines.

Such detailed scheduling requires far more information and a different type of information than is required to establish a production plan. It is necessary to know the capabilities of each machine, each fixture, each operator, each department, etc. These capabilities include the size and type of part that can be handled, the time for each operation, the time available, the time for maintenance, the time for change-over and many other, perhaps small, but no less important pieces of information. To be effective in this job, the scheduler must be a highly competent individual acquainted with all aspects of manufacturing.

9.2. Sequencing the Operations for One Product*

In Table 7.3, we made a production plan for the product of Example 1. The production plan called for seven men. In sequencing the production of this product, we should have seven work stations and assign the work to those stations in the most efficient manner. (We shall assume that this is an assembly operation and that one or several operations can be done at a single work station.)

To sequence the manufacturing of this product requires that we know the necessary operations and the possible order in which they can be done. The operations in the required order are shown in Fig. 9.1. There are a total of

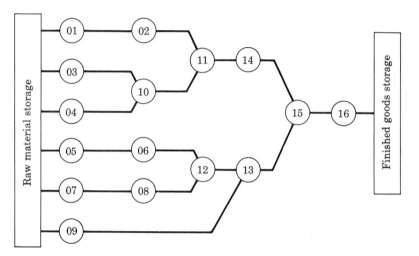

Fig. 9.1. Operations and sequences for Example 1.

16 operations, and the total time for one unit of product is 10 man-hours. The standard minutes for each operation are shown in Table 9.1.

The assignment of these operations can be done in a straightforward manner. The first step is to make a table such as Table 9.2 in which the operations are listed in numerical order. In the second column, enter the time remaining for the operations that follow the listed operation. For example, from Fig. 9.1, we see that operations 02, 11, 14, 15, and 16 must follow operation 01. The times for these operations (from Table 9.1) are 43, 22, 86, 21, and 63. The subsequent sequence time is the sum of these times, or 235 minutes. The operations that follow operation 02 are 11, 14,

*This material was adapted from W. B. Helgeson and D. P. Birnie, "Assembly Line Balancing Using the Ranked Positional Weight Technique" *The Journal of Industrial Engineering*, Volume XII, Number 6, November–December 1961, pages 394–398, by permission.

Table 9.1. Operation Times for
Example 1

Operation	Time	Operation	Time
01	20	09	45
02	43	10	22
03	23	11	22
04	90	12	22
05	30	13	22
06	33	14	86
07	21	15	21
08	37	16	63
		Total	600

Table 9.2. Subsequent Sequence Times and Preceding Operations in
Order of Operations

Operation	Subsequent Sequence Time	Operation/s That Must Immediately Precede
01	235	. . .
02	192	01
03	214	. . .
04	214	. . .
05	161	. . .
06	128	05
07	165	. . .
08	128	07
09	106	. . .
10	192	03, 04
11	170	02, 10
12	106	06, 08
13	84	09, 12
14	84	11
15	63	13, 14
16	0	15

15, and 16 with a subsequent sequence time of $22 + 86 + 21 + 63$, or 192
minutes. The remainder of the column is completed in the same manner.
The third column of Table 9.2 is determined from Fig. 9.1. We see that
there are no operations that must precede operation 01, so there is no entry
in the column "Operation/s That Must Immediately Precede." Since oper-

ation 02 must follow operation 01, an 01 is placed in the third column of Table 9.2 opposite the 02 in the first column. The remainder of the third column is completed similarly.

It is usually well to assign the operations with the largest subsequent sequence times to the first work station. To facilitate such an assignment, it may be helpful to rearrange the operations in descending size of the subsequent sequence time. This rearrangement is shown in Table 9.3. From

Table 9.3. Subsequent Sequence Times and Preceding Operations in Order of Sequence Times

Operation	Subsequent Sequence Time	Operation/s That Must Immediately Precede
01	235	. . .
03	214	. . .
04	214	. . .
02	192	01
10	192	03, 04
11	170	02, 10
07	165	. . .
05	161	. . .
06	128	05
08	128	07
09	106	. . .
12	106	06, 08
13	84	09, 12
14	84	11
15	63	13, 14
16	0	15

this table, we see that operation 01 has the longest subsequent sequence time and thus should be assigned to the first work station.

Before starting the actual assignment of operations to the work stations, we should determine a desirable cycle time. Since there are 600 minutes required and seven men, an optimum cycle time would be $\frac{600}{7}$ or 85.7 minutes. A look at Table 9.1 reveals that the longest operation is 90 minutes, so a cycle time of 90 minutes is the minimum we can expect to achieve.

If we start the assignment of operations to work stations on the basis of the order in Table 9.3 and a cycle time of 90 minutes, we can assign operation 01 to work station 1 and have a remaining time of 90 − 20 or 70 minutes. The next operation is 03, requiring 23 minutes. If we assign this operation to work station 1, the remaining or unused time is 70 − 23 or 47 minutes. From Table 9.3, we see that there are no preceding operations for operation 03, so it is an appropriate assignment. The next operation shown in Table 9.3 is 04, requiring 90 minutes. This operation cannot be assigned to work station 1, since the operation times would then exceed the 90-minute cycle time. Now, we should try operation 02 with a 43-minute time. Since there are still 47 minutes unused at work station 1, operation 02 can be assigned with four minutes of unused time at work station 1. There are no operations with a time of 4 minutes or less, so we start assignments to work station 2. We could not assign operation 04 to work station 1, so it is the first candidate for assignment to work station 2. Since the time for operation 04 is 90 minutes, it is the only operation assigned to work station 2. Proceeding in this way, we arrive at a possible solution, which is shown in Table 9.4. In this solution, the assignments are in the order of Table 9.3

Table 9.4. A Possible Assignment and Sequence of Operations for Example 1

Work Station	Operations Assigned	Time Assigned (Minutes)	Operation Efficiency (%)
1	01, 03, 02	20 + 23 + 43 = 86	95.5
2	04	90	100.0
3	10, 11, 07	22 + 22 + 21 = 65	72.2
4	05, 06	30 + 33 = 63	70.0
5	08, 09	37 + 45 = 82	91.1
6	12, 13	22 + 22 = 44	48.9
7	14	86	95.5
8	15, 16	84	93.3
Over-all Efficiency = 83.3%			

except for operation 04. The assignments call for eight work stations and, consequently, for eight men. The efficiency is only 83.3 per cent. If we could possibly rearrange some of the operations, maintain the precedence requirements, and use a 90-minute cycle with seven men, we would achieve an efficiency of 95.2 per cent.

The 95.2 per cent efficiency can be achieved by rearranging the order of operations 10, 11, 07, 05, 06, 08 to 05, 06, 07, 08, 10, 11. This has been done in Table 9.5. The operations will still be performed in a sequence that causes no conflicts. The assignments of Table 9.5 are an optimum solution to the problem.

It is possible to obtain an indication of the possibility of achieving the optimum solution by computing combinations of operation times that ap-

Table 9.5. An Optimum Assignment of Operations
for Example 1

Work Station	Operations Assigned	Time Assigned (Minutes)
1	01, 02, 03	20 + 43 + 23 = 86
2	04	90
3	05, 06, 07	30 + 33 + 21 = 84
4	08, 10, 11	37 + 22 + 22 = 81
5	09, 12, 13	45 + 22 + 22 = 89
6	14	86
7	15, 16	21 + 63 = 84
Over-all Efficiency = $\frac{600}{630} \times 100 = 95.2\%$		

proach the minimum cycle time. If we do this for the preceding example, we get the figures shown in Table 9.6. However, before going ahead with

Table 9.6. Combinations of Operation
Times that May Result in an
Optimum Assignment

Operations	Time (Minutes)
01, 02, 03	20 + 43 + 23 = 86
04	90
05, 06, 07	30 + 33 + 21 = 84
08, 09	37 + 45 = 82
10, 11, 12, 13	22 + 22 + 22 + 22 = 88
14	86
15, 16	21 + 63 = 84

this, we must check the precedence requirements. All such requirements have been met, and we have another optimum solution. The difference between the two solutions is in the assignment of operations 09, 10, and 11 to work stations 4 and 5. The solution of Table 9.6 might be preferable, since it tends to balance the work more evenly (only slightly, however).

In Chapter 7, the production plan of Table 7.3 was made on the basis of 100 per cent efficiency. We now find that we can achieve only 95.2 per cent efficiency. Instead of 10 man-hours per unit, it will require 10.5 man-hours per unit. Thus, the monthly forecast of demand must be increased to 1312.5 hours. The annual requirements under these conditions are 15,750 man-hours. Including overtime, seven men can provide 1944 (1.25)(7) or 17,010

Table 9.7. Revised Production Plan for Example 1

Month in Which Required	Man Hours Required		Month in Which									
			Jan.		Feb.		Mar.		Apr.		May	
			R.T.	O.T.	R.T.	O.T.	R.T.	O.T.	R.T.	O.T.	R.T.	O.T.
			1232	308	1064	266	1176	294	1232	308	1232	308
Jan.	1312.5	Available	1232	308								
		Cost	0	1.00								
		Planned	1232	80.5								
Feb.	1312.5	Available		227.5	1064	266						
		Cost		1.04	0	1.00						
		Planned		...	1064	248.5						
Mar.	1312.5	Available		227.5		17.5	1176	294				
		Cost		1.08		1.04	0	1.00				
		Planned		...		...	1176	136.5				
Apr.	1312.5	Available		227.5		17.5		157.5	1232	308		
		Cost		1.12		1.08		1.04	0	1.00		
		Planned		...		...		...	1232	80.5		
May	1312.5	Available		227.5		17.5		157.5		227.5	1232	308
		Cost		1.16		1.12		1.08		1.04	0	1.00
		Planned		...		...		...		...	1232	80.5
June	1312.5	Available		227.5		17.5		157.5		227.5		227.5
		Cost		1.20		1.16		1.12		1.08		1.04
		Planned		...		...		...		...		...
July	1312.5	Available		227.5		17.5		157.5		227.5		227.5
		Cost		1.24		1.20		1.16		1.12		1.08
		Planned		...		...		...		157.5		227.5
Aug.	1312.5	Available		227.5		17.5		157.5		70		
		Cost		1.28		1.24		1.20		1.16		
		Planned		...		...		...		...		
Sept.	1312.5	Available		227.5		17.5		157.5		70		
		Cost		1.32		1.28		1.24		1.20		
		Planned		...		...		...		...		
Oct.	1312.5	Available		227.5		17.5		157.5		70		
		Cost		1.36		1.32		1.28		1.24		
		Planned		...		...		...		...		
Nov.	1312.5	Available		227.5		17.5		157.5		70		
		Cost		1.40		1.36		1.32		1.28		
		Planned		...		...		...		...		
Dec.	1312.5	Available		227.5		17.5		157.5		70		
		Cost		1.44		1.40		1.36		1.32		
		Planned		...		...		...		...		
Total Production Planned	R.T.		1232		1064		1176		1232		1232	
	O.T.			80.5		248.5		136.5		238		308

'o Be Produced

	June		July		Aug.		Sept.		Oct.		Nov.		Dec.		Total Production Planned
	R.T.	O.T.	R.T.	O.T.	R.T.	O.T.	R.T.	O.T.	R.T.	O.T.	R.T.	O.T.	R.T.	O.T.	
	1120	280	672	168	1232	308	1120	280	1288	322	1064	266	1176	294	
															1312.5
															1312.5
															1312.5
															1312.5
															1312.5
	1120 0 1120	280 1.00 192.5													1312.5
		87.5 1.04 87.5	672 0 672	168 1.00 168											1312.5
					1232 0 1232	308 1.00 80.5									1312.5
					227.5 1.04 ...		1120 0 1120	280 1.00 192.5							1312.5
					227.5 1.08 ...		87.5 1.04 ...		1288 0 1288	322 1.00 24.5					1312.5
					227.5 1.12 ...		87.5 1.08 ...		297.5 1.08 ...		1064 0 1064	266 1.00 248.5			1312.5
					227.5 1.16 ...		87.5 1.12 ...				17.5 1.04 ...		1176 0 1176	294 1.00 136.5	1312.5
	1120	280	672	168	1232	80.5	1120	192.5	1288	24.5	1064	248.5	1176	136.5	13608.0 2142.0

man-hours. There is a possibility that we can make a production plan to meet the revised requirements with seven men. Before doing that, it may be possible to use only six men (six work stations) and achieve an efficiency in excess of 95.2 per cent, which is the best possible with seven men. But six men can provide only 14,580 man-hours in a year. At 100 per cent efficiency, we require 15,000 man-hours, so we must use seven men.

A revised production plan with seven men at 95.2 per cent efficiency is shown in Table 9.7. The incremental costs are now $2182.60, an increase of $762.28 over the incremental costs of the plan in Table 7.3. This is not a valid comparison, since we are adding 750 man-hours of work. Assuming that total overhead and other costs are not variable with variations in direct labor hours worked, at least, within the range of the two solutions, the second plan costs $2262.28 more. This is the cost of 750 overtime hours at $3.00 per hour plus the added inventory carrying cost of $12.28 ($40.60 − $28.32).

Now, we have even less possibility for variations in production to meet variations in demand. It is necessary to be rather cautious in any adjustments made to the production plan, since we are using 15,750 of the 17,010 man-hours available. Before we used only 15,000 of the 17,010 man-hours.

9.3. The Assignment of Orders to Machines

In a multiproduct operation, where there may be several machines that can do the same job, problems of the assignment of orders to machines may arise. The objective of any such assignment is to minimize the total costs. To do this exactly may require an extensive amount of data and an unjustifiable amount of time and calculations, particularly if such calculations must be done manually. However, if we assume that the cost of doing a job varies directly with the time to do the job, we can use a simple method called the *indicator method*.*

Again, an example will serve to illustrate this technique. Assume that the shop has four orders, as follows:

Order 1   100 pieces
Order 2   200 pieces
Order 3   50 pieces
Order 4   75 pieces

Any order can be done on any of four machines, but the time required for the order may vary with the machine. Each of the four machines has a limited amount of time available for doing this job. The pertinent data are summarized in Table 9.8.

*Adapted from Nyles V. Reinfeld and William R. Vogel, *Mathematical Programming*, Englewood Cliffs, N. J.: Prentice-Hall, Inc., 1958, pages 153–161.

Table 9.8. Standard Pieces per Hour for
Each Order on Each Machine

Order	Machine			
	A	B	C	D
1	1	$\frac{2}{3}$	$\frac{4}{5}$	$\frac{4}{3}$
2	2	1	$\frac{10}{11}$	$\frac{5}{3}$
3	2	$\frac{4}{3}$	1	$\frac{5}{2}$
4	1	$\frac{4}{5}$	$\frac{2}{3}$	$\frac{5}{4}$
Machine Hours Available	80	150	250	100

The first step is to determine the number of hours required to do a given order on a given machine. This has been done in Table 9.9 in the columns headed "Hours per Order."

The next step is to establish some measure of the efficiency of each machine in manufacturing each order. This is done by the indicator. The machine with the highest production rate for a given order is assigned an indicator of 1.00. The next machine, in order of production rate, is assigned an indicator of hours on this machine divided by hours on the best machine. For order 1, machine D, is best, so it should be given an indicator of 1.00; machine A is second best, so it gets an indicator of 1.33, etc. This is shown in the indicator columns of Table 9.9, which summarizes the problem. Orders should now be assigned to machines on the basis of the lowest indicators, if sufficient time is available.

Examination of Table 9.9 reveals that certain combinations are not possible (if we assume that an order must be done on only one machine). Orders 1 and 2 cannot be done on machine A. They require 100 hours each, and there are only 80 hours available. Likewise, order 2 cannot be assigned to machine B nor to machine D. Consequently, order 2 must be assigned to machine C even though it has the highest (least desirable) indicator. When the assignment is made, the hours per order should be circled (as the 220 hours for order 2 on machine C). Order 1 cannot be done on machine A. After the assignment of order 2 to machine C, there is insufficient time for order 1 on machine C. But order 1 has a 1.00 indicator on machine D and will be assigned there. Order 3 can also be assigned to machine D. Now, order 4 must be assigned to either machine A or machine B. Since machine A has the smaller indicator, order 4 will be assigned there. This completes the assignment. The table is completed by determining the "Machine Time Used" row. The total machine time to be used is 390 hours. Any other assignment will take more hours.

The indicator method is simple and easily used, but it does not directly

Table 9.9. An Example of the Indicator Method of Machine Assignment

Order	Order Size	Machine A			Machine B			Machine C			Machine D		
		Std. Pcs. per Hour	Indicator	Hours per Order	Std. Pcs. per Hour	Indicator	Hours per Order	Std. Pcs. per Hour	Indicator	Hours per Order	Std. Pcs. per Hour	Indicator	Hours per Order
1	100 pcs.	1	1.33	100	2/3	2.00	150	4/5	1.67	125	4/3	1.00	75
2	200 pcs.	2	1.00	100	1	2.00	200	10/11	2.20	220	5/3	1.20	120
3	50 pcs.	2	1.25	25	4/3	1.88	37½	1	2.50	50	5/2	1.00	20
4	75 pcs.	1	1.25	75	4/5	1.56	93¾	2/3	1.87	112½	5/4	1.00	60
Machine Time Available			80			150			250			100	
Machine Time Used			75			0			220			95	

consider the costs involved. It does indirectly consider costs by basing the indicator on the relative efficiency of the machines on each order.

9.4. The Use of Charts in Scheduling

Many times it is desirable to display schedules by charts. Most scheduling charts are based on the Gantt Chart. This chart can be illustrated by the order-assignment example. If we assume that the times used in the previous example were based on an eight-week period, we must have previously scheduled jobs on machine A for 8(40) — 80 or 240 hours — on machine B for 170 hours, on machine C for 70 hours, and on machine D for 220 hours. This is shown in Fig. 9.2. The previously scheduled times are

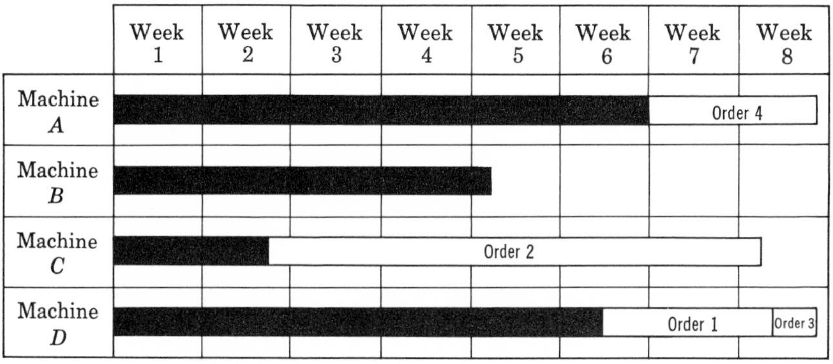

	Week 1	Week 2	Week 3	Week 4	Week 5	Week 6	Week 7	Week 8
Machine A							Order 4	
Machine B								
Machine C			Order 2					
Machine D						Order 1		Order 3

Fig. 9.2. Gantt load chart for order assignment.

shown by the solid blocks. To illustrate how the chart is used, the order assignments from Table 9.9 are shown by the open bars with the order number inside. Table 9.9 assigns order 4 to machine A and requires 75 hours. Order 2 is assigned to machine C and requires 220 hours, etc.

A similar chart can also be used to show the assignment of work to the work stations established in Table 9.5. Here, we must recognize that the operations on the same unit must follow (in time) from work station 1 to 2, etc. Since there are many units to be made, there will be a unit being assembled at each work station during each 90-minute cycle.

There are many forms of charts used and many commercially available charts, forms, boards, etc. Each system has its strong points and each its weak points. The general intent of charting is to show work that needs to be done, work that has been done, backlogs, etc.

9.5. The Schedule with Lead Times

In intermittent manufacturing and in continuous manufacturing where the product is made in large lots spaced in time, there will usually be lead times to consider. Suppose that a product consists of four parts. Each of the parts is purchased as a raw material and then is further processed in the plant. Part A-1 goes through two operations. Operation 01 requires 24 minutes, and operation 02 requires 48 minutes. The purchasing lead time for part A-1 is four weeks. There are similar conditions for the other three parts, as shown in Table 9.10. The product is on a special order of 100 units.

Table 9.10. Lead Times and Operation Times To Be Used in Scheduling

| | | In-Plant Operations | |
Part	Purchasing Lead Time for Raw Material (Weeks)	Operation Number	Operation Time (Minutes)
A-1	4	01	24.0
		02	48.0
A-2	6	03	48.0
		04	24.0
A-3	3	05	24.0
A-4	1	06	24.0

The 100 units of each part must be available as a lot and will be processed as a lot. Further, the parts will be processed through each operation as a lot. Operation 01 is a turning operation on part A-1, operation 02 is a milling operation on part A-1, operation 03 is a turning operation on part A-2, operation 04 is a milling operation on part A-2, operation 05 is the assembly of parts A-1, A-2, and A-3, and operation 06 is the assembly of part A-4 to the subassembly of parts A-1, A-2, and A-3. All turning operations will be on the same piece of equipment. The same holds for all milling operations.

Since the purchasing lead time for part A-2 exceeds that of part A-1 and they are made on the same equipment, we shall schedule part A-1 to be manufactured first, then part A-2, the subassembly, and the assembly in that order. The schedule including the purchasing lead times is shown in Fig. 9.3. The total elaspsed time, from placing the first order to the completion of the order, is 11 weeks. The operations cover six weeks of elapsed time.

The schedule in Fig. 9.3 gives the minimum total elapsed time under the given conditions, as well as minimum inventory. If we were to place all orders at the same time, we would have part A-1 in inventory for one week, part A-3 in inventory for six weeks, and part A-4 in inventory for nine weeks. This latter course has the advantage of incorporating a safety factor on the lead times of all parts except those which have the tightest schedules. However, it costs more, because there are more inventory carrying costs.

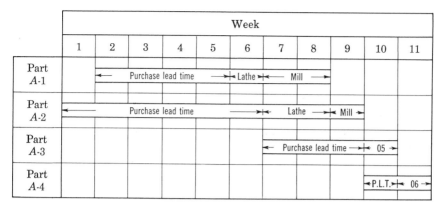

Fig. 9.3. A schedule with lead times.

The type of schedule shown in Fig. 9.3 is also applicable to the programming of production for new products and for plant expansions.

9.6. Scheduling Several Products

When several products are produced on the same production line it is necessary to establish the quantity of each product to be produced in any given time period (assuming that we are not using economic fractions of yearly demand) and the order in which the products are to be scheduled. The quantities to be produced can be determined by using the ratio of the total quantities available through the scheduling period to the total expected usage during the scheduling period. This ratio will be called the available-usage ratio. The order in which the products are to be scheduled is determined by the product inventory to product usage ratio which will be shortened to the inventory-usage ratio. When products are scheduled in economic fractions of yearly demand, the inventory-usage ratio will determine the order of scheduling.

9.6.1. Scheduling by the Available-Usage Ratio

Again, we use Examples 1, 2, 3, and 4. Assume that we have the following inventories on January 1:

Example 1	85 units or 850 hours
Example 2	55 units or 1320 hours
Example 3	65 units or 1170 hours
Example 4	55 units or 825 hours

This is a total of 4165 hours in inventory on January 1. From Table 7.9, we find that 10,560 hours should be scheduled in January. Also, as previously determined in Chapter 3, the expected usage is 10,277 hours. The available-usage ratio is

$$\frac{4165 + 10{,}560}{10{,}277} = 1.43$$

The quantity of each product to be scheduled is the expected monthly demand multiplied by the available-usage ratio minus the inventory on hand at the beginning of the month. The planned ending inventory of each product is the expected monthly demand multiplied by the available-usage ratio minus the expected monthly demand. These calculations are shown in Table 9.11.

Table 9.11. Determination of the Number of Units to be Scheduled

Product	Expected Usage	Total Requirements	Inventory on Hand	Production To Be Scheduled		Planned Ending Inventory
(Example)	(Hours)	(Hours)	(Hours)	Hours	Units	(Hours)
1	1,250	1,792	850	942	94.2	542
2	2,136	3,061	1,320	1,741	72.5	925
3	3,366	4,822	1,170	3,652	202.9	1,456
4	3,525	5,050	825	4,225	281.7	1,525
Total	10,277	14,725	4,165	10,560		4,448

The order of scheduling should be Example 4,3,2, and 1. The inventory-usage ratios are 0.23, 0.35, 0.62, and 0.68, respectively. (See Table 9.12)

At the end of January, another determination of the available-usage ratio should be made. This new ratio would be used to establish the production schedule for February.

9.6.2. The Use of the Inventory-Usage Ratio to Determine the Sequence of the Production Schedule

When several products are to be scheduled, the inventory-usage ratio can be used to establish the order or sequence of scheduling when attempting to achieve equal inventory-usage ratios at the end of the scheduling period or when producing the products in economic fractions of yearly demand. In Table 5.2, we established that we should produce 0.0557 of the yearly demand in each production cycle. The necessary computations are shown in Table 9.12.

Before the next cycle is scheduled, new inventory-usage ratios should be computed. Since demand is a dynamic thing, the demand situation is constantly changing and it is only through the continual checking of the

Table 9.12. Run-out Times for Several Products

Product (Example)	Inventory on Hand (Hours)	Expected Usage (Hours)	Inventory-Usage Ratio	Order of Scheduling	Quantity to Schedule
1	850	1250	0.68	4	84
2	1320	2136	0.62	3	63
3	1170	3366	0.35	2	112
4	825	3525	0.23	1	151

current situation that we can accomplish a good job of controlling production and inventories.

9.7. Summary

There are many approaches that can be taken in establishing production schedules. There are also many methods of displaying the schedule. This is as it should be, because a variety of problems arise in scheduling production. There are several rather simple mathematical techniques which objectively evaluate the available scheduling data and reduce the risks involved.

10. Linear Programming Applied to Scheduling and Distribution

10.1. Introduction

There are several linear programming methods that are applicable to the problems of production and inventory planning and control. One of these methods, the indicator method, was used in Chapter 9. Another of these methods is the modi method. This method will be applied to two types of problems. The first application will be to the distribution of product between plants and warehouses in a multiplant, multiwarehouse operation. The second application is to a machine-order or machine-scheduling problem.

The modi method, when applied to the distribution problem, is generally called the transportation method. It is illustrated in the following example.

10.2. Setting up the Problem

The transportation method of solution to the distribution problem requires that the following information be known:

1. The cost of production at each plant.
    a. Regular time.
    b. Overtime.
2. The planned production at each plant.
    a. Regular time.
    b. Overtime.
3. The forecast requirements at each warehouse.
4. The cost of transporting the product from each plant to each warehouse.

An example of this type of data is given in Tables 10.1 and 10.2. In the example, all planned production is on regular time, and the per unit cost of

Table 10.1. Planned Production and Warehouse Requirements (in Units)

Plant	Planned Production	Warehouse	Forecast Requirements
A	8	1	10
B	7	2	8
C	9	3	9
D	4	4	1
Total Planned Production	28	Total Forecast Requirements	28

Table 10.2. Transportation Costs from Plants to Warehouses (in Dollars)

Warehouse	Plant			
	A	B	C	D
1	10	8	10	8
2	10	7	8	10
3	11	9	9	7
4	12	14	13	10

producing the product is the same at all plants. A further simplifying condition is that the planned production equals the forecast requirements. The above restrictions are not necessary and will be discussed later.

10.3. Solving the Problem

The solution to the transportation problem starts with the assignment of planned production at the various plants to fill the forecast requirements of the various warehouses. A systematic approach to this assignment can be made by use of the "northwest corner rule." This rule can be stated mathematically as follows

Assign output of plant P_r to warehouse W_s if

$$\sum_{i=1}^{r} (PP)_i > \sum_{j=1}^{s-1} (WR)_j \tag{a}$$

and if

$$\sum_{i=1}^{r-1} (PP)_i < \sum_{j=1}^{s} (WR)_j \tag{b}$$

where $(PP)_i$ = the planned production for the ith plant.

(WR_j) = the forecast requirement for the jth warehouse.

The use of the northwest corner rule is shown in Table 10.3, the assignment table.

Table 10.3. First Assignment

Warehouse	Plant				Total Forecast Requirements
	A	B	C	D	
1	8	2			10
2		5	3		8
3			6	3	9
4				1	1
Total Planned Production	8	7	9	4	28

In Table 10.3, all the output of plant A (8 units) was assigned to warehouse 1. Since warehouse 1 required 10 units, it was necessary to make a further assignment of 2 units from plant B. After this assignment, there were still 5 units of output from plant B to be assigned. In accordance with the northwest corner rule, these 5 units were assigned to warehouse 2. The remainder of the table was completed in a like manner. The assignments meet the requirements at each warehouse and still use the planned production from each plant.

The next step is to evaluate the assignments in the first assignment table. This is done by what we shall call the value table. But before constructing the value table, we shall revise the transportation costs by subtracting the smallest transportation cost (7 units) from all the costs in the transportation cost table. We get the revised transportation cost table as Table 10.4 (*Note* It is not necessary to make a revised cost table, but since the solution is based on incremental costs, it may simplify the arithmetic to do so. However, the total transportation cost must be used to determine the actual cost of the optimum assignment.)

Table 10.4. Revised Transportation Costs

Warehouse	Plant			
	A	B	C	D
1	3	1	3	1
2	3	0	1	3
3	4	2	2	0
4	5	7	6	3

Table 10.5. Partial First Value Table

	Warehouse	Plant	A	B	C	D
		Column Value / Row Value	2	0	1	−1
Value Cost Diff.	1	1	3	1		
Value Cost Diff.	2	0		0	1	
Value Cost Diff.	3	1			2	0
Value Cost Diff.	4	4				3

Now, we will make a value table. Table 10.5 is a part of this value table. Table 10.5 was constructed as follows:

1. In the "cost" rows, enter the revised transportation costs from Table 10.4 wherever an assignment has been made in Table 10.3.
2. Choose any row or column (preferably the row or column with the most entries) and assign it the value of zero (0) in the appropriate row value column or column value row. (We chose the second column, plant B, as zero.)
3. Complete the row and column values (rim values) so that the row value plus the column value equals the cost value at their row-column intersection.
   a. The row value for warehouse 1 is $1 - 0 = 1$.

b. The column value for plant A is $3 - 1 = 2$.
c. The row value for warehouse 2 is $0 - 0 = 0$.
d. The column value for plant C is $1 - 0 = 1$.
e. The row value for warehouse 3 is $2 - 1 = 1$.
f. The column value for plant D is $0 - 1 = -1$.
g. The row value for warehouse 4 is $3 - (-1) = 4$.

The next step is to determine the "value" to go into each box in Table 10.5. The values are determined by adding the respective row values and column values, as shown in Table 10.6. After this is done, enter the remain-

Table 10.6. First Value Table

Warehouse	Plant / Row Value / Column Value		A	B	C	D
			2	0	1	-1
Value	1	1	3	1	2	0
Cost			3	1	3	1
Diff.			0	0	-1	-1
Value	2	0	2	0	1	-1
Cost			3	0	1	3
Diff.			-1	0	0	-4
Value	3	1	3	1	2	0
Cost			4	2	2	0
Diff.			-1	-1	0	0
Value	4	4	6	4	5	3
Cost			5	7	6	3
Diff.			+1	-3	-1	0

ing revised cost values from Table 10.4. Then the costs are subtracted from the values. If all the differences are zero or negative, a minimum-cost solution has been found. If plus differences exist, a different assignment will result in a lower total cost. Before discussing this further, we shall check Table 10.6 for either a minimum-cost solution or for a reassignment to obtain a minimum-cost solution. We see a plus value from plant A to warehouse 4. Therefore, an assignment from plant A to warehouse 4 will reduce the total cost over the first assignments shown in Table 10.3. To obtain the new assignments, we use the "steppingstone method." To use this method, place a circle in the spot where the assignment is needed (plant A to warehouse 4), and place a small plus sign ($+$) in the lower right corner of the block. Next move horizontally to a block which has an assignment and where there is a block with an assignment either above it or below it in the same column (plant D to warehouse 4), circle this entry and place a small minus sign ($-$) in the lower right-hand corner of this block. Now move vertically to an assignment that has an assignment to the right or left of it (plant D to warehouse 3), circle this entry and place a small plus sign ($+$) in the lower right-hand corner of this block. Repeat this procedure until it is possible to return in a vertical direction to the starting point. This is shown in Table 10.7.

Table 10.7. Application of the Steppingstone Method

Warehouse	Plant				Total Forecast Requirements
	A	B	C	D	
1	⑧ ← ②				10
	− +				
2		⑤ ← ③			8
		− +			
3			⑥ ← ③		9
			− +		
4	○ → ①				1
	+ −				
Total Planned Production	8	7	9	4	28

The amount to be reassigned is the smallest value circled in a block with a minus sign ($-$) (plant D to warehouse 4). This quantity is added to each block with a plus sign ($+$) and subtracted from each block with a minus sign ($-$). Thus, we obtain Table 10.8.

Table 10.8. Second Assignment

Warehouse	Plant				Total Forecast Requirements
	A	B	C	D	
1	7	3			10
2		4	4		8
3			5	4	9
4	1				1
Total Planned Production	8	7	9	4	28

This reassignment must now be evaluated by a value table as before. The new value table is presented as Table 10.9.

Table 10.9. Second Value Table

Plant				A	B	C	D
Warehouse		Column Value		3	1	2	0
Value				3	1	2	0
Cost	1		0	3	1	3	1
Diff.				0	0	−1	−1
Value				2	0	1	−1
Cost	2		−1	3	0	1	3
Diff.				−1	0	0	−4
Value				3	1	2	0
Cost	3		0	4	2	2	0
Diff.				−1	−1	0	0
Value				5	3	4	2
Cost	4		2	5	7	6	3
Diff.				0	−4	−2	−1

Examination of Table 10.9 reveals that we have found a minimum-cost solution to this problem. (The differences are all zero or negative.) Let us retrogress for a minute. If we go back to Tables 10.6 and 10.8, we can determine the amount to be saved by the reassignment indicated in Table 10.6. The difference from plant A to warehouse 4 is + 1 (from Table 10.6), and the amount to be moved is 1 unit (from Table 10.8). Therefore, the savings expected are 1 × 1, or 1 unit of cost. This saving can be verified by finding the total differential costs from the assignments in Table 10.3. This cost is $(8)(3) + (2)(1) + (5)(0) + (3)(1) + (6)(2) + (3)(0) + (1)(3) = 44$. From this cost, we subtract the differential cost of Table 10.8. This cost is $(7)(3) + (3)(1) + (4)(0) + (4)(1) + (5)(2) + (4)(0) + (1)(5) = 43$. The difference between these costs is the 1 unit previously obtained. If it is desired to determine the total cost of this assignment, we would use the costs in Table 10.2 and the assignments shown in Table 10.8. This cost is $(7)(10) + (3)(8) + (4)(7) + (4)(8) + (5)(9) + (4)(7) + (1)(12) = 239$ units. This can also be determined by multiplying the total warehouse assignments (28) by the reduction in the transportation costs from Table 10.2 to Table 10.4 (7) and adding the incremental costs as determined above $(28 × 7 + 43 = 239)$.

10.4. More Than One Optimum Solution

The transportation method is more general than is indicated by the example given. To illustrate another feature of this method, suppose the transportation cost from plant C to warehouse 1 were nine units instead of ten units. The revised costs are shown in Table 10.10. The solution is

Table 10.10. Modified Transportation Costs

Plant Warehouse	Actual Costs				Revised Costs			
	A	B	C	D	A	B	C	D
1	10	8	9	8	3	1	2	1
2	10	7	8	10	3	0	1	3
3	11	9	9	7	4	2	2	0
4	12	14	13	10	5	7	6	3

shown in Table 10.11. (*Note* This table combines the assignment and value tables used before.) Table 10.11 is constructed by making the assign-

Table 10.11. An Optimum Solution to the Revised Problem

Plant Warehouse	3 A	1 B	2 C	0 D	Total Forecast Requirements
1	0 7	3 3	1	2	0	10
2	−1	2 4	0 4	1	−1	8
3	0	3	1 5	2 4	0	9
4	2 1	5	3	4	2	1
Total Planned Production	8	7	9	4	28

ments which are shown in the larger portions of the blocks, and the entries in the smaller upper right-hand corners of the blocks are the values (based on the revised incremental transportation costs) which are determined in the same way as in the value tables previously used. The differences (value − cost) are not shown in Table 10.11, but a comparison of the values with the costs shows that the cost and value for shipment from plant C to warehouse 1 are equal. This zero implies that a revision of the solution by an assignment from plant C to warehouse 1 would cost no more than the solution of Table 10.11. The incremental cost of the solution of Table 10.11 is 43. This is the same solution as Table 10.8 provides.

If we use the steppingstone method to make an assignment from plant C to warehouse 1, we get the solution of Table 10.12. The incremental cost of

Table 10.12. Another Optimum Solution to the Revised Problem

Warehouse \ Plant	1 A	−1 B	0 C	−2 D	Total Forecast Requirements
1	2 7	3	1 3	2	0	10
2	1	2 7	0 1	1	−1	8
3	2	3	1 5	2 4	0	9
4	4 1	5	3	4	2	1
Total Planned Production	8	7	9	4	28

this solution is also 43 units. Thus, either the solution of Table 10.11 or that of Table 10.12 can be used. Both have the same cost.

10.5. The Degenerate Case

Sometimes the previous method of solution becomes inadequate. Such cases arise (1) when the problem divides into two or more problems, and (2) when there are fewer assignments than the sum of the number of plants added to the number of warehouses minus one. In this example, such a situation would arise if the output of plant C were assigned to warehouse 3, as shown in Table 10.13, or if only six assignments were made, as in Table 10.14. In either situation, it is impossible to complete the value table. The relative costs for the assignments shown in Tables 10.13 and 10.14 are 51 and 67; both are higher than the 43 previously obtained for the minimum-cost solution.

Table 10.13. A Degenerate Case with Minimum Number of Assignments

Warehouse	Plant				Total Forecast Requirements
	A	B	C	D	
1	3	3		4	10
2	4	4			8
3			9		9
4	1				1
Total Planned Production	8	7	9	4	28

Table 10.14. A Degenerate Case with Too Few Assignments

Warehouse	Plant				Total Forecast Requirements
	A	B	C	D	
1		1	9		10
2	8				8
3		6		3	9
4				1	1
Total Planned Production	8	7	9	4	28

It is possible to make a revision to the data previously used and to develop a degenerate case. Such a revision is to increase the requirements of warehouse 4 to five units and to increase the planned output of plant D to 8 units and make the assignments as shown in Table 10.15. For an opti-

Table 10.15. Assignment Table

Warehouse \ Plant	A (3)	B (1)	C (2)	D (0)	Total Forecast Requirements
1 (0)	[3] 8	[1] 2	[2]	[0]	10
2 (−1)	[2]	[0] 5	[1] 3	[−1]	8
3 (0)	[3]	[1]	[2] 6	[0] 3	9
4 (3)	[6]	[4]	[5]	[3] 5	5
Total Planned Production	8	7	9	8	32

mum solution, we need an assignment from plant A to warehouse 4. This assignment is made according to the steppingstone method, and the new assignments are shown in Table 10.16. Note that there are only six assign-

Table 10.16. Degenerate Assignment

Warehouse \ Plant	A	B	C 0	D −2	Total Forecast Requirements
1	3	3 / 7 / 1			10
2	1		8	1	8
3	2		2 / 1	0 / 8	9
4	5	5			5
Total Planned Production	8	7	9	8	32

ments, and the problem is degenerate. (It is impossible to complete the table.)

When a degenerate situation occurs, one method of handling it is to enter a zero in one of the blocks from which the assignments were most recently removed. In Table 10.16 this would be either from plant B to warehouse 2 or from plant D to warehouse 4. The zero should be placed in the block which represents the least cost, which is plant B to warehouse 2. The new assignments are shown in Table 10.17. The optimum solution is shown

Table 10.17. Assignments To Avoid Degeneracy

Warehouse	Plant				Total Forecast Requirements
	A	B	C	D	
1	3	7			10
2		0	8		8
3			1	8	9
4	5				5
Total Planned Production	8	7	9	8	32

Table 10.18. Optimum Solution for a Degenerate Case

Warehouse \ Plant		A (3)	B (1)	C (2)	D (0)	Total Forecast Requirements
1	0	3	3 / 7	1	2	0	10
2	−1	2	0	0 / 8	1	−1	8
3	0	3	1	2 / 1	0 / 8	0	9
4	2	5 / 5	5	3	4	2	5
Total Planned Production		8	7	9	8	32

in Table 10.18. The zero is treated as an assignment. Our assignment of the product to be shipped from the plants to the warehouses is as follows:

Plant A to warehouse 1   3 units
Plant B to warehouse 1   7 units
Plant C to warehouse 2   8 units
Plant C to warehouse 3   1 unit
Plant D to warehouse 3   8 units
Plant A to warehouse 4   5 units

10.6. The Dummy Plant or Dummy Warehouse

When the planned production exceeds the forecast warehouse requirements, a dummy warehouse is entered to obtain the solution. This dummy warehouse will have zero transportation costs, and the production assigned to this warehouse is product that should not be produced. When the forecast warehouse requirements exceed the planned production, a dummy plant is entered. Again, the transportation costs are zero, and production from the dummy plant is a product not to be produced. Hence, the warehouse or warehouses scheduled to receive this output do not receive that amount of material. In the case of excess capacity, the most expensive product is deleted from the production plan. In the case of excess requirements, the least expensive distribution is made and the most expensive requirements are not supplied. An example of this type of problem and its

Table 10.19. Assignments with Dummy Warehouse

Warehouse	Plant				Total Forecast Requirements
	A	B	C	D	
1	8	2			10
2		5	3		8
3			6	3	9
4				1	1
Dummy				4	4
Total Planned Production	8	7	9	8	32

solution is given in Tables 10.19 and 10.20. Table 10.19 is the first assignment, using the northwest corner rule, and Table 10.20 is the optimum solution.

Table 10.20. Optimum Solution with Dummy Warehouse

Warehouse	Plant				Total Forecast Requirements
	A	B	C	D	
1	3	7			10
2			8		8
3			1	8	9
4	1				1
Dummy	4				4
Total Planned Production	8	7	9	8	32

The intervening steps have been omitted. In the final assignment of product to plants and shipment to warehouses, the four units from plant A to the dummy warehouse will not be produced. At this point, an interesting comparison is the total cost of the assignments in Tables 10.8 and 10.20. These costs are 43 and 31 units, respectively. In this instance, we see that a choice of production point can reduce total costs.

10.7. Unequal Production Costs

Thus far, we have discussed situations in which the only costs have been the transportation costs. The transportation method is more flexible, and production costs, as well as distribution costs from the warehouse to the customer, can also be included. Prior to this time we have implicitly assumed that the per unit cost of product at all plants was the same. Table

Table 10.21. Combined Data Table for Problem with Unequal Production Costs

| | Plant | | | | | | | | Warehouse Requirements |
	A	A-O.T.	B	B-O.T.	C	C-O.T.	D	D-O.T.	
Production Cost	$20.00	$30.00	$18.00	$27.00	$22.00	$33.00	$20.00	$30.00	
Capacity	20	5	24	6	32	8	16	4	
Warehouse 1	$10.00	$10.00	$ 9.00	$ 9.00	$12.00	$12.00	$13.00	$13.00	40
Warehouse 2	$ 8.00	$ 8.00	$11.00	$11.00	$10.00	$10.00	$12.00	$12.00	30
Warehouse 3	$11.00	$11.00	$10.00	$10.00	$13.00	$13.00	$ 7.00	$ 7.00	25
Warehouse 4	$14.00	$14.00	$ 9.00	$ 9.00	$ 8.00	$ 8.00	$10.00	$10.00	45

10.21 gives the capacity of several plants, the forecast requirements of several warehouses, and the production and shipping costs. (*Note* O.T. is the abbreviation for overtime.)

The minimum-cost solution to this problem is shown in Table 10.22.

Table 10.22. Solution to Unequal-Production-Cost Problem

	Plant								
	A	A-O.T.	B	B-O.T.	C	C-O.T.	D	D-O.T.	Dummy
Warehouse 1			24	1					15
Warehouse 2	20	5							5
Warehouse 3							16	4	5
Warehouse 4				5	32	8			

Note that only warehouse 4 is scheduled to receive enough material to fulfill its requirements. Because the total requirements exceed the planned production, a dummy plant was entered to obtain a solution, and, as a consequence, the requirements of warehouses 1, 2, and 3 will have to be reduced to obtain an optimum solution. This example illustrates the method of handling unequal costs as well as overtime and excess requirements.

10.8. The Modi Method Applied to the Assignment of Orders to Machines

To illustrate the use of the modi method for the solution of this type of problem, we shall use the data of the problem solved by the indicator method (see Section 9.3) and add cost and selling-price information. Because the solution of this problem requires the use of certain averages, it is not necessarily an exact solution.

The cost and price data, along with data given previously, are shown in Table 10.23. The order sizes, standard hours per piece, and machine time available are from the previous example (see Table 9.8).

From Table 10.23., we determine the equivalent average pieces per hour for each machine and for all of the machines combined. The equivalent average hours per piece for machines A, B, C, and D are 0.750, 1.125, 1.213, and 0.638, respectively. The grand average is 0.93 hours per piece. From these values, we can establish what can be called the equivalent standard hours available on each machine. The equivalent standard hours available on each machine are determined by multiplying the actual hours available by the equivalent average pieces per hour and then dividing by the grand

Table 10.23. Data for Modi Machine Assignment

Order	Order Size (pieces)	Selling Price (per piece)	Machine A			Machine B			Machine C			Machine D		
			Standard Pieces per Hour	Hours per Order	Cost per Piece	Standard Pieces per Hour	Hours per Order	Cost per Piece	Standard Pieces per Hour	Hours per Order	Cost per Piece	Standard Pieces per Hour	Hours per Order	Cost per Piece
1	100	$10.00	1	100	$7.00	2/3	150	$7.50	4/5	125	$7.20	4/3	75	$6.00
2	200	$ 6.00	2	100	$3.50	1	200	$5.00	10/11	220	$6.60	5/3	120	$4.80
3	50	$ 7.00	2	25	$3.50	4/3	37½	$3.75	1	50	$6.00	5/2	20	$3.20
4	75	$11.00	1	75	$7.00	4/5	93¾	$6.25	2/3	112½	$9.00	5/4	60	$6.40
Machine Time Available				80			150			250			100	

average pieces per hour. Computed in this manner, the equivalent standard hours available are:

Machine A	99 hours
Machine B	124 hours
Machine C	192 hours
Machine D	146 hours

We obtain the standard hours per order by dividing the order quantity by the equivalent pieces per hour. In this way, we find the equivalent standard hours per order as:

Order 1	106 hours
Order 2	212 hours
Order 3	53 hours
Order 4	80 hours

The profit per standard hour for each order on each machine is determined by multiplying the profit per piece by the standard pieces per hour. The profits per standard hour for each order on each machine are shown in Table 10.24.

Table 10.24. Profit Matrix for Modi Machine-Order Assignment

Order	Machine A	Machine B	Machine C	Machine D
1	$3.00	$1.67	$2.24	$5.33
2	$5.00	$1.00	−$0.55	$2.00
3	$7.00	$4.33	$1.00	$9.50
4	$4.00	$3.80	$1.33	$5.75

The optimum solution is shown in Table 10.25. In this solution, we have assumed that an order could be split; i.e., done on more than one machine. Since the modi method requires that the "Total Requirements" equal the "Total Capacity," it is necessary to add a dummy order for this problem. The assignments to the dummy order represent product that will *not* be made. If the capacity had been less than the requirements, a dummy machine would have been added, and any assignments to the dummy machine would represent ordered material that would not be delivered.

The optimum solution of Table 10.25 is determined by the methods used in the solution of the transportation method, with one exception: since the values used are profits and not costs, the differences between the "Value" and "Profit" should be zero or positive. The solution, in terms of units, is summarized in Table 10.26. The unit values in the upper right-hand corner of the blocks are the ones determined by dividing the standard hours of Table 10.25 by the index. Since the index is based on averages,

Table 10.25. Optimum Assignment of Orders to Machines

Machine \ Order	2.05 A	−1.95 B	−3.09 C	0.00 D	Total Equivalent Standard Hours Required
1 (cost)	5.33	7.38	3.38	2.24	5.33
1 (alloc)			27	66	93
2 (cost)	2.95	5.00	1.00	−0.14	2.95
2 (alloc)	99	87			186
3 (cost)	9.50	11.55	7.55	6.41	9.50
3 (alloc)				47	47
4 (cost)	5.75	7.80	3.80	2.66	5.75
4 (alloc)		37		33	70
Dummy (cost)	3.09	5.14	1.14	0.00	3.09
Dummy (alloc)			165		165
Total Equivalent Standard Hours Available	99	124	192	146	561

Table 10.26. Final Assignment of Orders

Order	A	B	C	D	Total Quantity Scheduled
1				75 / 100	100
2	80 / 160	32 / 32		$4\frac{8}{10}$ / 8	200
3				20 / 50	50
4		$93\frac{3}{4}$ / 75			75
Machine Time Used	80	$125\frac{3}{4}$		$99\frac{8}{10}$	

some adjustments are necessary. The adjusted assignment is shown in the lower left-hand corner of the blocks in Table 10.26.

The total profit is

Order 1:	100($4.00) =	$ 400.00
Order 2:	160($2.50) =	$ 400.00
	32($1.00) =	$ 32.00
	8($1.20) =	$ 9.60
Order 3:	50($3.80) =	$ 190.00
Order 4:	75($4.75) =	$ 356.25
Total profit		$1387.85

This solution does not include any setup costs.

Since the modi method is based on one cost or profit matrix, it is necessary to reduce the problem to:

1. A set of requirements.
2. A set of availabilities or capacities.
3. A cost or profit matrix.

If such a simplification is undesirable, the simplex method should be used.

10.9. Summary

The modified distribution (modi) method is only one of the tools of linear programming, a new mathematical approach to manufacturing problems. The modi method is one of the simpler methods to understand and is useful for the solution of the types of problems illustrated in this chapter. There are certain restrictions which must be placed on the problem, and, as a consequence, the solution reflects the restraints.

Linear programming is a useful tool for solving difficult problems and points the way toward an era of objective solutions rather than subjective solutions.

11. Where Today and Where Tomorrow?

11.1. Where Does Production and Inventory Control Stand Today?

The survey quoted in Chapter 1 provides considerable light on the nature of production and inventory control as it is practiced today.

11.1.1. Methods of Demand Forecasting

The current status of sales forecasting is shown by the following quotation from the *Factory*-APICS Survey.*

> *Good sales forecasting is still a matter of intuition — plus personal judgment. Many plants project only four months ahead, few beyond one year. If they do, statistics enter.*
>
> Dependable sales forecasts still elude most plants. Even though basic information starts with the sales department, it seldom winds up unaltered as production orders. In between come many changes. Opinion of top executives, comparison with company's share of the market, a market analysis — all alter the original sales estimate, each one trying to outguess the consumer's chameleon-like decision.

*"Exclusive Survey of Production and Inventory Control," *Factory* April 1961. Reprinted by permission.

Good sales forecasting is still a seat-of-the-pants area, most of it limited to less than four months in advance. About 40% try to extend it to a year. But few (17%) go out as far as five years.

From a majority of the plants (light assembly or fabrication) this is to be expected. But as [Table 11.1] verifies, the longer the period of forecasting,

Table 11.1. Current Methods of Sales Forecasting

| | Number of plants | For these time periods | | | Moving | |
		5-year	Annual	Quarterly	Monthly	12-month	3-month
By estimates from:							
Customers	81	6	63	27	38	15	27
Salesmen	118	15	96	50	45	20	25
Sales managers	186	49	163	71	70	31	34
Executives	150	65	135	42	51	20	32
Market analysis	119	61	104	36	35	21	26
Company's share of market	130	62	122	25	21	17	11
By statistical methods:							
Correlation with economic indicators	58	32	58	22	15	9	11
Trend and cycle analysis	69	27	49	22	33	24	20
Leading series	19	3	10	4	5	3	2
Charted control limits	34	17	17	11	23	7	16
By historical averages:							
Without adjustment	21	6	26	7	13	7	11
Adjusted for current demand of orders	104	10	51	50	73	19	39
Adjusted by latest sales information	138	21	84	66	91	26	36
Adjusted by statistical formula smoothing	33	5	23	13	16	19	15

the less intuitive it becomes. Statistics, rather than judgment, are more dependable on a long-range basis.

But no matter how much statistical methods or historical averages are consulted, final production plans come from someone's personal judgment. And not all figures receive the same judgment. Fewer than 20% place any faith in the customer's estimate. Most rely on information from their own sales departments. But even here 80% of the P&IC groups adjust this information in some manner before turning it into production plans.

One method of evaluating initial sales estimates is by charting historical averages. Adjustments for current orders or later information from the sales department is also used. A few plants use statistical smoothing techniques. Only 21 plants claim they use historical averages without some adjustment.

Correlation with economic indicators is another possibility. But the most widely used statistical method for evaluating sales estimates is analysis of business trends and cycles. Charting with control limits or comparison with a leading series (of economic indicators) is used only by a few to date.

Detailed production scheduling may also be a seat-of-the-pants art. Operations are scheduled by 55% of the plants only when large orders are in sight. On short runs, 55% plan on finishing one operation before beginning another one.

11.1.2. Basis for the Determination of Production and Inventory Levels

The same survey has some pertinent facts relating to the determination of production and inventory levels.*

The biggest factor in planning final production is the sales forecast [Table 11.2]. But it is not the only one. The opinion of many executives

Table 11.2. Methods of Establishing Production and Inventory Levels

This method	In these plants	Of raw materials	Of work in process	Of finished goods
Executive opinion	**171**	94	82	140
Over-all financial considerations	153	**164**	**116**	**172**
Employment level and seasonal fluctuations	156	44	82	109
Production plan related to:				
Over-all sales forecast	**191**	96	90	136
Details in sales forecast	160	100	**107**	140
Total plant load by applying re-order point on EOQ for each product	75	70	71	66
Optimum inventory calculation	63	69	50	64
Inventory turnover	83	**106**	80	117
Linear programing	23	13	16	13
Other calculations	12	7	8	8
Other methods	23	19	19	11

who carefully consider company financial condition, employment levels, and seasonal fluctuations remove over-all planning from the P&IC department.

Few plants rely heavily on linear programming or other mathematical techniques, although these assume greater importance in setting inventory levels. Inventory turnover is a large factor in establishing levels of raw

Ibid.

materials and in controlling finished goods inventory. Work in process still depends heavily on sales expectations.

A surprising discovery of the survey, related to inventory control, is the unexpected number (over 40%) of plants not using the well-recognized ABC classification of raw materials and supplies.

11.1.3. The Size of the Production and Inventory Control Department

The average number of people employed in this department is $3\frac{1}{2}$ per cent of the total number of employees. The range is from about one to ten per cent, but the maximum tends to decrease as the plant size increases. This is shown by Fig. 11.1.

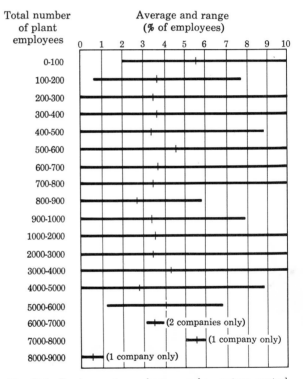

Fig. 11.1. Employees in production and inventory control departments.*

11.1.4. The Measures of the Effectiveness of Production and Inventory Control*

As shown by [Table 11.3], 80% of the plants measure effectiveness of inventory management. But 14% pay no attention to it. From keeping a

*Ibid.

Table 11.3. Measures of Production and
Inventory Control Effectiveness

Inventory		% of plants		% using
Inventory control?	Yes	80	Inventory turnover	86
	No	14	Dollar investment	89
	No answer	6	Return on investment	41
			Obsolescence	60
			Surplus	56
Production control?	Yes	72	Actual vs. planned	90
	No	17	Overtime (hourly workers)	75
	No answer	11	Machine utilization	39

close count of dollars invested in materials to computing return on inventory investment, good managers know how well inventory is being controlled. Inventory turnover is also used.

A smaller number (72%) keep an eye on production control. Comparison of actual with planned production is widely used. Overtime paid to hourly workers is next in popularity. Ratio of machine utilization to capacity is least used.

Surprising is the small number of plants (only 62%) concerned with meeting promised delivery dates. Apparently, customer service is a philosophy that has not yet soaked into 38% of P&IC departments.

11.1.5. Data Processing Methods Currently Used

*Most plants still cling to the old system of processing information by hand. In spite of this, the use of data-processing equipment has doubled in two years.**

Are data being processed efficiently? It depends on your viewpoint. Since *Factory's* survey two years ago, the use of tabulating equipment with punched cards have increased 30%. The use of computers has increased 100% in P&IC.

But as with all percentage comparisons, these hide low base figures. Less than 10% of all plants are using computers for controlling production orders and schedules. Only 5% use them for follow-up reporting on the progress of production schedules. In processing information on inventories, computers are used 10–15% of the time.

Punched cards and tabulating equipment are used to a greater extent — up to 34% in finished goods control and 24% in raw material and work in process. But in scheduling production, the use of tabulating equipment is again low.

Other mechanical or electronic tools find little use, either. Control boards are used by 11% for detailed production scheduling, but for little

Ibid.

else. Edge-notched cards are used the least. And some even report that they have no method for processing information.

Scheduled dispatching is 70% centralized, with schedules going directly from production control to the foreman. Only 27% go through a chief dispatcher, who then releases them to department dispatchers.

Resistance to change is an old story, one that affects even production and inventory control. But here it may stem from management inattention. As many as 21% have no formal organization, 27% have no adequate job descriptions, 51% have no formal training program for positions in their departments, 61% have no procedure manual — and 71% report that they operate their departments without clearly spelled-out poli ies for the management of production and inventories [see Table 11.4].

Table 11.4. Data Processing Methods Used*

	Manually	Control boards	Edge-notched cards	Punched card tab. equipment	Computer	No method
Customer delivery schedules and order backlog	58	7	2	27	10	4
Production order: Quantity and timing	66	8	1	15	11	1
Preparation	67	3	2	15	8	2
Detail schedules for production department	69	11	1	11	5	7
Follow-up reporting of progress on schedules	68	7	1	14	5	4
Inventory records: Finished goods	56	1	1	34	15	1
Work in process	59	3	3	24	9	5
Raw materials	67	1	1	23	10	1

11.1.6. The Quantitative Methods Currently Used

The various quantitative techniques that are available for the analysis and solution of production and inventory control problems are not used extensively. In fact, less than 40 per cent of the companies participating in the *Factory*-APICS survey used EOQ (economic order quantity) determinations (economic purchased lot sizes and economic manufactured lot sizes).

*Ibid.

Of the other quantitative techniques, none were used in more than 10 per cent of the plants (see Table 11.5).

Table 11.5. Quantitative Techniques Currently Used

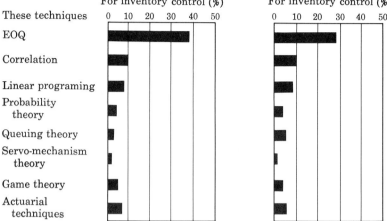

11.2. What Should Be Expected in the Future?

As time progresses, changes become more rapid. This will no doubt be true of production and inventory control. One change now in progress is the use of electronic data processing methods. As these installations become more numerous, there will be a switch from "seat-of-the-pants" methods to quantitative methods. With such systems comes the use of decision rules. As these decision rules are established, the machine can take over from the man and relieve him of the routine tasks. This will result in faster and perhaps more consistent decisions.

One can visualize an electronic system that completely controls a factory. But it controls the factory within the bounds (decision rules) established by man.

To make such an installation function properly, man must make a thorough study of all of the requirements of the factory. To be exact, man must apply systems engineering; from such an application, he can devise a control system which eliminates the manual elements now in use.

The above in no way implies the subjugation of man to machine. It does imply man's control of a machine which in turn controls the machines currently controlled by men. Man will really have moved one step up the intelligence ladder. As such progress is made, man becomes the thinker rather than the doer. It is not merely a necessity that production and inventory control people work toward such a goal, but it appears to be an obligation.

12. An Illustrative Case: The Paint and Allied Products Industry[*]

12.1. Introduction

The manufacture of paints and similar products is a batch or lot process. For any given batch, the manufacturing is of the process type; i.e., the materials follow through the required sequence without undue delays or storages between operations. The size of the lot is determined by the equipment available and is variable only within restricted limits. Thus, the flexibility of production plans and schedules as well as the inventory levels is limited.

In the paint manufacturing process, the pigment, in an agglomerated form, is dispersed in the vehicle (oil, varnish, alkyd resin, latex emulsion, etc.) by "grinding" or, more properly, dispersing in a mill. Mills of many types have been and are utilized for the dispersing process. In nearly all

[*]Author's Note: This material was supplied by the production manager and chief chemist of a paint company, but for obvious reasons, the figures given are illustrative only and are not actual production and sales figures for any known company.

cases, the pigment and a part of the vehicle are mixed to form a paste. This paste is processed through a mill, where it is subjected to high shear and impact, which reduces the agglomerates to fine, individual particles. Also, the milling process results in the wetting of the particles by the vehicle. The paste is then mixed with the remainder of the vehicle, solvent, and other necessary additives for the required application and drying properties.

The average small paint company manufactures and stocks from 80 to 100 different products. Many of these coatings are basically similar in formulation, but they differ in color and intended method of application. This variety of product requires a raw-material inventory of more than 100 different pigments, vehicles, solvents, and additives.

The number of items in the raw-materials and finished-goods inventories, the number of operations in processing, and the diversity of equipment used give rise to many production-control problems. Some of these problems will be discussed in the remainder of this chapter.

12.2. Forecasting

Many production-control problems arise from the sales forecast. The absence of a forecast, or the use of one which is inadequate or erroneous, necessitates the continual shift of production facilities from one product to another in an attempt to meet unexpected consumer demands. An accurate forecast, on the other hand, would provide the necessary information on which to base economic inventory levels, work force, production plans, and warehousing, as well as a practical maintenance schedule.

Traditionally, the paint industry is somewhat seasonal, and manufacturing for stock is done during the slower winter months. The forecast is of major importance during periods of extreme business fluctuations. An excess inventory during a period of recession could result in a considerable loss to the company. On the other hand, too small an inventory during a period of increasing business activity may result in the loss of customers.

In this company, the primary responsibility for the forecast rests with the sales department. A production manager is seldom aware of all sales policies and the conditions that exist in those industries that are served by the company. It is wise, however, for the production management to analyze the forecast and to question those items in which the forecast departs appreciably from past production records or their extrapolation into the future.

Information upon which to base the forecast is gathered from such sources as the historical record of past sales and trends, and a forecast of general economic conditions in the geographical sales area. Any apparent trend in potential sales may cause management to effect changes in marketing policy to obtain what appears to be the best over-all result from sales effort. The economic forecast for each industry and consumer group should be considered. Any apparent or expected change in the competitive situation must also be analyzed and taken into consideration.

The first step in developing a forecast for the paint company is an evaluation of sales for the preceding years. Yearly records for five years show a general downward trend in sales. The breakdown by user groups in Table 12.1 shows professional sales climbing slightly, industrials about level, trade

Table 12.1. Yearly Sales by User Group (In Gallons)

Source of Demand	Year				
	1	2	3	4	5
Industrial sales	16,660	10,420	16,000	10,680	12,760
Government sales	7,840	12,190	86,100	10,680	8,740
Professional sales	41,100	36,700	38,400	42,920	43,280
Trade	27,500	21,600	20,800	17,600	16,200
Special	4,900	6,090	3,200	7,120	7,020
Total	98,000	87,000	164,500	89,000	88,000

or retail sales down, government sales level with a large increase in the third year because of one large contract, and special coatings fluctuating from year to year.

In the paint industry, the consumers are from several distinct economic classifications. Industrial sales are to the larger companies who buy their paint, etc. direct from the manufacturer. The professional sales are to the painting contractors. The government and trade or retail sales are self-explanatory. Because the composition of the sales to each of these groups will vary, it is necessary to have such a breakdown to forecast the type and quantity of each product.

The general downward trend is believed to be the result of misplaced sales effort, poor economic conditions in the trading area, and a retardation of housing construction in the last three years. A heavy sales effort has been made in the industrial area, which a recent market survey has shown to be quite limited. Professional sales were shown to be the most profitable. Until recently the company had placed only a minor sales emphasis on this potentially expandable market area.

Trade sales are usually more stable than other groups, but they are also more expensive, because investment in a retail outlet is necessary, and because more service is required for each customer. A new retail outlet is expected to operate at a loss for two or three years. The company does not have the necessary capital to do an effective marketing job in the retail area and is not considering any additional effort in retail sales.

Table 12.2. Distribution of Sales by User Group and Type of Coating (In Gallons)

Source and Type of Demand	Year				
	1	2	3	4	5
Retail and professional					
Exterior:					
Oil base	22,940	16,860	16,440	14,770	14,320
Alkyd base	5,130	3,370	3,740	4,110	4,610
Latex base	2,110	2,250	4,720	5,330	6,650
Total exterior	30,180	22,480	24,900	24,210	25,580
Interior:					
Alkyd base	17,670	14,690	13,380	14,160	12,200
Latex base	20,750	21,130	20,920	22,150	21,700
Total interior	38,420	35,820	34,300	36,310	33,900
Total retail and professional	68,600	58,300	59,200	60,520	59,480
Industrial					
Primers	7,160	5,000	7,320	4,270	5,230
Enamels	9,500	5,420	8,680	6,410	6,130
Lacquers	...	...	...	...	1,400
Total industrial	16,660	10,420	16,000	10,680	12,760
Government					
Stock	2,590	3,660	2,580	2,990	3,150
Bid	5,250	8,530	83,520	7,690	5,590
Total government	7,840	12,190	86,100	10,680	8,740
Total special	4,900	6,090	3,200	7,120	7,020
Yearly totals	98,000	87,000	164,500	89,000	88,000

In the past, government business has not been given adequate consideration. By taking advantage of the volume which government contracts offer, plant efficiency can be maintained, and overhead expenses per unit volume can be controlled. Competition for government contracts varies for several reasons. During good business periods many companies do not have manufacturing capacity for the increased volume. During slow periods competition may be keener, because manufacturers are attempting to maintain volume. In general, government business is quite competitive and shows a low margin of profit as compared with other sales. However, if properly planned, this type of trade can be used to stabilize the level of activity of the company and probably increase the per unit profit margin and the total profit margin.

Special coatings are manufactured as a consideration to valued or prospective customers. They require special handling from engineering through manufacturing and are seldom a direct profit-making item.

Further analysis of records shows a definite trend in the sales of certain types of paint to each user group. Table 12.2 shows a decline in sales of exterior oil-base paints and an increase in sales of latex for both interior and exterior. This company has just entered the lacquer field; although there is no history of lacquer sales, it is expected that they will increase. Government coatings carried in stock for use by the painting contractor on government construction have remained quite stable.

The seasonal aspect of paint sales is depicted in Table 12.3. Production is normally one to three months ahead of sales from December through

Table 12.3. Total Sales by Months (In Gallons)

Month	Year				
	1	2	3	4	5
Jan.	7,400	8,300	21,300	7,000	6,700
Feb.	7,000	8,500	30,000	8,800	6,600
Mar.	7,600	7,900	23,500	9,000	7,200
Apr.	7,500	7,900	23,600	7,400	6,100
May	9,100	7,100	16,000	8,100	6,700
June	9,500	8,300	8,000	8,700	8,200
July	10,000	8,200	7,900	9,600	7,800
Aug.	9,600	7,200	8,300	8,400	8,400
Sept.	9,700	6,900	7,800	6,900	8,600
Oct.	8,600	6,200	7,200	5,300	7,700
Nov.	6,300	5,600	5,600	5,500	7,100
Dec.	5,700	4,900	5,300	4,300	6,900
Total	98,000	87,000	164,500	89,000	88,000

March. By September much of the inventory has been depleted, and production is about even with sales. These seasonal changes may occur at
different times in different climates, or not at all within companies with a
greatly diversified product line or in those which specialize in coatings for a
particular industry. As revealed in Table 12.3, the company experienced a
variation in the seasonal fluctuation during the last half of the fifth year.
This upturn during the latter months of the year can be attributed to two
principal factors: an increased prosperity in the general economy of the
trading area, and greater sales and service effort during the entire year.

There are a number of things to consider in developing a forecast for the
sixth year. A company as small as this is very flexible. Sales policy, prices,
direction of sales effort, inventories and manufacturing procedures can be
changed in a rather short time to meet changing economic situations. Also,
it is the only manufacturer of paint in the immediate geographical area and,
consequently, is able to give immediate technical and material service.
These advantages should indicate that the consumers most in need of such
services are the industrial firm and the painting contractor. The forecast
for the sixth year should show an expected increase in sales to those consumers. Pricing policies and sales effort are now such that a 15 per cent
increase in sales is expected, as well as one government contract in February,
March, and April for 40,000 gallons.

12.2.1. Annual Forecasts by User Group

Since there are five distinct user groups, a forecast should be made for
each group. Industrial sales showed no distinct trends, but appear to fall
about an average value with large fluctuations. The average industrial
sales over the five years were 13,300 gallons. The market survey revealed
that sales to this user group would probably not expand, but might contract if sales emphasis were shifted to other areas. It appears logical to assume a relatively steady demand and to forecast 13,300 gallons.

Government sales are extremely difficult to forecast, since much of this
volume is by contract as a result of bids. We shall defer the discussion of
possible methods of handling this group until later.

Professional sales indicate an upward trend since the second year. The
regression line based on the last four years is $x' = 41{,}540 + 2430t$ ($t = 0$
for the fourth year). Thus, these sales increased at an average rate of 2430
gallons per year. Based on the historical data, the forecast for the next year
would be 46,400 gallons.

Trade or retail sales show a downward trend over the last four years. The
regression line for this user group is $x' = 18{,}280 - 2040t$ ($t = 0$ for the
fourth year). The forecast based on this would be 14,200 gallons.

The special sales do not appear to have any trend, but since they are essentially a customer-service item, an attempt should be made to correlate these sales to some other group. With the limited amount of data available, it would appear that an average might be best, but, with an expanded sales effort, it should probably be modified by the elimination of the two lowest values or perhaps by averaging only the last two years. For the last two years the average is 7070 gallons.

To summarize the forecasts to this point, we have the following:

Industrial sales:	13,300 gallons
Professional sales:	46,400 gallons
Trade sales:	14,200 gallons
Special sales	7,070 gallons
Total (less government)	80,970 gallons

If the redirected sales effort might result in a 15 per cent increase in professional sales, we should then increase that forecast to 53,360 gallons. This increase in professional sales could result in a lesser increase in special sales, say 5 per cent, increasing sales in that area to 7420 gallons. The annual forecast now becomes 88,280 gallons, excluding government sales.

With this forecast, it becomes necessary to evaluate the company's production capacity and profit position before a forecast of government sales is considered. Knowledge of past records, both public and company, will reveal the timing and size of various government contracts that might be available. If the timing and size of such possible contracts are compatible with the production and profit positions, the company should make every attempt to obtain this business. The sales records (Table 12.3) reveal that the company can operate at a capacity of 30,000 gallons per month. This is 360,000 gallons per year, or four times the present production level. The desirability of this type of operation must yet be evaluated. If the company continues at the level of government business shown for the years 1, 2, 4, and 5, the forecast based on the average for those years is 9860 gallons. This puts the forecast at 98,140 gallons.

12.2.2. Annual Forecast by Type

In Table 12.2, we have a breakdown of sales by the type of coatings sold to each user group. During the last four years, the sales to the professional group increased at nearly the same rate (2790 gallons per year) as the sales to the trade group decreased (2660 gallons per year). The sales of interior and exterior coatings were also fairly constant, but the type of coatings within these groups changed decidedly. In the exterior type, the sales of oil-base coatings decreased, the sales of alkyd-base coatings remained fairly constant, and the latex-base sales increased at a rate which approximately equals the decrease in oil-base volume. In the interior-type coatings, the alkyd- and latex-base products remained relatively constant. The industrial sales remained stable in their compositions. Although the effect of the introduction of lacquers to this group is still undetermined, it might be expected to increase the industrial sales volume (and perhaps the sales volume in the other categories) because of expanded service to this user group.

The composition of sales within these groups (based on historical data) can be forecast as follows:

Retail and Professional Users (based on the last four years)

Exterior Coatings

Oil base ($x' = 15{,}130 - 930t$ $t = 0$ for 4th yr.)	13,270 gallons
Alkyd base ($x' = 4150 + 410t$ $t = 0$ for 4th yr.)	4,970 gallons
Latex base ($x' = 5430 + 1380t$ $t = 0$ for 4th yr.)	8,190 gallons

Total   26,430 gallons

Interior Coatings

Alkyd base ($x' = 13{,}060 - 1090t$ $t = 0$ for 4th yr.)	10,880 gallons
Latex base ($x' = 21{,}620 + 290t$ $t = 0$ for 4th yr.)	22,200 gallons

Total   33,080 gallons

Industrial Users

Primers ($x' = 5780$)	5,780 gallons
Enamels ($x' = 7230$)	7,230 gallons
Lacquers ($x' = 1400$)	1,400 gallons

Total   14,410 gallons

Special Users   7,070 gallons

Grand Total (Less gov't.)   80,990 gallons

The forecast, in total, is quite close to the previous forecast made by user group. It is now necessary to assign the expected increases to types of coatings. Under the assumption that latex-base coatings will increase more rapidly than the others, the 15 per cent might be forecast for these types. This percentage, when apportioned between exterior and interior types, gives a forecast of $8190 + 1870$ or 10,060 gallons of exterior latex-base paints and $22{,}200 + 5090$ or 27,290 gallons of interior latex-base paints For purposes of production planning, the annual forecasts are summarized in Table 12.4.

Table 12.4. Forecast by Type of Coating

Exterior Coatings	Oil base	13,270 gallons	
	Alkyd base	4,970 gallons	
	Latex base	10,060 gallons	
Total			28,300 gallons
Interior Coatings	Alkyd base	10,880 gallons	
	Latex base	27,290 gallons	
Total			38,170 gallons
Primers			5,780 gallons
Enamels			7,230 gallons
Lacquers	Stock items		1,400 gallons
Government			2,990 gallons
Special			7,420 gallons
Total (Less government contract sales)			91,290 gallons

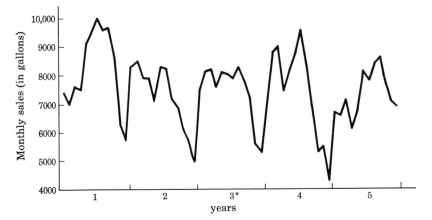

Fig. 12.1. Paint sales for past five years.

*Adjusted for large contract during January through May.

12.2.3. Monthly Forecast of Total Volume

If linear regression lines are applied to the data of Table 12.3, which data are shown in graphical form in Fig. 12.1, the regression line for January through July is

$$x' = 7150 + 195t, \quad t = 1, 2, \ldots, 7$$

and for August through December the regression line is

$$x' = 13,980 - 705t, \quad t = 8, 9, \ldots, 12$$

The monthly and cumulative monthly forecasts are summarized in Table 12.5.

Table 12.5. Unadjusted Monthly Sales Forecasts

| Month | Forecast (gallons) | |
	Monthly	Cumulative Monthly
Jan.	7,345	7,345
Feb.	7,540	14,885
Mar.	7,735	22,620
Apr.	7,930	30,550
May	8,125	38,675
June	8,320	46,995
July	8,515	55,510
Aug.	8,340	63,850
Sept.	7,635	71,485
Oct.	6,930	78,415
Nov.	6,225	84,640
Dec.	5,520	90,160

The adjustments made in Section 12.2.1 brought the total forecast to 98,140 gallons. Thus, the forecasts should be increased by a factor of 7980/90,160 per month. The adjusted values will be used for production-planning purposes.

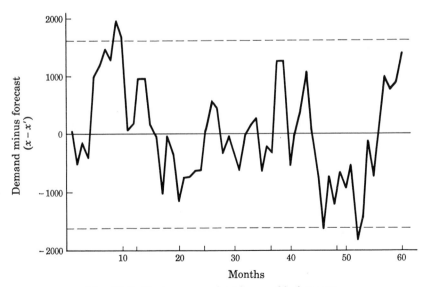

Fig. 12.2. Moving-range chart for monthly forecasts.

12.3. Control Charts on the Monthly Forecast

The moving-range chart for the data of Table 12.3 is shown in Fig. 12.2. There are many points outside the limits, runs, etc. on either side of the center line. Examination of Figs. 12.1 and 12.2 shows that the best regression lines may be derived from the last year. These regression lines are

$$x' = 6030 + 260t, \quad t = 1, 2, \ldots, 8$$

and

$$x' = 13,560 - 570t, \quad t = 9, 10, \ldots, 12$$

12.3.1. Revised Forecast Based on Analysis of Control Chart

Since the chart of Fig. 12.3, for the fifth year, is in control, we probably have a reasonable forecast procedure. The revised forecasts are presented in Table 12.6. Again, the forecasts of Table 12.6 need to be adjusted for the

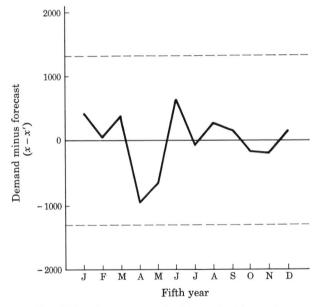

Fig. 12.3. Moving-range chart for revised forecasts.

anticipated increases in sales. This adjustment factor is $10,240/87,900 = 0.1165$.

12.4. Economic Lot-Size Determination

In order to maintain adequate working capital and flexibility, it is essential that both raw-materials and finished-goods inventories be held to an economic optimum level.

Table 12.6. Revised Monthly Forecasts Based on Fifth Year

Month	Forecast Monthly	Forecast Cumulative
Jan.	6,290	6,290
Feb.	6,550	12,840
Mar.	6,810	19,650
Apr.	7,070	26,720
May	7,330	34,050
June	7,590	41,640
July	7,850	49,490
Aug.	8,110	57,600
Sept.	8,430	66,030
Oct.	7,860	73,890
Nov.	7,290	81,180
Dec.	6,720	87,900

The average inventory turnover rate for the coatings industry is estimated to vary from four to seven times per year. The rate for the company we are analyzing has been six times per year for several years. This rate is dictated to some extent by available capital. It is quite possible that a lower turnover rate would pay dividends by allowing the company to take advantage of quantity discounts on raw materials and to reduce processing costs by producing paints in larger lot sizes. Inventories make up more than 60 per cent of the net worth of the company. It is readily apparent that excessive or slow-turning inventories could endanger the liquidity of the company. Expressing inventory investment in another way, the company is storing a two-months stock, or one-sixth of the cost of goods sold is invested in inventory.

The objectives to keep in mind in setting inventory levels are as follows: keeping the investment as low as possible, maintaining stocks adequate to supply customer needs immediately, economical purchasing, and efficient processing. In determining economic lot sizes, the availability and cost of capital must be considered, as well as raw-material and freight-rate quantity discounts.

As the manufacturing lot size increases, the processing cost per gallon decreases because of a minimum setup and quality-control testing time for each batch. Practical and economic lot sizes may vary from a one year's supply of some items to a few weeks' supply of others. Maximum and minimum inventory levels may also vary during certain seasons of the year. The maximum would ordinarily be reached during the spring and early summer, and a lower inventory would be carried during the fall and winter. This practice allows a lower labor force during low-income periods. There are certain advantages and disadvantages resulting from this practice. Payrolls and inventory investment are lower during periods of slower cash flow. The greatest disadvantages are labor turnover and training.

Cost data peculiar to this company are

Order cost for raw material	$22.00
Order cost for finished goods	$ 7.00
Setup time per batch	$36.00
Inventory carrying charge per year	18 per cent

Other company data required for inventory and lot size problem solutions (using information in Chapter 5) are

Maximum batch size   180 gallons

Lot size distribution for the past year has been

25 gallons or less	19% of all batches processed
26 to 50 gallons	18% of all batches processed
51 to 75 gallons	15% of all batches processed
76 to 150 gallons	36% of all batches processed
151 gallons or more	12% of all batches processed
	100%

Average freight-in rates:

Minimum (regardless of quantity)	$2.50
Up to 4000 pounds	$2.50/cwt
4000 to 20,000 pounds	$2.00/cwt
20,000 to RR carload	$1.25/cwt
RR carload	$ .75/cwt

Lead time required for raw materials:

Less than truck load	1 to 5 days
Truck load	10 to 14 days

Lead time required for finished goods is discussed under production planning.

The raw-material usage during the fifth year is shown in Table 12.7. The economic lot sizes were based on these values rather than extending them for the expected increase in sales in the sixth year. The average increase in usage would be 0.115, which would increase the economic lot sizes by 5.6 per cent.

The economic purchased lot sizes are shown in Table 12.8. In the same table, the number of orders per year is also shown. These lot sizes are calculated from the average price plus transportation cost and then rounded to the nearest purchased unit. (All quantities are computed at 8 pounds per gallon.) The "Cans and pails" and "Boxes or cartons" should probably be purchased by the truck load. The economic lot sizes give an average inventory turnover of about four times, which is less than the desired six

Table 12.7. Raw-Material Usage During Fifth Year

Raw Material	Fifth Year Usage	No. of Products	Average Unit Cost	Package	No. of Suppliers	Minimum Possible No. of Suppliers
Resins and resin solutions	170,000 lb.	26	$0.23/lb.	55 gal drum or 4000 gal tank truck	9	3
Oils	33,000 lb.	10	$0.18/lb.	55 gal drum or 4000 gal tank truck	3	1
Latex emulsions	78,000 lb.	3	$0.18/lb.	55 gal drum or 4000 gal tank truck	3	1
Petroleum solvents	30,000 gal	6	$0.28/gal	55 gal drum or 4000 gal tank truck	2	1
Lacquer solvents	10,000 gal	9	$1.30/gal	55 gal drum or 4000 gal tank truck	3	1
Metallic pigments	2,400 lb.	3	$0.48/lb.	50, 100, 200 lb drum	1	1
Titanium pigments	154,000 lb.	6	$0.20/lb.	50 lb. bags	2	1
Lead pigments	3,000 lb.	6	$0.18/lb.	50 lb. bags	1	1
Zinc oxide pigments	5,000 lb.	2	$0.15/lb.	50 lb. bags	1	1
Dry colors	6,000 lb.	11	$0.60/lb.	50 lb. bags	3	2
Iron oxide pigments	7,000 lb.	7	$0.15/lb.	50 lb. bags	2	1
Extender pigments	264,000 lb.	8	$0.04/lb.	50 lb. bags	5	4
Driers	8,000 lb.	7	$0.32/lb.	55 gal drum	3	1
Miscellaneous additives	8,000 lb.	36	$0.40/lb.	5 and 55 gal drums	10	6
Cans and pails*	117,000	10	$0.24/gal	cartons	2	2
Cartons or boxes	20,000	4	$0.03/gal		1	1

*Containers may be purchased in truck loads or less. A truck load of gallon and quart cans would provide containers for 11,000 to 12,000 gallons of paint. A truck load of 5 gallon pails would provide containers for 9000 to 10,000 gallons of paint.

Table 12.8. Economic Purchased Lot Sizes and
Number of Orders per Year

	Economic Purchased Lot Size	Number of Orders per Year
Resins and resin solutions	29 drums	133.1
Oils	14 drums	5.4
Latex emulsions	22 drums	8.0
Petroleum solvents	80 drums	6.8
Lacquer solvents	24 drums	7.6
Metallic pigments	5 drums	2.4
Titanium pigments	262 bags	11.8
Lead pigments	38 bags	1.6
Zinc oxide pigments	55 bags	1.9
Dry colors	31 bags	3.9
Iron oxide pigments	62 bags	2.3
Extender pigments	7012 bags	0.8
Driers	5 drums	3.6
Miscellaneous additives	5 drums	3.6
Cans and pails	10,918	10.7
Cartons or boxes	12,758	1.6

times. In only one instance is there less than one order per year (extender pigments, with an annual usage of 264,000 pounds). In the case of resins and resin solutions, an order would be placed about every other day.

12.5. Production Planning

In manufacturing for stock, the sales forecast becomes the production forecast. We have included special orders in the forecast, and we know that in planning production the company must remain flexible to make possible the manufacture of special items at any time, one of its greatest competitive advantages.

The plant has been set up to meet a cyclic demand. There is dispersion equipment available to manufacture up to 400,000 gallons per year under maximum utilization. This excess production capacity is present not only to meet a cyclic demand, but also because of a need for specialized dispersion equipment.

It has been found that two men in the processing department can produce and package paint ready for labeling and warehousing at the average rate of 14 gallons per man-hour worked. As the direct labor force is increased, the rate per man-hour decreases somewhat until it has reached 11 gallons per man-hour with six men working. This downward trend is due to inadequate production scheduling and an occasional wait for certain pieces of equipment, such as vehicle pumps, hoists, and elevator. Six production men is the maximum number who can work in the plant with any degree of efficiency. When additional production is necessary, it is more desirable to work either a split shift or two eight-hour shifts than to increase the work force per shift.

The gallons-per-man-hour rate indicates that, to meet the production forecast during the early months of the sixth year, a split or double shift will be necessary. The 40,000 gallon government contract will be produced at a higher gallons-per-man-hour rate, because it is all the same type of paint and the same color. Also, the entire amount will be packaged in five-gallon pails. Setup time per batch will decrease to one-half the standard time, since one batch after another can be run with less mill and tank clean-up. The expected gallons-per-man-hour rate is 38 for this contract.

The lead time required for manufactured goods will be determined by the lot sizes produced, inventory levels, and the flexibility of the production plan.

Since the forecast calls for 98,140 gallons of paint, and the company has a 40,000 gallon contract to be manufactured in February, March, and April, the total production which must be planned is not less than 138,140 gallons. If we assume 2000 working hours per man per year, at the rate of 14 gallons per man-hour on regular production and 38 gallons per man-hour on contract production, the company requires about 8060 man-hours, or approximately four men. For the current planning year there are 2040 working hours. Two production plans were made. One plan was based on the use of four men during January through April and three men for the remainder of the year. The number of hours available was reduced by the efficiency of three and four men compared to two men. The man-hours required in each month were based on 14 gallons per man-hour for 98,140 gallons and 38 gallons per man-hour for 40,000 gallons. This plan, which is shown in Table 12.9, has an incremental cost of $3303.46 over the cost of two men. The man-hours required are shown in Table 12.10.

The production plan in Table 12.9 requires considerable overtime. A comparison plan was made, using five men during the first four months and four men during the last eight months. This plan, shown in Table 12.11, has an incremental cost of $3320.83 plus the wages paid to one extra employee throughout the year. The decrease in efficiency increases the cost, and the use of overtime proves to be advantageous over a larger work force.

The production plan of Table 12.9 is summarized in Table 12.12. Because of the large variety of products and the fairly high inventories plus short purchasing and lead times, no consideration has been given to safety stocks. The inventories normally carried far exceed safety stock requirements.

Table 12.9. Production Plan for Sixth Year

			Month in Which									
			Jan.*		Feb.*		Mar.*		Apr.*		May**	
Month in Which Required	Man Hours Required		R.T.	O.T.	R.T.	O.T.	R.T.	O.T.	R.T.	O.T.	R.T.	O.T.
			629	315	572	286	629	315	600	300	499	250
Jan.	502	Available	629	315								
		Cost	.24	1.36								
		Planned	502	...								
Feb.	874	Available	127	315	572	286						
		Cost	.69	1.81	.24	1.36						
		Planned	127	...	572	175						
Mar.	894	Available	...	315	...	111	629	315				
		Cost		2.26		1.81	.24	1.36				
		Planned		...		...	629	265				
Apr.	915	Available		315		111	...	50	600	300		
		Cost		2.71		2.26		1.81	.24	1.36		
		Planned		...		...		15	600	300		
May	585	Available		315		111		35	...	...	499	250
		Cost		3.16		2.71		2.26			.11	1.17
		Planned		...		...		...			499	86
June	605	Available		315		111		35			...	164
		Cost		3.61		3.15		2.71				1.59
		Planned		...		...		...				...
July	626	Available		315		111		35				164
		Cost		4.06		3.61		3.16				2.01
		Planned		...		...		...				...
Aug.	647	Available		315		111		35				164
		Cost		4.51		4.06		3.61				2.43
		Planned		...		...		...				...
Sept.	672	Available		315		111		35				164
		Cost		4.96		4.51		4.06				2.85
		Planned		...		...		...				...
Oct.	627	Available		315		111		35				164
		Cost		5.41		4.96		4.51				3.27
		Planned		...		...		...				...
Nov.	582	Available		315		111		35				164
		Cost		5.86		5.41		4.96				3.69
		Planned		...		...		...				...
Dec.	536	Available		315		111		35				164
		Cost		6.31		5.86		5.41				4.11
		Planned		...		...		...				...
Total Production Planned	R.T.		629		572		629		600		499	
	O.T.			...		175		280		300		86

*Four men at $12\frac{1}{2}$ gallons per man-hour. Their efficiency is 12.5/14.0 or 0.893. Thus, the number of hours available is equivalent to 0.893 of the hours available with two men, and the costs are revised accordingly.

To Be Produced														
June**		July**		Aug.**		Sept.**		Oct.**		Nov.**		Dec.**		Total Pro-duction Planned
R.T.	O.T.	R.T.	O.T.	R.T.	O.T.	R.T.	O.T.	R.T.	O.T.	R.T.	O.T.	R.T.	O.T.	
477	239	477	239	522	261	431	216	522	261	477	239	454	227	
														502
														874
														894
														915
														585
477 .11 477	239 1.17 128													605
...	111 1.59 ...	477 .11 477	239 1.17 149											626
	111 2.01 ...	...	90 1.59 ...	522 .11 522	261 1.17 125									647
	111 2.43 ...		90 2.01 ...	...	136 1.59 25	431 .11 431	216 1.17 216							672
	111 2.85 ...		90 2.43 ...		111 2.01 ...	...	...	522 .11 522	261 1.17 105					627
	111 3.27 ...		90 2.85 ...		111 2.43 ...			...	156 1.59 ...	477 .11 477	239 1.17 105			582
	111 3.69 ...		90 3.27 ...		111 2.85 ...				156 2.01 ...	...	134 1.59 ...	454 .11 454	227 1.17 82	536
477	128	477	149	522	150	431	216	522	105	477	105	454	82	6289 1776

**Three men at 13¼ gallons per man-hour at an efficiency of 0.946 compared to two men.

Table 12.11. An Alternative but Less Efficient Production Plan

Month in Which Required	Man Hours Required		Jan.* R.T. 738	Jan.* O.T. 184	Feb.* R.T. 671	Feb.* O.T. 168	Mar.* R.T. 738	Mar.* O.T. 184	Apr.* R.T. 705	Apr.* O.T. 176	May** R.T. 629	May** O.T. 157
Jan.	502	Available	738	184								
		Cost	.38	1.58								
		Planned	502	...								
Feb.	874	Available	236	184	671	168						
		Cost	.86	2.06	.38	1.58						
		Planned	203	...	671	...						
Mar.	894	Available	33	184		168	738	184				
		Cost	1.34	2.54		2.06	.38	1.58				
		Planned	33	...		...	738	123				
Apr.	915	Available	...	184		168	...	61	705	176		
		Cost		3.02		2.54		2.06	.38	1.58		
		Planned		...		...		34	705	176		
May	585	Available		184		168		27	...	...	629	157
		Cost		3.50		3.02		2.54			.24	1.36
		Planned		...		...		...			585	...
June	605	Available		184		168		27			44	157
		Cost		3.98		3.50		3.02			.69	1.81
		Planned		...		...		...			5	...
July	626	Available		184		168		27			39	157
		Cost		4.46		3.98		3.50			1.14	2.26
		Planned		...		...		...			26	...
Aug.	647	Available		184		168		27			13	157
		Cost		4.94		4.46		3.98			1.59	2.71
		Planned		...		...		...			...	...
Sept.	672	Available		184		168		27			13	157
		Cost		5.42		4.94		4.46			2.04	3.16
		Planned		...		...		...			...	...
Oct.	627	Available		184		168		27			13	157
		Cost		5.90		5.42		4.94			2.49	3.61
		Planned		...		...		...			...	...
Nov.	582	Available		184		168		27			13	157
		Cost		6.38		5.90		5.42			2.94	4.06
		Planned		...		...		...			...	...
Dec.	536	Available		184		168		27			13	157
		Cost		6.86		6.38		5.90			2.39	4.51
		Planned		...		...		...			...	...
Total Production Planned	R.T.		738		.671		738		705		616	
	O.T.			...		...		157		176		...

*Five men at an efficiency of 0.839 when compared to two men. Adjustment is made to the man hours and costs.

To Be Produced

June**		July**		Aug.**		Sept.**		Oct.**		Nov.**		Dec.**		Total Production Planned
R.T.	O.T.	R.T.	O.T.	R.T.	O.T.	R.T.	O.T.	R.T.	O.T.	R.T.	O.T.	R.T.	O.T.	
600	150	600	150	657	164	543	136	657	164	600	150	572	143	
														502
														874
														894
														915
														585
600 / .24 / 600	150 / 1.36 / ...													605
...	150 / 1.81 / ...	600 / .24 / 600	150 / 1.36 / ...											626
	150 / 2.26 / ...	...	150 / 1.81 / ...	657 / .24 / 647	164 / 1.36 / ...									647
	150 / 2.71 / ...		150 / 2.26 / ...	10 / .69 / 10	164 / 1.81 / ...	543 / .24 / 543	136 / 1.36 / 119							672
	150 / 3.16 / ...		150 / 2.71 / ...	...	164 / 2.26 / ...	...	17 / 1.81 / ...	657 / .24 / 627	164 / 1.36 / ...					627
	150 / 3.61 / ...		150 / 3.16 / ...		164 / 2.71 / ...		17 / 2.26 / ...	30 / .69 / ...	164 / 1.81 / ...	600 / .24 / 582	150 / 1.36 / ...			582
	150 / 4.06 / ...		150 / 3.61 / ...		164 / 3.16 / ...		17 / 2.71 / ...	30 / 1.14 / ...	164 / 2.26 / ...	18 / .69 / ...	150 / 1.81 / ...	572 / .24 / 536	143 / 1.36 / ...	536
600	...	600	...	657	...	543	119	627	...	582	...	536	...	7613 / 452

**Four men at an efficiency of 0.893.

Table 12.10. Man-Hours Required at Maximum Efficiency

Month	Regular Production		Contract Production	
	Gallons	Man-Hours	Gallons	Man-Hours
Jan.	7,028	502	. . .	. . .
Feb.	7,312	523	13,333	351
Mar.	7,606	543	13,333	351
Apr.	7,892	564	13,334	351
May	8,182	585	. . .	. . .
June	8,472	605	. . .	. . .
July	8,762	626	. . .	. . .
Aug.	9,052	647	. . .	. . .
Sept.	9,412	672	. . .	. . .
Oct.	8,776	627	. . .	. . .
Nov.	8,140	582	. . .	. . .
Dec.	7,506	536	. . .	. . .
Total	98,140	7,012	40,000	1,053

Table 12.12. Summary of Production Plan

Month	Production			Inventory
	Actual Man-Hours			
	R.T.	O.T.	Gallons	(Gallons)
Jan.	704	0	11,849	4,821
Feb.	640	196	15,821	13,330
Mar.	704	302	21,511	27,235
Apr.	672	336	20,657	. . .
May	528	91	8,182	. . .
June	504	135	8,472	. . .
July	504	158	8,762	. . .
Aug.	552	159	9,364	312
Sept.	456	228	9,100	. . .
Oct.	552	111	8,776	. . .
Nov.	504	111	8,140	. . .
Dec.	480	87	7,506	. . .
Total	6,800	1,914	138,140	

Further, any determination of safety stocks would necessitate a detailed examination of the sales of each product and the availability of raw materials and equipment. Such a study is beyond the space available in this book.

12.6. Production Scheduling

Perhaps more detail is involved in production scheduling than in any other phase of manufacturing. In this plant there are four different types of dispersion equipment:

1. Ball Mill. A hollow steel cylinder filled approximately one-third full of $\frac{5}{8}$ inch steel balls. The mill is charged to the two-thirds level with pigment and vehicle to form a heavy paste. The steel balls are lifted up by the rotation of the mill, and they fall back; dispersion is accomplished by the shearing action of the cascading balls and by the impact of the balls striking each other and the sides of the mill. The paste usually makes up one-fifth to one-third of the batch. A ball mill with total capacity of approximately 125 gallons can grind 65 to 70 gallons of paste, which will make up to 400 gallons of finished product, depending upon the type of product. The grinding cycle varies from 16 to 40 hours, depending upon the degree of dispersion required and the dispersion characteristics of the pigment.

2. Kinetic Dispersion Mill. A vertical, cylindrical tank with a vertical shaft attached to an impeller and a rotor driven at very high speeds. Surrounding the rotor, which is quite small in comparison to the tank, is a steel stator. A low solids-vehicle-solvent combination is charged into the mill. The pigment is added slowly, with the mill running, and is drawn into the rotor-stator by the impeller. Pigment agglomerates are thrown at high velocities into the stator and are broken by the collision. Dispersion is also accomplished by the shearing action created by the high velocity.

3. High-Speed Stone Mills. A pigment-vehicle paste is passed between two circular carborundum stones, one of which is rotating at a speed of approximately 3600 rpm. Fineness of grind is determined by the distance between the two stones.

4. High-Speed Dispersers. A specially designed circular impeller driven at high speed in a tank containing vehicle and solvent. The shearing action accomplishes adequate dispersion for some products. This equipment is also used to premix paste for the high-speed stone mills, to mix finished batches while the paste is being thinned with solvent and vehicle, and to mix shading colors into a finished paint.

This plant has one 125-gallon ball mill, one 100-gallon kinetic dispersion mill, two high-speed stone mills, and one high-speed disperser. In scheduling production we can assume that, in general, the following types of products are processed most efficiently on the indicated dispersion equipment:

Exterior oil base	High-speed stone mill
Exterior alkyd base	High-speed stone mill

Exterior latex base	High-speed disperser
Interior alkyd base	High-speed stone mill
Interior latex base	High-speed disperser
Industrial primers	Kinetic dispersion mill, ball mill, or high-speed stone mill
Industrial enamels	Kinetic dispersion or ball mill
Industrial lacquers	Kinetic dispersion or ball mill
Government stock	All produced on high-speed stone mill
Government bid	Depends on specific product. We must plan on some time on all mills.

The average production capacities of each mill are

Ball mill	Two 180-gallon batches per day.
Kinetic dispersion mill	Four 150-gallon batches per day.
High-speed stone mill	Two 150-gallon batches per day. Used in conjunction with the high-speed disperser.
High-speed disperser	Three 180-gallon batches per day. Not available when the high-speed stone mill is in use.

At the present time, storage tanks, mixers for thinning finished mill pastes, and filling equipment is not available to take advantage of the maximum capacity of all dispersion equipment. As was stated in an earlier paragraph, six men producing 11 gallons per man-hour would be the maximum efficient production. This maximum has been determined from the manufactured lot size distribution of previous years and would increase with an increase in lot size. The company has dispersion equipment available to produce approximately 1500 to 1600 gallons of finished product daily, and space and accessory equipment to produce 550 gallons during an eight-hour shift unless one product is being manufactured in large quantities. Because of the large number of variations possible for any given product, no attempt will be made to show the detail scheduling and flow of individual products.

12.7. Summary

The analysis of the data in this chapter has been rather abbreviated, because of the very large number of variables that must be considered. However, an attempt has been made to show the application of the techniques presented in the earlier chapters. The material illustrates the difficulty of applying quantitative techniques but also the advantages of such techniques.

Problems

Problem Group 1

Chapter 3

1. Records show that your company has had the following demand for one of its products:

	Demand	
Month	First Year	Second Year
Jan.	80	90
Feb.	100	105
Mar.	79	97
Apr.	98	100
May	95	117
June	104	101
July	80	103
Aug.	98	95
Sept.	102	87
Oct.	96	80
Nov.	115	78
Dec.	88	79

a. Establish a monthly sales forecast for the third year.
b. Establish the expected maximum and minimum demands (assuming that the same cause system exists) for 95 out of 100 months. For 997 out of 1000 months.
c. Establish cumulative forecasts for each month of the third year, starting with January as the first month.
d. Establish the expected range of the cumulative forecast through December of the third year.
e. Establish forecasts for January of the third year by use of the moving averages. Use $n = 3$, $n = 5$, and $n = 7$.
f. Establish forecasts for January of the third year by the weighted-average method. Use $w = 0.2$, $w = 0.5$, and $w = 0.8$.
g. Compare the forecasts from (a), (e), and (f). Which is best? Why?

Chapter 4

2. The sales during the third year are given below

Month	Sales	Month	Sales	Month	Sales
Jan.	97	May	75	Sept.	117
Feb.	100	June	84	Oct.	91
Mar.	104	July	94	Nov.	104
Apr.	98	Aug.	100	Dec.	105

a. Make a moving-range chart for the demands of the first two years. (Leave space to add the demands of the third year.) Is the chart in control? Why? If not, why not?
b. Add the demands from the third year to your moving-range chart. Does the chart still show control? What is your forecast for January of the fourth year?
c. In Prob. 1(e), you determined moving-average forecasts for January of the third year. Extend these moving-average forecasts ($n = 3$, $n = 5$, and $n = 7$) through the third year on a month-by-month basis. (Remember, the moving average you get is the forecast for the next month.) Determine $\Sigma \mid x - x' \mid$ (actual minus forecast demand) for each value of n for these twelve months. Compare these sums with $\Sigma \mid x - \bar{x} \mid$ for the same period. Which of the four procedures gives the best forecast based on the criteria that the $\Sigma \mid x - x' \mid$ or $\Sigma \mid x - \bar{x} \mid$ should be a minimum? Plot these absolute differences against time.
d. Repeat Prob. 2(c), but use the weighted-average forecasts as in Prob. 1(f).

e. Why would it be inappropriate to use a regression line as a fore-casting procedure in this problem?

Chapter 5

3. This product is made from several components. One of these com-ponents is purchased. The average cost of placing an order is $72.00. The average cost of carrying one component in inventory for one year is $1.81.
   a. Determine the economic purchased lot size for this component: (1) graphically and (2) by Eq. (5.2).
   b. What is the total variable annual cost and the unit variable annual cost of purchasing this component in economic lot sizes?
   c. The supplier has asked you to consider purchasing this component in lots of 500 units, rather than in the lot size determined in Prob. 3(a). If you do so, he will reduce his per unit price. Your carrying charges are 25 per cent of the material cost. How much must the supplier reduce his price (per unit) so that your costs remain the same as they were for the lot size determined in Prob. 3(a)?
   d. Suppose you can manufacture this same component in your own plant at the rate of 3133 units per year. If your setup cost is equal to your order cost, what is your economic manufactured lot size?
   e. Repeat Prob. 3(b) for the conditions of Prob. 3(d).

4. Your company manufactures five other products. The demand, pro-duction, and cost data are given below.

Product	Sales (Units/Yr)	Production (Units/Yr)	Inventory Cost (per Unit/Mo)	Setup Cost (per Time)
A	10,000	80,000	$0.12	$20.00
B	20,000	80,000	$0.15	$30.00
C	15,000	75,000	$0.18	$16.00
D	30,000	120,000	$0.20	$17.50
E	17,000	136,000	$0.10	$25.00

   a. Determine the economic fraction of yearly demand.
   b. Determine the economic manufactured lot size for each product considered individually.
   c. Compare the annual costs under (a) and (b) above.
   d. Under (a), what quantity of each product will be manufactured during each run?

5. It costs you \$72.00 to place an order and 25 per cent of the material cost to carry an item in inventory for one year.

    a. Construct an economic purchased order quantity table for monthly usages of 100 to 200 units (in increments of 20 units) and per item costs from \$6.00 to \$20.00 (in increments of \$2.00).

    b. Interpolate in your order table to determine the economic order quantity for an item with a monthly usage of 134 units and a cost of \$7.87 per unit. Calculate the economic order quantity. What is your error? How much would this add to your total annual cost?

Chapter 6

6. a. Determine the reorder point for Prob. 3(a), when a fixed-order-size inventory system is used, if the lead time is 25 days. If the lead time is 100 days.

    b. Determine the order interval and reorder points, when a fixed-order-interval inventory system is used, for the conditions of Prob. 6(a).

    c. Determine the safety stock that should be used in Prob. 6(a).

    d. Determine the safety stock that should be used in Prob. 6(b).

    e. Set up the fixed-order-size inventory control system of Prob. 6(a) and 6(c). Assume that an order is placed in inventory on the first of January. On the last day of the preceding December, you had exactly the safety stock in inventory. Assume 21 days per month, and show how your inventory system works for the demands of the third year (see Prob. 2). Determine the inventory at the reorder point and just before replenishment, if an order is placed at the end of the day in which the inventory reaches the reorder point. Further, assume that back orders are possible but must be filled as soon as stock is again available. (Use 25 day lead time only.)

    f. Repeat Prob. 6(e) under the same conditions, but use the fixed-order-interval inventory system and the results of Prob. 6(b) and 6(d).

Chapter 7

7. The product under consideration requires 20 man-hours to manufacture. There is no beginning inventory and no ending inventory. [Use your forecast from Prob. 1(a).]

    a. Determine the economic production plan for the current year if:

       (1) Any number of men may be used.

(2) The cost of labor is $2.00 per hour for regularly scheduled 40-hour-per-week shifts.

(3) Overtime pay is $1\frac{1}{2}$ times regular time pay.

(4) The plant closes for vacation during the first full two weeks in August.

(5) The company maintains a level work force for this product.

(6) Each production employee must be paid for 40 hours work each week.

(7) There are six paid holidays during the calendar year.

(8) Only 10 hours overtime per employee are permissible in any week.

(9) Cost of carrying material in inventory is $0.02/man-hr/month.

b. What are the anticipation stocks at the end of each month?

c. Repeat Prob. 7(a) if there are 300 units in inventory on January 1 and 100 units are desired on December 31.

d. What are the anticipation stocks in your solution to Prob. 7(c)?

e. Repeat Prob. 7(a), assuming that the plant does not cease operations for vacation but that each man is expected to miss six per cent of the working time due to illness, vacation, personal business, etc. This six per cent is distributed evenly throughout the year.

f. Determine the costs of your plans for Probs. 7(a), 7(c), and 7(e). Separate overtime costs, inventory carrying costs, and costs of regular time not worked.

g. If the 20 man-hours per unit represent the standard hours, but the plant operates at 125 per cent of standard, what is the required production plan?

Chapter 8

8. Use your production plan for Prob. 7(a) and the data of Prob. 2 and adjust your production plan as necessary. Adjustment is made in the third month (skip two months).

a. Adjust the production plan by leveling over one period.

b. Adjust the production plan by leveling over five periods.

c. Adjust the production plan by leveling over 10 periods.

d. Make a plot of the adjustment to the production plan against time from Probs. 8(a), 8(b), and 8(c).

e. Make a plot of the anticipation stocks against time from Probs. 8(a), 8(b), and 8(c).

f. Are the adjusted production plans of Probs. 8(a), 8(b), and 8(c) possible under the conditions of your plan in Prob. 7(a)?

g. Repeat Probs. 8(a) through 8(f) for a one-month lag, rather than a two-month lag, in the adjustment.

Chapter 9

9. The 20 man-hours to manufacture one unit of product are distributed as follows:

Operation	01	02	03	04	05	06	07
Time (hrs)	1.90	5.50	3.60	1.75	3.60	1.82	1.83

The sequence of manufacture is

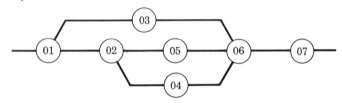

a. Determine the most efficient schedule for this product. [Use the number of men from Prob. 7(a).] What is the efficiency?

b. Is your production plan for Prob. 7(a) the most economical? If necessary, make a new plan with more men. After revising your production plan, repeat Prob. 9(a).

10. Your machine shop has received four orders. The order sizes are as follows:

Order	1	2	3	4
No. pieces	75	75	125	80

You have four machines on which you can do any one or all of the orders. The machine time available on each of the machines is shown below.

Machine	A	B	C	D
Time Available	65	90	105	110

The standard hours per piece are estimated to be

	Machine			
Order	A	B	C	D
1	0.75	0.80	0.65	0.70
2	0.90	0.70	0.75	0.85
3	0.70	0.65	0.80	0.80
4	0.85	0.75	0.80	0.75

a. Use the indicator method to make an optimum assignment of orders to machines.
b. How many machine hours are used?
c. If your average cost per machine hour is $7.50, what is the required average selling price of each item to yield a profit that is 40 per cent of the cost of manufacturing?

11. Make a Gantt Chart to show one cycle of your schedule sequence determined in Prob. 9(a). In Prob. 9(b).

12. At the beginning of the year, your inventories of the five products of Prob. 4 were 1000, 1000, 1500, 1500, and 1700 units for products A, B, C, D, and E, respectively.
a. Determine the quantity of each product to be scheduled during January to give equal inventory-usage ratios at the end of January.
b. Determine the sequence of scheduling the five products using the economic fraction of yearly demand determined in Prob. 4(a).
c. Schedule the quantities of each product as determined in Prob. 12(b).
d. Are your inventories sufficient to prevent run-out during the month of January (assume level or constant demand) under the schedule of (c) above?
e. Repeat Prob. 12(c) for the sequence determined in Prob. 12(b).
f. Repeat Prob. 12(d) under the schedule of Prob. 12(c).

Chapter 10

13. A large, multiplant, multiwarehouse operation distributes one product from four plants to four warehouses. For the coming year, the forecast requirements and the planned productions are as follows:

Plant	Planned Production	Warehouse	Forecast Requirements
A	5,000	1	5,500
B	6,000	2	6,800
C	5,000	3	7,700
D	6,500	4	2,500
Total	22,500	Total	22,500

The transportation costs are

| | Plant | | | |
Warehouse	A	B	C	D
1	1.25	1.35	1.20	1.40
2	1.15	1.20	1.35	1.25
3	1.35	1.40	1.10	1.20
4	1.20	1.45	1.35	1.25

a. Determine an optimum distribution of product.
b. Is there another optimum? If so, what is it?
c. Change the planned production at plant A to 6000 units. Now determine an optimum distribution.
d. Change the forecast requirements of warehouse 4 to 3000 units. Determine the optimum solution under these conditions. [Include the change in Prob. 13(c) also.]
e. The production costs at the plants are not equal. The cost per unit at each of the plants is

Plant	A	B	C	D
Cost	$10.50	$11.25	$10.75	$11.00

Determine the optimum distribution under these conditions. [Use data of Prob. 13(a).]

14. The selling price of each of the items on the orders of Prob. 10 is

Order	1	2	3	4
Selling Price	$10.00	$8.75	$7.80	$9.20

The cost of operating the machines is

Machine	A	B	C	D
Cost/hour	$8.00	$7.50	$8.00	$8.50

a. Determine an optimum assignment of orders.
b. What is the total profit under your assignment?
c. Can you increase your total profit by not producing any of the product? What is the increase in profit?

Problem Group 2

Chapter 3

1. Records show that your company has had the following demand for one of its products.

Month	First Year	Second Year
Jan.	117	120
Feb.	124	118
Mar.	95	104
Apr.	228	240
May	274	222
June	248	250
July	220	240
Aug.	130	135
Sept.	109	127
Oct.	128	130
Nov.	125	147
Dec.	134	131

a. Establish a monthly sales forecast for the third year.

b. Establish the expected maximum and minimum demands (assuming that the same cause system exists) for 95 out of 100 months. For 997 out of 1000 months.

c. Establish cumulative forecasts for each month of the third year, starting with January as the first month.

d. Establish forecasts for January of the third year by use of moving averages. Use $n = 3$, $n = 5$, and $n = 7$.

e. Establish forecasts for January of the third year by use of weighted averages. Use $w = 0.2$, $w = 0.5$, and $w = 0.8$.

f. Compare the forecasts from (a), (d), and (e). Which is best? Why?

Chapter 4

2. The sales during the third year are given below.

Month	Sales	Month	Sales
Jan.	110	July	252
Feb.	143	Aug.	110
Mar.	128	Sept.	145
Apr.	250	Oct.	108
May	264	Nov.	118
June	234	Dec.	109

    a. Make a moving-range chart for the demands of the first two years. (Leave space to add the demands of the third year.) Is the chart in control? Why? If not, why not?

    b. Add the demands of the third year to your moving-range chart. Does the chart still show control? What is your forecast for January of the fourth year?

    c. In Prob. 1(d), you determined moving-average forecasts for January of the third year. Extend these moving-average forecasts ($n = 3$, $n = 5$, and $n = 7$) through the third year on a month-by-month basis. (Remember, the moving average you get is the forecast for the next month.) Determine $\Sigma \mid x - x' \mid$ (actual minus forecast demand) for each value of n for these twelve months. Determine the sum of the absolute deviations from your forecasts of Prob. 1(a). Which of the four procedures gives the best forecast, based on the criterion that the sum of the absolute deviations should be a minimum? Plot these absolute differences as a function of time.

    d. Repeat Prob. 2(c), but use the weighted-average forecasts as in Prob. 1(e).

    e. Why would it be inappropriate to use a regression line as a forecasting procedure in this problem?

Chapter 5

3. This product is made from several components. One of these components is purchased. The average cost of placing an order is $68.00. The average cost of carrying one component in inventory for one year is $1.56.

    a. Determine the economic purchased lot size for this component: (1) graphically, and (2) by Eq. (5.2).

    b. What is the total variable annual cost of purchasing this component in economic lot sizes? The unit variable annual cost?

    c. The supplier has asked you to consider purchasing this component in lots of 500 units, rather than in the economic lot size determined in Prob. 7(a). If you do so, he will reduce his unit price. Your carrying charges are 35 per cent of the material cost. How much must the supplier reduce his per unit price so that your costs remain the same as they were for Prob. 7(a)?

    d. Suppose you can manufacture this same component in your own plant at the rate of 10,000 units per year. If your setup cost is equal to your order cost, what is your economic manufactured lot size?

    e. Repeat Prob. 3(b) for the conditions of Prob. 3(d).

4. Your company manufactures five other products. The demand, production, and cost data are given below.

Product	Sales (Unit/Yr)	Production (Units/Yr)	Inventory Cost (per Unit/Yr)	Setup Cost (per Time)
A	20,000	160,000	$2.88	$40.00
B	40,000	160,000	$3.60	$60.00
C	30,000	150,000	$4.32	$32.00
D	60,000	240,000	$4.80	$35.00
E	34,000	272,000	$2.40	$50.00

a. Determine the economic fraction of yearly demand.
b. Determine the economic manufactured lot size for each product considered individually.
c. Compare the annual costs under (a) and (b) above.
d. Under (a), what quantity of each product will be manufactured during each run?

5. It costs you $50.00 to place an order and 24 per cent of the material cost to carry an item in inventory for one year.
a. Construct an economic purchased order quantity table for monthly usages of 400 to 800 units (in increments of 100 units) and for per item costs of $12.00 to $26.00 per unit (in increments of $2.00 per unit).
b. Interpolate in your table to determine the economic order quantity for an item with a monthly usage of 525 units and a cost of $13.24 per unit. Calculate the economic order quantity. What is your error? How much would this add to your total annual cost?

Chapter 6

6. a. If the product of Prob. 3(a) were controlled by a fixed-order-size inventory control system, determine the reorder point if the lead time is 20 days. If the lead time is 75 days.
b. Determine the order interval and the reorder point for the conditions of (a) above, if you were using a fixed-order-interval inventory system.
c. Determine the safety stock that should be used in Prob. 6(a).
d. Determine the safety stock that should be used in Prob. 6(b).

e. Set up the fixed-order-size inventory control system of Probs. 6(a) and 6(c). Assume that an order is placed in inventory on the first of January. On the last day of the preceding December, you had exactly the safety stock in inventory. Assume 21 days per month, and show how your inventory system works for the demands of the third year (see Prob. 2). Determine the inventory at the reorder point, just before replenishment and just after replenishment, if an order is placed at the end of the day in which the inventory reaches the reorder point. Further, assume that back orders are possible but must be filled as soon as stock is again available. (Use 20-day lead time).

f. Repeat Prob. 6(e) under the same conditions, but use the fixed-order-interval inventory system and the results of Prob. 6(b) and 6(d).

Chapter 7

7. The product under consideration requires 30 man-hours to manufacture. There is no beginning inventory and no ending inventory. [Use your forecast from Prob. 1(a).]

a. Determine the economic production plan for the current year if:
   (1) Any number of men may be used.
   (2) The cost of labor is $2.40 per hour for regularly scheduled 40-hour-per-week shifts.
   (3) Overtime pay is $1\frac{1}{2}$ times regular time pay.
   (4) The plant closes for vacation during the first two full weeks in August.
   (5) The company maintains a level work force for this product.
   (6) Each production employee must be paid for 40 hours work each week.
   (7) There are six paid holidays during the calendar year.
   (8) Only 10 hours overtime per employee are permissible in any week.
   (9) The cost of carrying material in inventory is $0.052 per man-hour per year.

b. What are the anticipation stocks at the end of each month?

c. Repeat Prob. 7(a) if there are 200 units in inventory on January 1 and no units are desired on December 31.

d. What are the anticipation stocks in your solution to Prob. 7(c)?

e. Repeat Prob. 7(a), assuming that the plant does not cease operations for vacation but that each man is expected to miss seven per cent of the working time due to illness, vacation, personal business, etc. This seven per cent is distributed evenly throughout the year.

f. Determine the costs of your plans for Prob. 7(a), 7(c), and 7(e). (Separate overtime costs, inventory costs, and the cost of regular time paid for but not worked.)

g. If the 30 hours per unit represents the standard time per piece, but the average output per hour is 120 per cent of standard, what is the revised production plan?

Chapter 8

8. Use your production plan for Prob. 7(a) and adjust it as necessary according to the data of Prob. 2. Adjustment is made in the third month following (skip two months).

a. Adjust the production plan by leveling over one period.

b. Adjust the production plan by leveling over five periods.

c. Adjust the production plan by leveling over 10 periods.

d. Make a plot of the variation in demand from forecast and the adjustments to the production plan [Probs. 8(a), 8(b), and 8(c)] against time.

e. Make a plot of the actual minus planned inventories and the variation of demand from forecast against time [from Probs. 8(a), 8(b), and 8(c)].

f. Are the adjusted production plans of Probs. 8(a), 8(b), and 8(c) possible under the conditions of your plan in Prob. 7(a)?

g. Repeat Probs. 8(a) through 8(f) for a one-month lag, rather than a two-month lag in adjustment.

Chapter 9

9. The 30 man-hours to manufacture one unit of product are distributed as follows:

Operation	01	02	03	04	05	06	07	08
Time (hrs)	3.8	7.5	1.8	3.7	1.9	7.4	2.0	1.9

The sequence of manufacture is

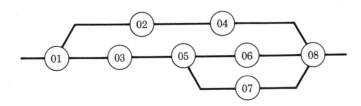

a. Determine the most efficient schedule for this product. [Use the number of men from Prob. 7(a).] What is the efficiency?
b. Is your production plan for Prob. 7(a) still the most efficient? If necessary, make a new plan with more men. After revising your production plan, repeat Prob. 9(a).

10. Your machine shop has received four orders. The order sizes are as follows:

Order	1	2	3	4
No. pieces	200	250	175	400

You have four machines on which you can do any one or all of the orders. The machine time available on each of the machines is

Machine	A	B	C	D
Time Available	200	400	200	150

The standard hours per piece are estimated to be:

Order	Machine			
	A	B	C	D
1	0.75	1.25	0.95	0.50
2	0.60	1.00	0.90	0.40
3	0.50	0.90	0.80	0.45
4	0.70	0.90	0.95	0.40

a. Use the indicator method to make an optimum assignment of orders to machines.
b. How many machine hours are used?
c. If your average cost per machine hour is $9.00, what is the required selling price of each item to yield a profit that is 60 per cent of the cost of manufacturing?

11. Make a Gantt Chart to show one cycle of your schedule sequence determined in Prob. 9(a). In 9(b).

12. At the beginning of the year, your inventories of the five products of Prob. 4 were 500, 600, 800, 800, and 1000 units for products A, B, C, D, and E, respectively.
a. Determine the quantity of each product to be scheduled during January to give equal inventory-usage ratios at the end of January.

b. Determine the sequence of scheduling the five products using the economic fraction of yearly demand determined in Prob. 4(a).
c. Schedule the quantities of each product as determined in (a) above.
d. Are your inventories sufficient to prevent run-out during the month of January (assume level or constant demand) under the schedule of (c) above?
e. Repeat Prob. 12(c) for the sequence determined in Prob. 12(b).
f. Repeat Prob. 12(d) under the schedule of Prob. 12(c).

Chapter 10

13. A large, multiplant, multiwarehouse operation distributes one product from four plants to four warehouses. For the coming year, the forecast requirements and the planned productions are as follows:

Plant	Planned Production	Warehouse	Forecast Requirements
A	10,000	1	15,000
B	12,000	2	9,000
C	7,000	3	4,000
D	13,000	4	14,000
Total	42,000	Total	42,000

The transportation costs are

Warehouse	Plant			
	A	B	C	D
1	$12.00	$11.00	$13.00	$14.00
2	$14.00	$15.00	$16.00	$15.00
3	$16.00	$14.00	$11.00	$13.00
4	$13.00	$11.00	$10.00	$12.00

a. Determine an optimum distribution of product.
b. Is there another optimum? If so, what is it?
c. Change the planned production at plant B to 10,000 units. Now determine an optimum distribution.
d. Change the forecast requirements of warehouse 1 to 14,000 units. Determine the optimum solution under these conditions. [Do not include the change in (c).]

e. The production costs at the plants are not equal. The cost per unit at each of the plants is

Plant	A	B	C	D
Cost	$10.00	$13.00	$11.00	$13.00

Determine the optimum distribution under these conditions.

14. The selling price of each of the items on the orders of Prob. 10 is

Order	1	2	3	4
Selling Price	$14.00	$16.00	$17.00	$15.00

The cost of operating the machines is

Machine	A	B	C	D
Cost/hour	$8.00	$7.00	$10.00	$11.00

a. Determine an optimum assignment of orders.
b. What is the total profit under your assignment?
c. Can you increase your total profit by not producing any of the product? What is the increase in profit?

Problem Group 3

Chapter 3

1. Records show that your company has had the following demand for one of its products.

Month	First Year	Second Year
Jan.	67	50
Feb.	53	61
Mar.	60	66
Apr.	79	81
May	102	105
June	118	125
July	135	138
Aug.	162	165
Sept.	70	59
Oct.	53	54
Nov.	68	53
Dec.	63	47

a. Establish a monthly sales forecast for the third year.
b. Establish the range between the expected maximum and minimum monthly demands (assuming that the same cause system exists) for 95 out of 100 months. For 997 out of 1000 months.
c. Establish cumulative forecasts for each month of the third year, starting with January as the first month.
d. Establish the expected range of the cumulative forecast through March of the third year.
e. Establish forecasts for January of the third year by use of moving averages. Use $n = 3$, $n = 5$, and $n = 7$.
f. Establish forecasts for January of the third year by use of weighted averages. Use $w = 0.2$, $w = 0.5$, and $w = 0.8$.
g. Compare the forecasts from (a), (e), and (f). Which is best? Why?

Chapter 4

2. The sales during the third year are given below:

Month	Sales	Month	Sales
Jan.	78	July	146
Feb.	71	Aug.	174
Mar.	89	Sept.	85
Apr.	100	Oct.	110
May	127	Nov.	120
June	140	Dec.	94

a. Make a moving-range chart for the demands of the first two years. (Leave space to add the demands of the third year.) Is the chart in control? Why? If not, why not?
b. Add the demands of the third year to your moving-range chart. Does the chart still show control? What is your forecast for January of the fourth year?
c. In Prob. 1(e), you determined moving-average forecasts for January of the third year. Extend these moving-average forecasts ($n = 3$, $n = 5$, and $n = 7$) through the third year on a month-by-month basis. (Remember, the moving average you get is the forecast for the next month.) Determine $\Sigma \, | \, x - x' \, |$ (actual minus forecast demand) for each value of n for these twelve months. Determine the sum of the absolute deviations from your forecasts of Prob. 1(a). Which of the four procedures gives the best forecast based on the criterion that the sum of the absolute deviations should be a minimum? Plot these absolute differences as a function of time.

d. Repeat Prob. 2(c), but use the weighted-average forecasts as in Prob. 1(f).

e. Why would it be inappropriate to use the arithmetic average as a forecasting procedure in this problem?

Chapter 5

3. This product is made from several components. One of these components is purchased. The average cost of placing an order is $87.00. The average cost of carrying one component in inventory for one year is $1.30.

a. Determine the economic purchased lot size for this component: (1) graphically, and (2) by Eq. (5.2).

b. What is the total variable annual cost of purchasing this component in economic lot sizes? The unit variable annual cost?

c. The supplier has asked you to consider purchasing this component in lots of 750 units, rather than in the lot size determined in Prob. 3(a). If you do so, he will reduce his unit price. Your carrying charges are 30 per cent of the material cost. How much must the supplier reduce his per unit price for your costs to remain the same as they were for the lot size determined in Prob. 3(a)?

d. Suppose you can manufacture this same component in your own plant at the rate of 5000 units per year. If your setup cost is equal to your order cost, what is your economic manufactured lot size?

e. Repeat Prob. 3(b) for the conditions of Prob. 3(d).

4. Your company manufactures five other products. The demand, production, and cost data are given below.

Product	Sales (Units/Yr)	Production Rate (Units/Mo)	Inventory Cost (per Unit/Yr)	Setup Cost (per Time)
A	60,000	20,000	$4.80	$17.50
B	20,000	13,333	$2.88	$20.00
C	34,000	22,667	$2.40	$25.00
D	40,000	13,333	$3.60	$30.00
E	30,000	12,500	$4.32	$16.00

a. Determine the economic fraction of yearly demand.

b. Determine the economic manufactured lot size for each product considered individually.

c. Compare the annual costs under (a) and (b) above.

d. Under (a), what quantity of each product will be manufactured during each run?

5. It costs you $87.00 to place an order and 30 per cent of the material cost to carry an item in inventory for one year.

    a. Construct an economic-purchased-order-quantity table for monthly usages of 150 to 250 units (in increments of 20 units) and for per item costs of $4.00 to $16.00 per unit (in increments of $2.00 per unit).

    b. Interpolate in your table to determine the economic order quantity for an item with a monthly usage of 187 units and a cost of $7.25 per unit. Calculate the economic order quantity. What is your error? How much would this add to your total annual cost?

Chapter 6

6. a. If the product of Prob. 3(a) is controlled by a fixed-order-size inventory-control system, determine the reorder point if the lead time is 20 days. If the lead time is 60 days.

    b. Determine the order interval and the reorder point for the conditions of (a) above if you were using a fixed-order-interval inventory system.

    c. Determine the safety stock that should be used in Prob. 6(a).

    d. Determine the safety stock that should be used in Prob. 6(b).

    e. Set up the fixed-order-size inventory-control system of Probs. 6(a) and 6(c). Assume that an order is placed in inventory on the first of January. On the last day of the preceding December, you had exactly the safety stock in inventory. Assume 21 days per month, and show how your inventory system works for the demands of the third year (see Prob. 2). Determine the inventory at the reorder point, just before replenishment and just after replenishment if an order is placed at the end of the day in which the inventory reaches the reorder point. Further, assume that back orders are possible but that they must be filled as soon as stock is again available. (Use 20-day lead time only.)

    f. Repeat Prob. (6e) under the same conditions, but use the fixed-order-interval inventory system and the results of Probs. 6(b) and 6(d).

Chapter 7

7. The product under consideration requires 25 man-hours to manufacture. There is no beginning inventory and no ending inventory. [Use your forecast from Prob. 1(a).]

    a. Determine the economic production plan for the current year if:

        (1) Any number of men may be used.

        (2) The cost of labor is $3.00 per hour for regularly scheduled 40-hour-per-week shifts.

(3) Overtime pay is $1\frac{1}{2}$ times regular time pay.

(4) The plant closes for vacation during the first two full weeks in August.

(5) The company maintains a level work force for this product.

(6) Each production employee must be paid for 40 hours work each week.

(7) There are six paid holidays during the calendar year.

(8) Only ten hours overtime per employee are permissible in any week.

(9) Cost of carrying material in inventory is $0.48 per man hour per year.

b. What are the anticipation stocks at the end of each month?

c. Repeat Prob. 7(a) if there are 500 units in inventory on January 1 and 200 units are desired on December 31.

d. What are the anticipation stocks in your solution to Prob. 7(c)?

e. Repeat Prob. 7(a), assuming that the plant does not cease operations for vacation but that each man is expected to miss 5 per cent of the working time because of illness, vacation, personal business, etc. This 5 per cent is distributed evenly throughout the year.

f. Determine the costs of your plans for Probs. 7(a), 7(c), and 7(e). (Separate overtime costs, inventory costs, and the cost of regular time paid for but not worked.)

g. If the 25 hours per unit represents the standard time per piece, but the average output per hour is 130 per cent of standard, what is the revised production plan?

Chapter 8

8. Use your production plan for 7(a) and adjust it as necessary according to the data of Prob. 2. Adjustment is made in the third month following (skip two months).

a. Adjust the production plan by leveling over one period.

b. Adjust the production plan by leveling over five periods.

c. Adjust the production plan by leveling over 10 periods.

d. Make a plot of the variation in demand from forecast and the adjustments to the production plan [Probs. 8(a), 8(b), and 8(c)] against time.

e. Make a plot of the actual minus planned inventories and the variation of demand from forecast against time [From Probs. 8(a), 8(b), and 8(c)].

f. Are the adjusted production plans of Probs. 8(a), 8(b), and 8(c) possible under the conditions of your plan in Prob. 7(a)?

g. Repeat Probs. 8(a) through 8(f) for a one-month lag, rather than a two-month lag in adjustment.

Chapter 9

9. The 25 man-hours to manufacture one unit of product are distributed as follows:

Operation	01	02	03	04	05
Time (hrs)	5.9	2.9	3.0	1.1	12.1

The sequence of manufacture is

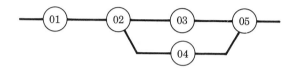

a. Determine the most efficient schedule for this product. [Use the number of men from Prob. 7(a).] What is the efficiency?

b. Is your production plan for Prob. 7(a) still the most economical? If necessary, make a new plan with more men. After revising your production plan, repeat Prob. 9(a).

10. Your machine shop has received five orders. The order sizes are as follows:

Order	1	2	3	4	5
No. pieces	50	75	60	80	100

You have four machines on which you can do any one or all of the orders. The machine time available on each of the machines is

Machine	A	B	C	D
Time Available	75	80	96	88

The standard pieces per hour are estimated to be

Order	Machine			
	A	B	C	D
1	1	$\frac{3}{2}$	2	$\frac{5}{4}$
2	2	$\frac{5}{4}$	2	$\frac{3}{2}$
3	2	$\frac{5}{2}$	$\frac{5}{2}$	1
4	$\frac{3}{2}$	1	2	1
5	1	$\frac{3}{2}$	$\frac{3}{2}$	$\frac{3}{2}$

a. Use the indicator method to make an optimum assignment of orders to machines.
b. How many machine hours are used?
c. If your average cost per machine hour is $10.00, what is the required selling price of each item to yield a profit that is 25 per cent of the cost of manufacturing?

11. Make a Gantt Chart to show one cycle of your schedule sequence determined in Prob. 9(a). In Prob. 9(b).

12. At the beginning of the year, your inventories of the five products of Prob. 4 were 5000, 7000, 9000, 8000, and 3000 units for products A, B, C, D, and E, respectively.
a. Determine the quantity of each product to be scheduled during January to give equal inventory-usage ratios at the end of January.
b. Determine the sequence of scheduling the five products, using the economic fraction of yearly demand determined in Prob. 4(a).
c. Schedule the quantities of each product as determined in (a) above.
d. Are your inventories sufficient to prevent run-out during the month of January (assume level or constant demand) under the schedule of (c) above?
e. Repeat Prob. 12(c) for the sequence determined in Prob. 12(b).
f. Repeat Prob. 12(d) under the schedule of Prob. 12(c).

Chapter 10

13. A large, multiplant, multiwarehouse operation distributes one product from five plants to five warehouses. For the coming year, the forecast requirements and the planned productions are as follows:

Plant	Planned Production	Warehouse	Forecast Requirements
A	1200	1	3000
B	1400	2	1300
C	1600	3	900
D	2000	4	800
E	2500	5	2700
Total	8700	Total	8700

The transportation costs are

Warehouse	Plant				
	A	B	C	D	E
1	$4.00	$3.00	$5.00	$2.50	$3.50
2	$3.00	$6.00	$5.00	$2.00	$5.00
3	$2.00	$4.00	$4.50	$2.00	$5.00
4	$2.50	$4.50	$4.50	$3.50	$6.00
5	$5.00	$3.50	$6.00	$2.00	$3.50

a. Determine an optimum distribution of product.
b. Is there another optimum? If so, what is it?
c. Change the planned production at plant C to 2000 units. Determine an optimum distribution.
d. Change the forecast requirements of warehouse 2 to 1100 units. Determine the optimum solution under these conditions. [Include the change in (c).]
e. The production costs at the plants are not equal. The cost per unit at each of the plants is

Plant	A	B	C	D	E
Cost	$20.00	$21.00	$17.00	$21.00	$19.00

Determine the optimum distribution under these conditions.

14. The selling price of each of the items on the orders of Prob. 10 is

Order	1	2	3	4	5
Selling Price	$13.00	$14.00	$12.50	$12.00	$13.00

The cost of operating the machines is

Machine	A	B	C	D
Cost/hour	$8.00	$12.00	$9.00	$11.00

a. Determine an optimum assignment of orders.
b. What is the total profit under your assignment?

c. Can you increase your total profit by not producing any of the product? What is the increase in profit?

Problem Group 4

Chapter 3

1. Records show that your company has had the following demand for one of its products.

Month	First Year	Second Year
Jan.	179	150
Feb.	148	143
Mar.	127	128
Apr.	114	93
May	86	90
June	47	70
July	53	57
Aug.	74	102
Sept.	99	118
Oct.	141	120
Nov.	146	133
Dec.	161	167

a. Establish a monthly sales forecast for the third year.
b. Establish the range between the expected maximum and minimum monthly demands (assuming that the same cause system exists) for 95 out of 100 months. For 997 out of 1000 months.
c. Establish cumulative forecasts for each month of the third year, starting with January as the first month.
d. Establish the expected range of the cumulative forecast through October of the third year.
e. Establish forecasts for January of the third year by use of moving averages. Use $n = 3$, $n = 5$, and $n = 7$.
f. Establish forecasts for January of the third year by use of weighted averages. Use $w = 0.2$, $w = 0.5$, and $w = 0.9$.
g. Compare the forecasts from (a), (e), and (f). Which is best? Why?

Chapter 4

2. The sales during the third year are given below.

Month	Sales	Month	Sales
Jan.	158	July	70
Feb.	165	Aug.	98
Mar.	136	Sept.	112
Apr.	92	Oct.	122
May	82	Nov.	125
June	55	Dec.	153

   a. Make a moving-range for the demands of the first two years.
      (Leave space to add the demands of the third year.) Is the chart
      in control? Why? If not, why not?
   b. Add the demands of the third year to your moving-range chart.
      Does the chart still show control? What is your forecast for Janu-
      ary of the fourth year?
   c. In Prob. 1(e), you determined moving-average forecasts for
      January of the third year. Extend these moving-average forecasts
      ($n = 3$, $n = 5$, and $n = 7$) through the third year on a month-by-
      month basis. (Remember, the moving average you get is the fore-
      cast for the next month.) Determine $\Sigma \mid x - x' \mid$ (actual minus
      forecast demand) for each value of n for these twelve months.
      Compare these sums with $\Sigma \mid x - x' \mid$ from Prob. 1(a) for the same
      period. Which of the four procedures gives the best forecast based
      on the criterion that the $\Sigma \mid x - x' \mid$ should be a minimum? Plot
      these absolute differences against time.
   d. Repeat Prob. 2(c), but use the weighted-average forecasts, as in
      Prob. 1(f).
   e. Why would it be inappropriate to use an average as a forecasting
      procedure in this problem?

Chapter 5

3. This product is made from several components. One of these components is purchased. The average cost of placing an order is $65.00.
   The average cost of carrying one component in inventory for one year
   is $1.44.
   a. Determine the economic purchased lot size for this component: (1)
      graphically, and (2) by Eq. (5.2).

b. What is the total variable annual cost of purchasing this component in economic lot sizes? The unit variable annual cost?

c. The supplier has asked you to consider purchasing this component in lots of 600 units, rather than in the lot size determined in Prob. 3(a). If you do so, he will reduce his unit price. Your carrying charges are 20 per cent of the material cost. How much must the supplier reduce his per unit price for your costs to remain the same as they were for the lot size determined in Prob. 3(a)?

d. Suppose that you can manufacture this same component in your own plant at the rate of 8000 units per year. If your setup cost is equal to your order cost, what is your economic manufactured lot size?

e. Repeat Prob. 3(b) for the conditions of Prob. 3(d).

4. Your company manufactures five other products. The demand, production, and cost data are given below.

Product	Sales (Units/Yr)	Production Rate (Units/Yr)	Inventory Cost (per Unit/Yr)	Setup Cost (per Time)
A	2,000	8,000	$1.35	$45.00
B	3,000	12,000	$1.80	$26.25
C	1,700	13,600	$0.90	$37.50
D	1,000	8,000	$1.08	$30.00
E	1,500	7,500	$1.62	$24.00

a. Determine the economic fraction of yearly demand.

b. Determine the economic manufactured lot size for each product considered individually.

c. Compare the annual costs under (a) and (b) above.

d. Under (a), what quantity of each product will be manufactured during each run?

5. It costs you $65.00 to place an order and 20 per cent of the material cost to carry an item in inventory for one year.

a. Construct an economic-purchased-order-quantity table for monthly usages of 200 to 400 units (in increments of 50 units) and for per item costs of $3.00 to $5.00 per unit (in increments of $0.25 per unit).

b. Interpolate in your table to determine the economic order quantity for an item with a monthly usage of 288 units and a cost of $4.16 per unit. Calculate the economic order quantity. What is your error? How much would this add to your total annual cost?

Chapter 6

6. a. If the product of Prob. 3(a) were controlled by a fixed-order-size inventory-control system, determine the reorder point if the lead time is 30 days. If the lead time is 90 days.

b. Determine the order interval and the reorder point for the conditions of (a) above if you were using a fixed-order-interval inventory system.

c. Determine the safety stock that should be used in Prob. 6(a).

d. Determine the safety stock that should be used in Prob. 6(b).

e. Setup the fixed-order-size inventory-control system of Probs. 6(a) and 6(c). Assume that an order is placed in inventory on the first of January. On the last day of the preceding December, you had exactly the safety stock in inventory. Assume 21 days per month, and show how your inventory system works for the demands of the third year (see Prob. 2). Determine the inventory at the reorder point, just before replenishment and just after replenishment if an order is placed at the end of the day in which the inventory reaches the reorder point. Further, assume that back orders are possible but that they must be filled as soon as stock is again available. (Use 30-day lead time only.)

f. Repeat Prob. 6(e) under the same conditions, but use the fixed-order-interval inventory system and the results of Probs. 6(b) and 6(d).

Chapter 7

7. The product under consideration requires 15 man-hours to manufacture. There is no beginning inventory and no ending inventory. [Use your forecast from Prob. 1(a).]

a. Determine the economic production plan for the current year if:

   (1) Any number of men may be used.

   (2) The cost of labor is $2.40 per hour for regularly scheduled 40 hour per week shifts.

   (3) Overtime pay is $1\frac{1}{2}$ times regular time pay.

   (4) The plant closes for vacation during the first two full weeks in August.

   (5) The company maintains a level work force for this product.

   (6) Each production employee must be paid for 40 hours work each week.

   (7) There are six paid holidays during the calendar year.

   (8) Only 10 hours overtime per employee are permissible in any week.

   (9) The cost of carrying a unit in inventory is $0.05 per man hour per month.
b. What are the anticipation stocks at the end of each month?
c. Repeat Prob. 7(a) if there are 400 man-hours in inventory on January 1 and 100 man-hours are desired on December 31.
d. What are the anticipation stocks in your solution to Prob. 7(c)?
e. Repeat Prob. 7(a), assuming that the plant does not cease operations for vacation but that each man is expected to miss 6 per cent of the working time due to illness, vacation, personal business, etc. This 6 per cent is distributed evenly throughout the year.
f. Determine the costs of your plans for Probs. 7(a), 7(c), and 7(e). (Separate overtime costs, inventory costs, and the cost of regular time paid for but not worked.)
g. If the 15 hours per unit represents the standard time per piece but the average output per hour is 120 per cent of standard, what is the revised production plan?

Chapter 8

8. Use your production plan for 7(a) and adjust it as necessary according to the data of Prob. 2. Adjustment is made in the third month following (skip two months).
a. Adjust the production plan by leveling over one period.
b. Adjust the production plan by leveling over five periods.
c. Adjust the production plan by leveling over 10 periods.
d. Make a plot of the variation in demand from forecast and the adjustments to the production plan [Probs. 8(a), 8(b), and 8(c)] against time.
e. Make a plot of the actual minus planned inventories and the variation of demand from forecast against time [from Probs. 8(a), 8(b), and 8(c)].
f. Are the adjusted production plans of Probs. 8(a), 8(b), and 8(c) possible under the conditions of your plan in Prob. 7(a)?
g. Repeat Probs. 8(a) through 8(f) for a one-month lag, rather than a two-month lag in adjustment.

Chapter 9

9. The 15 man-hours to manufacture one unit of product are distributed as follows:

Operation	01	02	03	04	05	06	07	08	09	10	11
Time (min)	40	90	35	38	167	45	58	165	30	80	152

The sequence of manufacture is

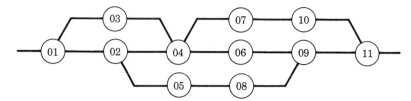

a. Determine the most efficient schedule for this product. [Use the number of men from Prob. 7(a).] What is the efficiency?
b. Is your production plan for Prob. 7(a) still the most economical? What is the required beginning inventory to meet the revised requirements?

10. Your machine shop has received five orders. The order sizes are as follows:

Order	1	2	3	4	5
No. pieces	80	75	100	120	60

You have six machines on which you can do any one or all of the orders. The machine time available on each of the machines is

Machine	A	B	C	D	E	F
Time Available	65	82	70	95	150	50

The standard pieces per hour are estimated to be

Order	Machine					
	A	B	C	D	E	F
1	$\frac{5}{4}$	$\frac{4}{4}$	$\frac{3}{2}$	$\frac{3}{4}$	$\frac{3}{4}$	$\frac{3}{2}$
2	$\frac{3}{2}$	2	$\frac{5}{4}$	$\frac{7}{4}$	$\frac{9}{4}$	2
3	$\frac{5}{4}$	$\frac{3}{4}$	$\frac{3}{2}$	$\frac{5}{4}$	$\frac{5}{4}$	2
4	$\frac{3}{2}$	1	2	1	$\frac{3}{2}$	$\frac{3}{2}$
5	1	$\frac{3}{4}$	$\frac{3}{4}$	$\frac{1}{2}$	$\frac{3}{4}$	$\frac{5}{4}$

a. Use the indicator method to make an optimum assignment of orders to machines.
b. How many machine hours are used?
c. If your average cost per machine hour is $8.00, what is the required average selling price of each item to yield a profit that is 50 per cent of the cost of manufacturing?

11. Make a Gantt Chart to show one cycle of your schedule sequence determined in Prob. 9(a).

12. At the beginning of the year, your inventories of the five products of Prob. 4 were 400, 400, 175, 125, and 100 units for products A, B, C, D, and E, respectively.
a. Determine the quantity of each product to be scheduled during January to give equal inventory-usage ratios at the end of January.
b. Determine the sequence of scheduling the five products, using the economic fraction of yearly demand determined in Prob. 4(a).
c. Schedule the quantities of each product as determined in (a) above.
d. Are your inventories sufficient to prevent run-out during the month of January (assume level or constant demand) under the schedule of (c) above?
e. Repeat Prob. 12(c) for the sequence determined in Prob. 12(b).
f. Repeat Prob. 12(d) under the schedule of Prob. 12(e).

Chapter 10

13. A large, multiplant, multiwarehouse operation distributes one product from five plants to five warehouses. For the coming year, the forecast requirements and the planned productions are

Plant	Planned Production	Warehouse	Forecast Requirements
A	15	1	5
B	12	2	25
C	19	3	17
D	10	4	14
E	8	5	6
Total	64	Total	67

The transportation costs are

Warehouse	Plant				
	A	B	C	D	E
1	$10.00	$12.00	$11.00	$12.00	$ 9.00
2	$11.00	$13.00	$10.00	$ 8.00	$11.00
3	$ 7.00	$10.00	$13.00	$10.00	$ 9.00
4	$12.00	$10.00	$ 9.00	$13.00	$13.00
5	$ 8.00	$14.00	$12.00	$10.00	$10.00

a. Determine an optimum distribution of product.
b. Is there another optimum? If so, what is it?
c. Change the planned production at plant A to 25 units. Now determine an optimum distribution.
d. Change the forecast requirements of warehouse 2 to 22 units. Determine the optimum solution under these conditions.
e. The production costs at the plants are not equal. The cost per unit at each of the plants is

Plant	A	B	C	D	E
Cost	$10.00	$9.00	$11.00	$8.00	$9.00

Determine the optimum distribution under these conditions.

14. The selling price of each of the items on the orders of Prob. 10 is

Order	1	2	3	4	5
Selling Price	$10.00	$9.00	$11.00	$8.00	$10.00

The cost of operating the machines is

Machine	A	B	C	D	E	F
Cost/hour	$8.00	$7.00	$8.00	$9.00	$10.00	$10.00

a. Determine an optimum assignment of orders.
b. What is the total profit under your assignment?
c. Can you increase your total profit by not producing any of the product? What is the increase in profit?

Problem Group 5

Chapter 3

1. Records show that your company has had the following demand for one of its products.

Month	First Year	Second Year
Jan.	101	159
Feb.	125	178
Mar.	108	174
Apr.	131	181
May	132	202
June	145	190
July	125	196
Aug.	147	192
Sept.	155	188
Oct.	163	185
Nov.	176	187
Dec.	153	192

a. Establish a monthly sales forecast for the third year.

b. Establish the range between the expected maximum and minimum monthly demands (assuming the same cause system exists) for 95 out of 100 months. For 997 out of 1000 months.

c. Establish cumulative forecasts for each month of the third year, starting with January as the first month.

d. Establish the expected range of the cumulative forecast through September of the third year.

e. Establish forecasts for January of the third year by use of moving averages. Use $n = 3$, $n = 5$, and $n = 7$.

f. Establish forecasts for January of the third year by use of weighted averages. Use $w = 0.2$, $w = 0.5$, and $w = 0.8$.

g. Compare the forecasts from (a), (e), and (f). Which is best? Why?

Chapter 4

2. The sales during the third year are given below.

Month	Sales	Month	Sales
Jan.	214	July	235
Feb.	221	Aug.	245
Mar.	229	Sept.	266
Apr.	227	Oct.	244
May	208	Nov.	261
June	221	Dec.	266

a. Make a moving-range chart for the demands of the first two years. (Leave space to add the demands of the third year.) Is the chart in control? Why? If not, why not?

b. Add the demands of the third year to your moving-range chart. Does the chart still show control? What is your forecast for January of the fourth year?

c. In Prob. 1(d), you determined moving-average forecasts for January of the third year. Extend these moving-average forecasts ($n = 3$, $n = 5$, and $n = 7$) through the third year on a month-by-month basis. (Remember, the moving-average you get is the forecast for the next month.) Determine $\Sigma \mid x - x' \mid$ (actual minus forecast demand) for each value of n for these twelve months. Determine the sum of the absolute deviations from your forecasts of Prob. 1(a). Which of the four procedures gives the best forecast based on the criterion that the sum of the absolute deviations should be a minimum? Plot these absolute differences as a function of time.

d. Repeat Prob. 2(c) but use the weighted average forecasts as in Prob. 1(f).

Chapter 5

3. This product is made from several components. One of these components is purchased. The average cost of placing an order is $100.00. The average costs of carrying one component in inventory for one year is $2.00.

a. Determine the economic purchased lot size for this component: (1) graphically, and (2) by Eq. (5.2).

b. What is the total variable annual cost of purchasing this component in economic lot sizes? The unit variable annual cost?

c. The supplier has asked you to consider purchasing this component in lots of 2500 units, rather than in the economic lots determined Prob. 3(a). If you do so, he will reduce his unit price. Your carrying charges are 25 per cent of the material cost. How much must the supplier reduce his per unit price so that your costs remain the same as they were for the economic lots of Prob. 3(a)?

d. Suppose you can manufacture this same component in your own plant at the rate of 15,000 units per year. If your setup cost is equal to your order cost, what is your economic manufactured lot size?

e. Repeat Prob. 3(b) for the conditions of Prob. 3(d).

4. Your company manufactures five other products. The demand, production and cost data are given below.

Product	Sales (Units/Mo)	Production (Units/Mo)	Inventory Cost (per Unit/Mo)	Setup Cost (per Time)
A	10,000	80,000	$0.12	$20.00
B	20,000	80,000	$0.15	$30.00
C	15,000	75,000	$0.18	$16.00
D	30,000	120,000	$0.20	$17.50
E	17,000	136,000	$0.10	$25.00

   a. Determine the economic fraction of yearly demand.
   b. Determine the economic manufactured lot size for each product considered individually.
   c. Compare the annual costs under (a) and (b) above.
   d. Under (a), what quantity of each product will be manufactured during each run?

5. It costs you $100.00 to place an order and 25 per cent of the material cost to carry an item in inventory for one year.
   a. Construct an economic purchased order quantity table for monthly usages of 10,000 to 20,000 units (in increments of 2000 units) and for per item costs of $20.00 to $40.00 per unit (in increments of $4.00 per unit).
   b. Interpolate in your table to determine the economic order quantity for an item with a monthly usage of 15,500 units and a cost of $22.50 per unit. Calculate the economic order quantity. What is your error? How much would this add to your total annual cost?

Chapter 6

6. a. If the product of Prob. 3(a) were controlled by a fixed-order-size inventory control system, determine the reorder point if the lead time is 10 days. If the lead time is 25 days.
   b. Determine the order interval and the reorder point for the conditions of (a) above if you were using a fixed-order-interval inventory system.
   c. Determine the safety stock that should be used in Prob. 6(a).
   d. Determine the safety stock that should be used in Prob. 6(b).
   e. Set up the fixed order size inventory control system of Probs. 6(a) and 6(c). Assume an order is placed in inventory on the first of

January. On the last day of the preceding December, you had exactly the safety stock in inventory. Assume 20 days per month, show how your inventory system works for the demands of the third year (see Prob. 2). Determine the inventory at the reorder point, just before replenishment and just after replenishment if an order is placed at the end of the day in which the inventory reaches the reorder point. Further, assume back orders are possible but must be filled as soon as stock is again available. (Use 10 day lead time.)

f. Repeat Prob. 6(e) under the same conditions except use the fixed-order-interval inventory system and the results of Probs. 6(b) and 6(d).

Chapter 7

7. The product under consideration requires 24 man-hours to manufacture. There is no beginning inventory and no ending inventory. [Use your forecast from Prob. 1(a).]

  a. Determine the economic production plan for the current year if:
   (1) Any number of men may be used.
   (2) The cost of labor is $2.50 per hour for regularly scheduled 40-hour-per-week shifts.
   (3) Overtime pay is $1\frac{1}{2}$ times regular time pay.
   (4) The plant closes for vacation during the first full two weeks in August.
   (5) The company maintains a level workforce for this product.
   (6) Each production employee must be paid for 40 hours work each week.
   (7) There are 6 paid holidays during the calendar year.
   (8) Only 10 hours overtime per employee are permissible in any week.
   (9) The inventory carrying charges are $1.00 per unit per month.
  b. What are the anticipation stocks at the end of each month?
  c. Repeat Prob. 7(a) if there are 1000 units in inventory on January 1 and 1700 units are desired on December 31.
  d. What are the anticipation stocks in your solution to Prob. 7(c)?
  e. Repeat Prob. 7(a), assuming that the plant does not cease operations for vacation but that each man is expected to miss 8 per cent of the working time due to illness, vacation, personal business etc. This 8 per cent is distributed evenly throughout the year.
  f. Determine the total costs of your plans for Probs. 7(a), 7(c), and 7(e). (Separate overtime costs, inventory costs, and the cost of regular time paid for but not worked.)

g. If the 24 hours per unit represent the standard time per piece, but the average output per hour is 110 per cent of standard, what is the revised production plan?

Chapter 8

8. Use your production plan for (7a) and adjust it as necessary according to the data of Prob. 2. Adjustment is made in the third month following (skip two months).
   a. Adjust the production plan by leveling over one period.
   b. Adjust the production plan by leveling over five periods.
   c. Adjust the production plan by leveling over 10 periods.
   d. Make a plot of the variation in demand from forecast and the adjustment to the production plan [Probs. 8(a), 8(b), and 8(c)] against time.
   e. Make a plot of the actual minus planned inventories and the variation of demand from forecast against time. [From Probs. 8(a), 8(b), and 8(c).]
   f. Are the adjusted production plans of Probs. 8(a), 8(b), and 8(c) possible under the conditions of your plan in Prob. 7(a)?
   g. Repeat Probs. 8(a) through 8(f) for a month lag, rather than a two-month lag in adjustment.

9. The 24 man-hours to manufacture one unit of product are distributed as follows:

Operation	01	02	03	04	05
Time (hrs)	6	12	2	2	2

The sequence of manufacture is

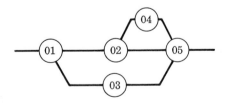

   a. Determine the most efficient schedule for this product. (Use the number of men from Prob. 7(a). What is the efficiency?
   b. Is your production plan for Prob. 7(a) still the most economical? If necessary, make a new plan with more men. After revising your production plan, repeat Prob. 9(a).

10. Your machine shop has received four orders. The order sizes are

Order	1	2	3	4
No. pieces	50	50	40	20

You have three machines on which you can do any one or all of the orders. The machine time available on each machine is

Machine	A	B	C
Time Available	150	200	240

The standard pieces per hour are estimated to be

Order	A	B	C
		Machine	
1	$\frac{1}{2}$	$\frac{1}{3}$	$\frac{1}{4}$
2	$\frac{1}{3}$	$\frac{1}{3}$	$\frac{1}{5}$
3	$\frac{1}{3}$	$\frac{1}{4}$	$\frac{1}{6}$
4	$\frac{1}{4}$	$\frac{1}{4}$	$\frac{1}{6}$

a. Use the indicator method to make an optimum assignment of orders to machines.
b. How many machine hours are used?
c. If your average cost per machine hour is $7.00, what is the required selling price of each item to yield a profit that is 45 per cent of the cost of manufacturing?

11. Make a Gantt Chart to show one cycle of your schedule sequence determined in Prob. 9(a). In 9(b).

12. At the beginning of the year, your inventories of the five products of Prob. 4 were 15,000, 20,000, 20,000, 18,000, and 15,000 units for products A, B, C, D, and E, respectively.
a. Determine the quantity of each product to be scheduled during January to give equal available-usage ratios at the end of January.
b. Determine the sequence of scheduling the five products using the economic fraction of yearly demand determined in Prob. 4(a).
c. Schedule the quantities of each product as determined in (a) above.
d. Are your inventories sufficient to prevent run-out during the month of January (assume level or constant demand) under the schedule of (c) above?
e. Repeat Prob. 12(c) for the sequence determined in Prob. 12(b).
f. Repeat Prob. 12(d) under the schedule of Prob. 12(e).

Chapter 10

13. A large multiplant, multiwarehouse operation distributes one product from four plants to four warehouses. For the coming year, the forecast requirements and the planned productions are

Plant	Planned Production	Warehouse	Forecast Requirements
A	1000	1	800
B	1200	2	1500
C	900	3	700
D	1200	4	1300
Total	4300	Total	4300

The transportation costs are

Warehouse	Plant			
	A	B	C	D
1	3	6	4	3
2	4	5	5	2
3	5	2	6	3
4	6	7	8	7

a. Determine an optimum distribution of product.
b. Is there another optimum? If so, what is it?
c. Change the planned production at plant A to 900 units. Now determine an optimum distribution.
d. Change the forecast requirements of warehouse 2 to 2000 units. Determine the optimum solution under these conditions. [Include the change in (c).]
e. The production costs at the plants are not equal. The cost per unit at each of the plants is

Plant	A	B	C	D
Cost	$10.00	$10.00	$9.00	$11.00

Determine the optimum distribution under these conditions.

14. The selling price of each of the items on the orders of Prob. 10 is

Order	1	2	3	4
Selling Price	$10.00	$10.00	$11.00	$9.00

The cost of operating the machines is

Machine	A	B	C
Cost/hour	$8.00	$7.00	$6.00

a. Determine an optimum assignment of orders.
b. What is the total profit under your assignment?
c. Can you increase your total profit by not producing any of the product? What is the increase in profit?

Problem Group 6

Chapters 1 and 2

1. Study the *Factory*-APICS survey, "Exclusive Survey of Production and Inventory Control" (published in *Factory*, Vol. **119**, No. 4, April 1961, pages 80–87). Visit a local manufacturing company.
   a. Determine its relative position on each of the factors reported in the survey.
   b. Classify this company as to the type of manufacturing and substantiate your classification.
   c. Investigate the use of production and inventory control documents and make a table similar to Table 2.1.

Chapter 3

2. For this problem use the data from the latest edition of the *FAA Statistical Handbook of Aviation* published annually by the United States Federal Aviation agency.
   a. Make plots of:
      (1) Monthly revenue passenger miles flown on scheduled domestic flights.
      (2) Monthly revenue passenger miles flown on scheduled international flights.
      (3) Monthly revenue passenger seat-miles flown on scheduled domestic flights.
      (4) Monthly revenue passenger seat-miles flown on scheduled international flights.
   b. Use regression lines to establish a forecast for the latest year reported, based on the data of the previous three years.
   c. Use a trigonometric form of regression curve to make the forecasts for the latest year.

   d. Compare your forecasts with actual performance of the latest year
      reported. Which method gives the best forecast based on the mini-
      mum sum of squares of the deviations of forecast from actual?
   e. Make a weighted-average forecast on a month-by-month basis.
      Make a comparison with the other forecasts of parts (b) and (c)
      on the basis of minimum sum of squares of deviations.

3. Obtain data on the annual enrollment of engineering students from the
   latest annual reports of the American Society for Engineering Edu-
   cation.
   a. Make a forecast of the undergraduate engineering enrollment by
      class for the next five years for
      (1) All engineering disciplines.
      (2) For each engineering discipline.
   b. Make a forecast of the graduate engineering enrollment for the next
      five years for
      (1) Students enrolled in master's degree programs.
      (2) Students enrolled in doctor's degree programs.

4. Obtain data on the number of students enrolled in your university,
   college, or school. Make a forecast of the number in each class for the
   next five years.

5. Fit a trigonometric series to the data of Table 3.5. Does your trigonometric series give a better fit than the regression lines of Section
   3.8.2?

6. Derive Eq. (3.7) from Eq. (3.6).

Chapter 4

7. Make moving-range control charts for your forecasts of Probs. 2(b)
   and 2(c). Base your limits on the first three years data and also add
   the data of the latest year. Do you have a good forecasting technique?

Chapter 5

8. In Fig. 5.3, the inventory can be expressed as

$$I(t) = (p - s)t \quad \text{for} \quad o \leqslant t \leqslant q_m/p$$

and

$$I(t) = q - st \quad \text{for} \quad q_m/p \leqslant t \leqslant q_m/s$$

The inventory cost for one cycle is

$$C = i \int_o^{q/s} I(t) \, dt$$

From the above, obtain Eq. (5.2) and (5.4).

9. Assume that it is possible to back-order material (i.e., that delivery can be deferred) and that the penalty cost of each item back-ordered is b per unit time. Under these conditions the maximum inventory is $M (M < q_0)$. Determine the cost of such a policy. Compare this cost with the cost of a policy where back-ordering is not permissible.

10. Assume that order costs are $100.00 per order and carrying charges are $2.00 per unit per year. Determine the economic lot size.

   a. Demand is forecast to follow the regression lines:

$$x' = 1000 + 100t, \quad t = 1, 2, \ldots, 6$$

and

$$x' = 2300 - 100t, \quad t = 7, 8, \ldots, 12$$

   b. Demand is forecast to follow the trigonometric relationship:

$$x' = 200 + 5t + 40 \cos \frac{(2t - 1)\pi}{6}$$

for

$$t = 1, 2, \ldots, n$$

   c. Demand is forecast to follow the quadratic relationship:

$$x' = 100 + 20t + 10(t - 6)^2$$

for

$$t = 1, 2, \ldots, n$$

11. Construct an alignment chart for variable A, s, i, and p ($\$10 \leqslant A \leqslant \$100$, $1000 \leqslant s \leqslant 10{,}000$, $\$0.50 \leqslant i \leqslant \$15.00$, $10{,}000 \leqslant p \leqslant 100{,}000$).

Chapter 6

12. If the order cost, A, is $100.00, the annual forecast demand, s, is 2,000,000 units and the annual inventory carrying cost is $1.00 per unit per year, determine I_m and I_i in Fig. 6.10. (References: K. Arrow T. Harris, and J. Marschak, "Optimal Inventory Policy," *Econometrica*, Vol. **19**, No. 3, July 1951, pages 250–272. J. F. Magee, *Production Planning and Inventory Control*, New York: McGraw-Hill Book Co., Inc., 1958, pages 83–86.)

Chapter 7

13. Use your forecast from Prob. 4 to establish a five-year plan for

   a. The courses and number of sections to be offered each term.

   b. The number of faculty members required each term.

   c. The classroom space required each term.

Chapter 9

14. Make a course schedule for your department or school for the next year:
   a. For a typical freshman, sophomore, junior, and senior.
   b. For the department faculty.
   c. For the classrooms for department courses.
   d. Assuming that a sophomore fails to complete a required course, make a course schedule for him for the next year, using your schedule for the department.

Chapter 12

15. Make a January schedule for the paint company described in Chapter 12. Use the forecasts and production plan in the text.

Bibliography

Abramovitz, Moses, *Inventories and Business Cycles*. New York: National Bureau of Economic Research, 1950.

Ammer, Dean S., *Materials Management*. Homewood, Illinois: Richard D. Irwin, Inc., 1962.

Brown, Robert G., *Statistical Forecasting For Inventory Control*. New York: McGraw-Hill Book Company, Inc., 1959.

Charnes, A., W. W. Cooper, and A. Henderson, *An Introduction to Linear Programming*. New York: John Wiley & Sons, Inc., 1953.

Clark, Wallace, *The Gantt Chart*. London: Sir Isaac Pitman & Sons, 1938.

Ferguson, Robert O., and Lauren F. Sargent, *Linear Programming: Fundamentals and Applications*. New York: McGraw-Hill Book Company, Inc., 1958.

Fetter, Robert B., and Winston C. Dalleck, *Decision Models for Inventory Management*. Homewood, Illinois: Richard D. Irwin, Inc., 1961.

Gass, Saul I., *Linear Programming: Methods and Applications*. New York: McGraw-Hill Book Company, Inc., 1958.

Hanssmann, Fred, *Operations Research in Production and Inventory Control*. New York: John Wiley & Sons, Inc., 1962.

Hoel, Paul G., *Introduction to Mathematical Statistics*. New York: John Wiley & Sons, Inc., 1947.

Holt, Charles C., Franco Modigliani, John F. Muth, and Herbert A. Simon, *Planning Production, Inventories and Work Force*. Englewood Cliffs, New Jersey: Prentice-Hall, Inc., 1960.

Kendall, Maurice G., *The Advanced Theory of Statistics*, Vol. II. London: Charles Griffin & Company, Ltd., 1946.

Magee, John F., *Production Planning and Inventory Control*. New York: McGraw-Hill Book Company, Inc., 1958.

Metzger, Robert W., *Elementary Mathematical Programming*. New York: John Wiley & Sons, Inc., 1958.

Moore, Franklin G., *Production Control*, Second Edition. New York: McGraw-Hill Book Company, Inc., 1959.

Reinfeld, Nyles V. and William R. Vogel, *Mathematical Programming*. Englewood Cliffs, New Jersey: Prentice-Hall, Inc., 1958.

Voris, William, *Production Control: Text and Cases*, Revised Edition. Homewood, Illinois: Richard D. Irwin, Inc., 1961.

Whitin, Thomas M., *The Theory of Inventory Management*. Princeton, New Jersey: Princeton University Press, 1953.

Magazines and Journals

Advanced Management

American Production and Inventory Control Society (APICS) Quarterly

Econometrica

Factory

Harvard Business Review

Journal of Business

Journal of Industrial Engineering

Management International

Management Review

Management Science

Operations Research

Operations Research Quarterly

Nations Business

Naval Research Logistics Quarterly

Index

A

ABC classification, of raw materials and supplies, 152
Algebraic representation, of time series, 37
Alignment charts (*see* Order charts)
American Production and Inventory Control Society, survey conducted by, 2–4, 149–155
  referred to in problem, 217
Anticipation stock, 72, 94
  problems, 183, 190, 198, 206, 213
APICS (*see* American Production and Inventory Control Society)
Arithmetic average, 22–23
  as forecast method, 36
Assembly line, conveyor-controlled, 7
Assembly line manufacturing, 114
Assembly line operations, production scheduling for, 115–122

B

Ball mill, 177, 178
Batch process, paint manufacture as, 156
Buffer stock (*see* Safety stock)
Business activity, index of, forecast based on, 18, 19
Business trends and cycles, analysis of, for sales forecasting, 151

C

Capital position, and production control, 1
Column values, 133–134
Completion report, as document in manufacturing, 12
Computers:
  use in forecasts, 21
  use in production and inventory control, 153, 154
Control boards, 153–154
Control charts:
  to determine forecast accuracy, 44–54
  on monthly forecasts in paint industry, 166
Control functions in manufacturing, main purposes of, 10–11
Conversion process, 4–5
Cost:
  of product transportation, 131
  of production, 131
  total annual, 56
Cost control, control function in manufacturing, 10–11
Cost elements in manufacturing, 55, 57
  evaluation of effects of changes in, 62, 63
  (*see also* Item costs, Order costs, Storage costs)
Cost estimate, as document in manufacturing, 12–13
Cost estimating, engineering function in manufacturing, 9–10
Cost factors, in economic lot-size determination, 56
Costs:
  distribution (*see* Distribution costs)
  production (*see* Production costs)
  transportation (*see* Transportation costs)
  unequal, method of handling, 144

Curvilinear regression, 38–41
Customer demand:
    and inventory, 70–71
    in paint and allied products industry, 157
    and production control, 1
Customer service, 2, 3
    concern with, 153
    determining level, 76
Cycle stock, 72
Cycles, component of time series, 37
Cyclic demand (*see* Demand, cyclic)

D

Data processing methods, 153–154, 155
Decision rules, use of, 155
Degenerate assignment, 140
Degenerate case, in transportation method
    of distribution problem solution,
    138–141
Demand:
    actual, 44, 53, 103, 106
        variation with forecast demand, 76
    compared with forecast, 44
    cyclic, 29–31, 32–34, 85
        in paint and allied industry, 170
        pattern of, 20
        with random variations, forecasting,
            29–31
        variations in, 17
        and work force size, 89
    devices used to detect changes in, 44
    forecast of, 17, 37, 38, 72, 73, 103, 106
        and inventory control, 71
        methods of, 149–151
    and inventory systems, nature of, 80–85
    and production planning, 88–89
    and safety stock, 76
    upward trend with random variation,
        forecasting, 24–29
    variation of, 76, 112
    and work force, effects on, 89
Demand data, determination of periodici-
    ty of, 41
Demand pattern, and forecasts, 17
Demand variations, distribution of, 76
Dispersing process, in paint and allied
    products industry, 156
Dispersion equipment, in paint and allied
    products industry, 177–178
Distribution, linear programming methods
    applied to, 130–148
    problems, 186, 193–194, 200–201, 208–
        209, 216
Distribution costs, and transportation
    method of distribution problem
    solution, 142

Distribution   problem,   transportation
    method applied to, 130–148
Documents in manufacturing, 12–13
    interrelationship with functions, 13, 14
Dummy machine, assignments to, 146
Dummy order, 146
Dummy warehouse, use in distribution
    problem solution, 141–142

E

Economic indicators, use in sales forecast-
    ing, 151
Economic lot size, 2, 73, 79
    cost factors in, 56–57
    determination of, 55–69
        in paint and allied products industry,
            166–170
        problems, 181–182, 188–189, 196–197,
            211–212, 203–204, 218–219
        replenishment instantaneous, 55–60
        replenishment over finite time period,
            55, 58–60
        use of order charts, 66–69
        use of order tables, 66–69
    increase of, 59
    and inventory, 71, 72
    manufactured, determination of, 60
    purchased, in paint industry, 168, 170
    quantity factors in, 56–57
Economic order quantity, determination
    of, 5, 154, 155
    problems, 182, 189, 197, 204, 212
Edge-notched cards, 154
Electronic system, for factory control, 155
Engineering:
    methods and standards, 9–10
    systems, 155
Engineering functions in manufacturing,
    main purposes, 9–10
Engineering group, responsibilities of, 7

F

Facilities forecast, 18
Factory magazine, survey conducted by,
    2–4, 149–155
    referred to in problem, 217
Final inspection report, as document in
    manufacturing, 13
Finished-goods inventory (*see* Inventory,
    finished-goods)
Fixed-order-interval inventory control sys-
    tem (*see* Inventory control system,
    fixed-order-interval)
Fixed-order-interval reorder rule (*see* Re-
    order rule, fixed-order-interval)

Fixed-order-size inventory control system (*see* Inventory control system, fixed-order-size)
Fixed-order-size reorder rule (*see* Reorder rule, fixed-order-size)
Fluctuation stock, 72, 76–80
Forecast:
 facilities, 18
 long-range, 18
 moving-average, 34–35
  defined, 34
  problems, 180, 188, 195, 203, 211
 product, 18
 production planning, 17, 18
 total-demand, 43
 weighted-average, 35–36, 104
  problems, 180, 188, 196, 203, 211, 218
Forecast methods, 18–21, 34–36, 104
Forecast requirements, 131–132
 exceeded by planned production, 141–142
Forecasting, 16–43
 in paint and allied products industry, 157–166
  sources of information for, 157–158
 problems, 179–180, 186–187, 194–195, 202, 209–210, 217–218
 and production control, 2, 4
Forecasting equations, 45, 49, 53
Forecasts (*see also* Demand, forecasts of; Sales forecasts)
 compared with actual demand, 44, 53, 103
 control of, 44–54
  problems, 180–181, 187–188, 195–196, 203, 210–211, 218
 defined, 16
 estimate of error in, 23–24, 28, 31, 33
 examples of, based on arithmetic average, 22–23
  cyclic demand, following upward trend with random variations, 32–34
  cyclic demand, with random variations, 29–31
  level demand, with random variations, 22–24
  upward trend, with random variations, 24–29
 importance of accuracy, 21–22
 and production planning, problems, 191
 reasons for, 16
 sales characteristics affecting, 17
 statistical methods for, 16, 19, 20–21, 36–41, 43 (*see also* Forecast, moving-average; Forecast, weighted-average)
 types of, 18–21
 use of, 17–18

Functions, in manufacturing, 9–12
 interrelationship with documents, 13, 14

G

Gantt chart, 125
 problems, 185, 192, 200, 208, 215

H

High-speed disperser, 177, 178
High-speed stone mill, 177, 178
Historical averages, use in sales forecasting, 150

I

Indicator method, for solution of production scheduling problems, 130, 144
 use for assigning orders to machines, 122–124
 problems, 192, 200
In-process inspection report, as document in manufacturing, 13
Inspection, as control function in manufacturing, 10–11
Inventory, 70–87
 actual, 104, 106, 107, 110, 112
 defined, 70
 demand and production related to, 107
 finished-goods, 70–71, 72
 function of, 71–72
 holding of, 71
 in-process, 71
 lot-size, 72
 minus, 107
 optimum size of, 72
 patterns of:
  under fixed-order-interval system, 85
  under fixed-order-size system, 84
 planned, 104, 106, 110, 112
 problems, 182
 and production control, 71
 and production planning, 91, 95
  adjustment of plan, 103
 and production scheduling, problems, 185, 192–193
 raw-materials, 70–71
 reorder rules, 75–76
 types of, 72–73
 under constant usage and instantaneous replenishment, 59
 under constant usage and replenishment over finite time period, 59
Inventory carrying costs, 111, 126
Inventory control (*see also* Production and inventory control)
 future changes expected in, 155
 linear programming methods applicable to, 130
 as practiced today, 149–155

Inventory control: (*Cont.*)
  problems, 189–190, 197, 205, 212–213, 219
  responsibilities of, 2–4
Inventory control department, 3
Inventory control system, fixed-order-interval, 73, 75, 77
  and demand, 80–81
  problems, 182, 189–190, 197, 205, 212–213
  safety stock in, 78, 79, 80
  stock levels under, 83
  variation of, 85–86
Inventory control system, fixed-order-size, 73, 74, 76
  problems, 182, 189–190, 197, 205, 212–213
  safety stock in, 76–78, 79
  stock levels under, 82
  use, when demand not level, 80
Inventory control systems, 55
  basic types, 73–76
  when demand not level, 80–85
  and order quantities, 57–58
  "two bin," 73
Inventory investment, in paint industry, 167
Inventory levels, 2
  determination of, 151–152
  methods of establishing, 151
  in paint industry, 156
  and production plan, 98
  variable, cost of, 112
Inventory planning, 20
Inventory problems, in paint and allied products industry, 157
Inventory record, as document in manufacturing, 12
Inventory turnover, 151–152
  and inventory control, 153
  rate, in paint and allied products industry, 167
Inventory-usage ratio, 127, 128–129
Item cost, 56, 57

J

Job order, as document in manufacturing, 12
Job shop manufacturing operation, 114
Job standard, as document in manufacturing, 13

K

Kinetic dispersion mill, 177, 178

L

Lead time, 72, 73
  in paint industry, 171
  production scheduling with, 125–127
  and safety stock, 76–77, 78
Level demand (*see* Demand, level)
Leveling method, of production plan adjustment, 104
  effect of number of periods used, 112–113
  example of, 104–111
  objective of, 106
Linear programming methods, 151 (*see also* Indicator method)
  applied to distribution, 130–148
  applied to production and inventory planning and control, 130
  applied to scheduling, 130, 144–148
  problems, 185–186, 193–194, 200–202, 208–209, 216–217
Linear regression, 36 (*see also* Regression line)
Long-range forecast, 18
Lot process (*see* Batch process)
Lot size, economic (*see* Economic lot size)

M

Machine-scheduling, modi method applied to, 130, 144–148
Machines, assignment of orders to, 122–125, 144–148
  problems, 184–185, 192–193, 199–200, 207, 215
Man, and machines, 155
Man-hours, scheduling of:
  in paint industry production plan, 170–171, 176, 178
  problems, 184, 192, 199–200, 207–208
  and production planning, 89–91
Manpower, and production control, 1
Manufacturing:
  continuous, 125–126
    production control requirements, 7
  control of, and forecasts, 21
  cost elements, 55
  documents used for production control, 8, 12–13
  problem, 217
  functions in, 8–15
    responsibilities of, 9
  importance of inventory in, 70
  as input-output process, 4–5
  intermittent, 125–126
    production control requirements, 7
  linear programming methods applied to problems in, 130–148

Manufacturing (*Cont.*)
and production control, 1, 6
problem, 217
types of, and production scheduling, 114
Manufacturing process, described, 4
Market research, as type of forecast, 21
Material cost (*see* Item cost)
Mean (*see* Arithmetic average)
Milling operations, 126
Minimum-cost determinations, for more than one product, 62–66
Minimum-cost lot size, 56 (*see also* Economic lot size)
Minimum-cost order quantity (*see* Economic lot size)
Modi method of production and inventory control, 130 (*see also* Transportation method)
applied to distribution problem, 130–144
applied to machine-order assignments, 144–148
Modified distribution method (*see* Modi method)
Movement inventories, 72
Moving average, 20
Moving-range chart:
construction of, 45
for controlling forecast, 54
to detect demand changes, 44–53
to determine appropriateness of forecasting equations, 53–54
for forecasts, in paint industry, 165, 166
Moving-average forecast (*see* Forecast, moving-average)

N

Northwest corner rule, 132, 142

O

Order charts, for determining economic lot sizes, 66–69
manufactured-lot-size, 68–69
purchased-lot-size, 67, 68–69
Order costs, 55–56
annual, 57
Order interval, 79
Order quantity, 79
economic (*see* Economic order quantity)
Order tables, for determining economic lot sizes, 66–69
manufactured-lot-size, 67
purchased-lot-size, 66–67
Orthogonal polynomials, 39
Oscillations (*see* Cycles)
Overtime, 153

P

Paint and allied products industry, illustrative case, 156–178
average inventory turnover rate, 167
consumer groups, 158–160
dispersion equipment, 177–178
economic lot-size determination, 166–170
purchased lot sizes, 168, 170
forecasting in, 157–161, 166, 171
annual, by type of coating, 162–164
annual, by user groups, 161–162
comparison, of users and types of coating, 163
information sources for, 157–158
monthly control charts, 166
monthly forecasts, of total volume, 164–165
steps in developing, 158–161
inventory investment in, 167
inventory levels in, 167
manufacturing process described, 156–157
production planning in, 170–176
man-hours required, 170–171, 176, 178
production scheduling in, 171, 177–178
problem, 220
raw-material usage, 168–169
sales trends in, 158–159, 161
Paint manufacture, as batch process industry, 156
Personnel, support function in manufacturing, 11
Plant engineering, engineering function in manufacturing, 9–10
Price break, 56
Problems, for study and solution, 179–220
Procedures control, control function in manufacturing, 10–11
Process description, as document in manufacturing, 12
Process design, engineering function in manufacturing, 9–10
Processing industries, production control problems in, 6
Procurement, support function in manufacturing, 11
Product, nature of, and forecasts, 17
Product demand, forecast of, 2
Product description, as document in manufacturing, 12
Product design, engineering function in manufacturing, 9
Product distribution, 2
Product drawings, as documents in manufacturing, 12

Product forecast, 18
Product inventory to product usage ratio
(*see* Inventory-usage ratio)
Product specification, as document in
manufacturing, 12
Product units, converted to man-hours,
89–91, 98
Production:
actual, 103, 110, 112
compared with planned, 153
main purposes in manufacturing, 9
planned, 103, 110, 153
assignment of to plants, 131–132
exceeding forecast requirements, 141–
142
variation in, 112
Production control (*see also* Production
and inventory control)
control function, in manufacturing, 10
determining major emphasis of, 7
and forecasting, 4
functions of, 2–4
future changes expected in, 155
and inventory, 71
linear programming methods applicable
to, 130
in manufacturing organization, place of, 1
and manufacturing process, 4
nature of, 1–7
objective of, 1
as practiced today, 149–155
principles of, 6
problem, 217
Production control department:
assignments, 4
responsibilities, 2–4
Production control function, related to
other manufacturing functions, 8
Production control group, responsibilities
of, 7
Production control problems, 57
illustration of, 5–6
in paint and allied products industry,
157
Production costs, unequal, 142–144
Production forecast, 170
in paint and allied products inventory,
170, 171
Production and inventory control:
major responsibilities, 3–4
measures of effectiveness, 152–153
quantitative methods used for analysis
and solution of problems, 154–155
resistance to change in, 154
survey of, 2–4
Production and inventory control department, size of, 152
Production line, 7

Production levels:
determination of, 151–152
methods of establishing, 151
Production manager, and forecasting, in
paint and allied products industry,
157
Production plan, 88–89
adjusted, reconciliation with available
hours, 111–112
adjustment of, 103–113
methods for, 104
problems, 183, 191, 206, 214
reasons for, 103
and demand, 88–89
as document in manufacturing, 12
example of, 89–95
revised, 119–121
with safety stocks, 95–98
minimum cost, 91–98
in paint industry, 156
purposes, 88
for several products, 98–102
variable, cost of, 112
Production planning, 2, 88–102
and inventory control, 71
in paint and allied products inventory,
170–176
problems, 182–183, 190–191, 197–198,
205–206, 213–214
applied to enrollment forecasts, 219
total-demand forecast in, 43
Production planning forecast, 17, 18
Production program, as document in
manufacturing, 12
Production rate:
and economic lot size, 61
and sales rate, 62
Production schedules, 2, 104
as document in manufacturing, 12
in paint industry, 156
Production scheduling, 114–129, 151
by available-usage ratio, 127–128
with lead times, 125–127
machine order assignment, in multiproduct operation, 122–125
of one product, 115–122
in paint and allied products industry,
171, 177–178
problems, 184–185, 191–193, 199–200,
206–208, 214–215
application to enrollment forecasts,
220
of several products, 127–129
and type of manufacturing, 114
use of charts, 125
Productive capacity, and production control, 1
Punched cards, 153, 154

Purchase cost (*see* Order cost)
Purchase orders, 56
  as document in manufacturing, 13
Purchase requisition, as document in manufacturing, 13
Purchased goods, routing of, 2, 3
Purchasing, support function in manufacturing, 11

Q

Quality control, control function in manufacturing, 10, 11
Quantity discounts, 56
Quantity factors, in economic lot-size determinations, 56

R

Random variations, 36–37
Raw-materials inventory (*see* Inventory, raw-materials)
Receiving, main purposes in manufacturing, 9
Receiving inspection report, as document in manufacturing, 13
Receiving report, as document in manufacturing, 13
Regression:
  curvilinear (*see* Curvilinear regression)
  linear (*see* Linear regression)
Regression lines, 26–28, 29, 32
  defined, 26
  establishing, 30–31, 33
  estimate of future demand, 25–26
  in paint industry forecast tables, 164
  simplified calculations for, 26–28
  standard deviation of variations, 28
  use, with cyclic demand, 29–31, 32–34
Reorder rules:
  fixed-order-interval, 76
  fixed-order-size, 75–76
Replenishment:
  instantaneous, 55–58, 59, 61–62, 73
  over finite period of time, 55, 58–60, 61–62
Rim values, 133
Row values, 133–134

S

Safety stock, 72, 73, 74, 75, 76–80
  and demand, 76, 80, 81
  determination of, 112
  economic level of, 79
  in paint industry production plan, 171, 176
  problems, 182, 189, 197, 205, 212–213
  production plan with, 95–98
  quantities, determination of, 78

Sales:
  actual, 106, 107
  characteristics affecting forecasts, 17
  support function, in manufacturing, 11
Sales data:
  averages of, forecast based on, 18–19, 20
  statistical analysis of forecast based on, 19, 20–21
Sales department, responsibility for forecast, in paint industry, 157
Sales forecast:
  as document in manufacturing, 12
  in paint and allied products industry, 157
  problems, 180, 187, 195, 202, 210
  production forecast, in manufacturing for stock, 170
Sales forecasting:
  current methods of, 150
  current status of, 149–151
Sales order, as document in manufacturing, 13
Sales trends, in paint and allied products industry, 158–159, 161
Sample, accuracy of, in predicting, 23
Scheduled dispatching, 154
Scheduling (*see also* Man-hours, scheduling of; Production scheduling)
  linear programming applied to, 130, 144–148
  problems, 194, 201–202, 209, 217
  of production, 114–129
School enrollments, forecasts of, as problem, 218, 219–220
Service industries, production control problems in, 6
Shipping, main purposes in manufacturing, 9
Shipping report, as document in manufacturing, 13
Shipments, routing of, 2, 3
Simplex method, 148
Standard deviation, 23–24
  defined, 23
  of variation about regression line, 28
Statistical methods, use in forecasting, 16, 20–21, 34–43, 149, 150, 151
Steppingstone method, of production assignments, 134–135, 138, 140
Stock:
  anticipation (*see* Anticipation stock)
  replenishment of, and economic lot-size problem, 55
  safety (*see* Safety stock)
Storage costs, 56, 57
Subjective opinions, forecast based on, 18, 19

Support functions, in manufacturing, 11–12

Systems engineering, 155

T

Tabulating equipment, 153, 154
Time periods, changes in, 62
Time series:
  algebraic representation, 37
  in forecasts, 36–37
  trigonometric representation, 37–38
Tool design, engineering function in manufacturing, 9–10
Total-demand forecast, 43
Traffic department, 2, 3
Transportation, main purposes in manufacturing, 9
Transportation costs, 132, 137, 141
Transportation method, applied to distribution problem, 130–144
  information needed for solution, 130–131
Trend, upward, 32–34
Trend line, establishing in forecast, 25–28
Trends, component of time series, 37
Trigonometric representation, 40–41
  of time series, 37–38
Turning operations, 126

U

Usage, expected, 78
  maximum, 78
Usage raito, available, 127–128
Use, forecast based on, 18

V

Value table, 136, 137
  construction of, 132, 133

W

Warehousing, main purposes in manufacturing, 9
Weighted-average forecast (*see* Forecast, weighted-average)
Weighted-average method, of production plan adjustment, 104
Work force (*see also* Man-hours, scheduling of)
  in paint industry production plan, 170–171
  and production planning, 89

RUNEL   ITY LIBRARY

OAN

60 4123634 3